Culture Shock
& Canapés

Culture Shock & Canapés

PAMELA O'CUNEEN

QUARTET BOOKS

First published in 2012 by
Quartet Books Limited
A member of the Namara Group
27 Goodge Street, London WIT 2LD

A catalogue record for this book
is available from the British Library

ISBN 978 0 7043 7254 2

Typeset by Antony Gray
Printed and bound in Great Britain by
T J International Ltd, Padstow, Cornwall

Contents

Introduction

When I was a teenager in Western Australia, a new International Airport was built in Perth, complete with black swans on a pond and a 'viewing gallery'. Families would go there on Sunday afternoons in the hope of seeing a flight take off to Europe. We would watch the plane rise into the air like a magic carpet – who knew where it might come to land, or what marvels those people might see? I doubted that I would ever be among them, but couldn't help dreaming.

Life often takes us further than we could ever have imagined, to places beyond any dreams of strangeness. As a 'trailing spouse' or diplomat's wife, there were crises, times of wonder and delight, times of loss, and times of loneliness, but the overwhelming memory of those unexpected adventures is of rich human encounters. A colourful procession of domestic helpers became brothers, sisters and friends, and warm people from every walk of life welcomed and supported us in each country. Even if you are not mentioned in the book, thank you.

Thank you too to all of those who inspired, and helped in the writing of this book. To my friend Mary Dwyer, who kept the hundreds of letters we wrote over twenty years and produced them when needed, to the friends who fell about laughing at bulletins of domestic disasters, and to those who read and critiqued early chapters. Thank you to Richard Addis, mentor and media man extraordinary, without whose constant support the book would never have reached publication, to Naim Attallah, who saw something in the original manuscript (and fortunately insisted that it be reduced by half), and to my delightful editor Anna Stothard, whose perspicacity improved the book so much. And to my loyal and loving husband KJ, without whom the story would never have happened.

My Mother often said, 'Pam has led a charmed life'. While I stoutly denied it at the time, she was right, in the sense that travel unrolls a series of magical places before us. The magic may not be initially evident but with time, endurance and love, it always appears. Mother also said, many times: 'Pam, you could write some beaut books!' Here is the first one, Mother. I hope you find it 'beaut'!

The Strangeness of a Mountain Kingdom

The tall African warrior in front of us was wearing only a *beshu* round his waist, of skins and monkey-tails. Strings of beads stretched diagonally across his smooth brown chest. As he talked, he gesticulated with the hand holding his spears and shield.

We took in the spectacle. KJ was relaxed but I could see that my mother, a well-brought up Australian matron, was half fascinated, half afraid. So was I. Was it safe? What might he do next?

What he did next could not have been predicted. The near-naked warrior leaned back to speak to the person on our right, saying in an Oxford accent: 'Good afternoon. How do you do. I'm the Minister of Agriculture.'

We gasped. This was modern Africa. It was the last place I had ever expected to find myself. How had it happened?

KJ and I had driven in to Swaziland from South Africa. The Drakensberg Mountains appeared on the left, folding into the distance like an immense blanket abandoned by a giant – blues, purples, pinks and browns. The range tailed into Swaziland, a country of dramatic peaks, hillsides that could be green or purple or parched, mountain streams, and little clustered kraals of grass-roofed huts. Oeshoek, the border town, was a con-glomeration of huts and bottle stores with names like the 'Heavenly Glory Bottle Shop'. There were goats and cows straggling on the road, and glowing braziers roasting corn cobs, stalls of carvings and beads and baskets. The Swazi people, small and sturdy, walked along the roads, or drove beaten up *bakkies* (small utility trucks) wearing their orange, black and red cloth *amahiyas* across one shoulder, golden brown skins shining in the evening light. It was '*libantu bahle*' – 'the time when the people are beautiful'.

In this tiny kingdom, King Sobhuza still reigned. In his eighties now, he had been king for sixty years. The first time we met him he was sitting on the ground among his ministers and counsellors. He was a small, thin, brown-skinned old man with a pointed beard, and a penetrating gaze. He had fine features, and the three royal red Lourie feathers in his hair. He wore skins and a thick rug around his shoulders. His courtiers knelt reverently before him, then backed away, saluting respectfully with the right hand, left hand under the right elbow. He was legendary for his Solomon-like wisdom and his Solomon-like harem. He probably had, at any one time, seventy or eighty wives and two or three times that number of concubines. His cattle were uncountable. In a polygamous society, where wealth was measured in cattle, this was true greatness. He walked his small country, dispensing justice, visiting his wives and here and there recognising pretty girls in the time-honoured way. Loved by the people, he was in every way the 'Father of the Nation' and with the process of natural increase over a reign of sixty years, the king's issue was 'numberless as the stars in the sky'.

The king saw the wisdom of binding the nation together with tradition. National costume was encouraged. People walked the roads wearing the red or orange *amahiya*. Seasonal rituals and ceremonies were seriously carried out. Sometimes the Royal Regiments appeared on the road near one of the palaces, trotting fast, brown chests shining as they exercised, carrying a forest of long spears and warrior-sized cowhide shields. Swaziland was in a changing world where an old African culture, powered by ancestor worship and animism, was in headlong collision with the modern world of moral relativism and technology.

To an Australian working girl fresh from London, this was another planet. Granted, English was spoken and traffic drove on the left but everything else was new. Sights, sounds and smells were colourful, stimulating, exciting and sometimes threatening. Added to that, KJ and I were newly married, unused to each other and trying not to step on each other's toes. He had spent sixteen years in Africa as a missionary priest. Now, after much soul-searching, with a combination of talent, panache and a modicum of divine intervention, he found himself working as Regional Training Advisor for the Commission of the European Communities, fire-fighting regional training projects in five southern African countries. Speaking fluent Zulu as he did, KJ hopped from car to plane to donkey cart and loved it. I was not so sure.

My parents announced that they were coming from Australia to inspect their new son-in-law. I wondered if these would be six weeks of unalloyed joy. We planned a trip to Johannesburg to meet them in our first car, our pride and joy. It was a Colt Galant in a peculiar colour between orange and mustard, called 'caramel' and it was polished to a high shine for the occasion. Champagne was placed in their room. KJ wanted to make a good impression.

They were duly impressed. We set out on the long drive back to Swaziland, conversing politely as we went. The first surprise came when Dad saw the name for 'High School' written on a signboard in Afrikaans. 'Hoerskoel', it said.

'Whore school?' he said. It was too much for his quiet Australian sense of humour and he cracked up with laughter.

As we approached the Swazi border, Mother was reduced to awed silence by the huge magnificence of the Drakensberg mountains unfolding in the setting sun. Her artist's eye drank it in. Mile after mile of changing landscape unrolled in the distance; blues, pinks, dark greens, violets and purple colours painting the peaks and shadows, back-lit and haloed by a peach and orange African sunset.

A day or two after the arrival of the parents, we went to the town of Mbabane to look at the Swazi markets and shops, and to get a feel for the pulse of this minuscule metropolis. Mother was very quiet on the drive, as she looked at the eucalyptus forests, the goats on the road, the tiny huts. In town there was the usual mild chaos on the sidewalks, people ambled across at the traffic lights – or not – as they felt inclined, a couple of cows grazed on the verge, an old utility truck stopped in the middle of the road while its owner did business with a friend in an adjoining car. Mother observed all of this with wonderment. I was waiting for her comment. When it came, even I was taken by surprise: 'Pam, there are a lot of African people here!' she said.

What could I say but, 'Yes Mother, it's their country!'

Darling Mother. It was all a bit threatening for her. I'm not sure that she was fully satisfied with the answer.

Soon the Reed Dance was announced, calculated as it is by the phases of the moon. Every year the event took place in the Ezulwini Valley near the Queen Mother's home. Ten thousand Swazi maidens danced before the king, wearing tiny beaded skirts well hitched up to show buttocks that could survive a drought. Bare-breasted, their torsos were tantalisingly adorned with brilliantly coloured skeins of wool, tied and tasselled and beaded and swinging with the rhythm of the dance, in time with the stomp and rattle of seed-pod anklets. It was a mesmerising sight, this sea of girls, dancing in formation to drums and slow, growling chants. They were kept in strict order by solid woman police, and each girl carried a flashing knife to cut new reeds for the Queen Mother's kraal. Traditionally the king could, if he wished, choose a new wife or wives from all the eligible virgins of the nation, although by then he rarely did.

Not wanting them to miss such a sight, we settled the parents on the benches reserved for visitors and VIPs. They were impressed with the overwhelming dull roar as phalanxes of unclad girls approached in dancing lines. The numbers grew, dancing past us in their brightly coloured thousands. Bare-chested warriors dashed out in front of the lines, and paid homage by banging down their spears and shields before the girls, whistles were blown, old women in heavy black cowhide skirts ululated above the din, and danced so that their massive hips jiggled under the pleats.

Mother watched these goings-on with widening eyes. She was already bereft of her comfortable certainties, as I was, feeling that the ground was less than solid under her feet in this strange and threatening environment. And it was then, in the roaring, chanting, ululating din, that the spear-brandishing Swazi minister of agriculture made his appearance. This was culture shock with a vengeance.

As the dancing progressed, it turned cold. Swaziland can be frosty in winter. Even the male guests, who might have been in danger of over-excitement at the close proximity of several thousand semi-naked nubile young maidens, were beginning to welcome the maidens chiefly as an effective human windbreak.

When it was over the girls broke ranks and went off to queue for buses back home to their rural areas. Our thoughts turned to warm drinks, and we made for the Swazi Sun hotel. We found a traditional British afternoon tea, then KJ suggested a visit to the hotel casino, set up to cater for virtuous South African visitors unable to indulge their desires for gambling and other wickedness in the God-fearing atmosphere of their republic.

Mother looked askance. In her mind, a casino was a den of vice. I should explain that on our rare visits, we allowed ourselves 2 Rand each – in those days about $US2 – and played with the slot machines until the money ran out. With some reassurance Mother accepted her 2 Rand in tokens, put money in the slot and turned the handle. On this, her first trial, bells rang, and a shower of coins tumbled out into the tray, clattering onto her feet.

Not for this lady the way of the compulsive gambler. She had no thoughts of putting her winnings back into the machine. Gathering everything up she clasped her handbag like the Queen and said: 'Well, that's good. I'll shout you all dinner!' And she did.

The next evening, though, when we were up the hill in Mbabane, on a cold and misty night, Mother had a sudden thought.

'Could we go back down to that casino again? That was a pretty good place.'

The 'Swazi Inn' was our home for the first weeks; a hotel where the rooms were thatched rondavels smelling of straw and creosote. It had been Rider Haggard's home overlooking the Ezulwini Valley – the Valley of Heaven – made famous by Haggard in his novels *King Solomon's Mines*, and *She*, as the 'valley of the mists'. It was well named – thick mists could rise within minutes. Clouds would roll in to envelop the 50-kilometre view down the valley to the two mountain peaks known as Sheba's Breasts. And in the Mdzimba mountains the Swazi kings really were buried sitting up in caves, though not perhaps encrusted with gold and diamonds.

Exploring, we drove down the Malagwane Hill into the Valley of Heaven. Along the roadside were sellers of carvings and curios, woven baskets and grass mats. And fruit – oranges and avocados sold, not singly for pounds, but in sackfuls for pennies. We went into the Malkerns valley and saw pineapples for sale, heaped green and gold treasure on the ground. KJ bought one and we drove to the Mantenga Falls. Mother and Dad had tea while KJ and I lay under the waterfall, letting the water-massage flow over us. And then we sat on a rock, watching Swazi children shouting in the shallows. With a pocketknife KJ dismantled the pineapple. We bit into it and the sweet liqueur of the tropical juice dripped down our chins and into the water.

Eventually we moved into our new house, a cream house with

an immense, bare garden, fenced only by barbed wire. Passers-by called in for a drink from the tap, local dogs used it as a short cut and sundry cows and donkeys found the garden flowers a pleasant change from their usual diet.

Then one morning our goods arrived.

Two Swazi faces, grinning broadly, looked down from the cabin of a truck: 'The goods, they are here from Durban, Boss.' The men gestured at a large wooden crate behind them.

We looked at the truck. There was no lifting tackle. We looked at each other, and at the truck-drivers.

'How are you going to unload it?' asked KJ. The grins broadened.

A second truck roared along the gravel of the Golf Course Road, a dozen workmen singing lustily on the back. In a flash KJ was in the car, off in pursuit, followed by a cloud of white dust. Five minutes later they were back. Twelve men tumbled out and scrambled onto the waiting goods truck with great good humour. A rhythmic work song began, and with heaves and a crash, the crate containing all our worldly goods was wrestled from the truck, slid off and landed squarely on top of a flower-bed, accompanied by loud cheers and thumbs-up signs.

'Oh my God! The flowers, the china, the glassware, the harp!' I thought.

Everyone else seemed delighted. Swapping jokes in fluent Zulu, KJ handed over some beer money and the twelve husky workers jumped back into their truck and sang off towards Mbabane, immensely pleased with this little diversion on the way to work.

Life in Africa introduced me to the concept of 'help in the house'. Up to that time, working in London, any flat of mine was lucky to see the business end of a broom once a week. Laundry meant a long slog on foot to a launderette and an hour or so in the steam with a book, surrounded by bits of other people's underwear. My first indication of what might be in store came in Lesotho when the wife of a technical assistant said blithely: 'I don't need a washing machine in Africa, I've got a "blackmatic"!'

By the time I realised what she meant, I was too speechless with shock to say anything.

In Swaziland, when we moved into our new cream house on Golf Course Road, the idea of 'help in the house' was mooted by KJ's driver, Mr Dlamini. His niece had become pregnant in her teens, had left school, and was looking for work. Could she come? A young egalitarian Australian, I felt uncomfortable with the concept of having someone work while I sat by and watched. Nevertheless, here was a person who really needed the job. So Mr Dlamini's niece would come for two days a week.

Thembeni was a tiny, pretty young Swazi girl, with enormous smiling eyes, and innocent willingness. She set to work in her own inimitable style. She began by dismantling the house. Every article, and every piece of furniture in every room was piled up high or put away, no matter where. Thembeni would get out her brooms, her polish and her cloths, and all surfaces would be scoured and cleaned. She eyed the vacuum cleaner suspiciously, and preferred the stiff brush and dustpan she was accustomed to. This way of working meant that even if I had not been too embarrassed to sit down, there was, for the entire day, nowhere to sit. All the chairs were on the tables. And in any case, we didn't have much furniture yet. At the end of the day, just as Thembeni was due to be taken to town to catch the Oeshoek bus, I would turn my back, and with less than five minutes to go, the entire house would return to its original order. I never saw it happen, but it always did, and there as if by magic stood Thembeni, bag in hand, changed out of her working clothes and dressed immaculately and fashionably for the journey home.

Thembeni gave me an early insight into the language. When our goods arrived she helped carry them into the house. There were several boxes of shoes. As she carried them in, she remarked: 'Madam, you have too many shoes!'

I was incensed, the more so because I knew it was true, but what business was it of Thembeni's to tell me so?

When KJ arrived home I told him about it. He burst out laughing and said: 'That wasn't criticism, that was admiration! Thembeni just meant "a lot of". Zulu doesn't have a specific expression for too much or too many of anything!'

In this society where prosperity has always depended on the seasons and there were traditionally few ways of preserving food, the concept of a surplus barely exists. When you have a lot of anything you eat it up, and when times are lean, you make do. But in the past, as in the present, only Europeans had 'too much!' I felt ashamed.

Thembeni had high standards. Glasses and windows were polished with old newspaper to a high shine; at her insistence sheets were folded in the correct hotel manner, dropping the sides and reversing the fold, beds were made with immaculate hospital corners. She loved to tidy the kitchen cupboards too, and I became confident enough to go to town to the OK Bazaar for the shopping while she was in charge. One day when I returned, she was looking particularly pleased with herself and had obviously been working very hard indeed.

'What have you been doing, Thembeni?' I asked as I put down the shopping.

'Oh Madam,' she said, 'I have been scrubbing the saucepans today. I managed to get all that nasty black stuff off them.'

And indeed she had. The entire black coating of the Teflon saucepans had gone and the interiors shone like mirrors.

Thembeni taught me my first lessons about housekeeping in Africa, and broke me in gently to the experience of rarely being alone in the house. As the 'mistress of the house', there was a subtle pressure to be relatively well dressed, well behaved and not lounge around too much. On Thembeni days, I felt morally obliged to work at least as hard as she did – sitting down with a book was impossible – so that at the end of the day the house was doubly gleaming, perfectly clean surfaces scrubbed and polished to a state beyond brand new. After she left I had to find where she had 'put away' all the objects that impeded her cleaning. Letters were folded into books, ashtrays tucked into drawers, books stuffed into shelves, sometimes upside down. Another aspect of being 'Thembeni'd'.

At first we had sandwiches for lunch on Thembeni days. Then I made a discovery. Swazi food was delicious and Thembeni could cook it. She made Uphuthu – mealie meal stirred with water in a pot, and cooked to a dry consistency so that it formed chewy lumps, like pasta but far tastier. It was served with a relish made of tomatoes, onions and green peppers and occasionally a small amount of meat. We became addicted to Uphuthu on Tuesdays and Fridays. It ruined the saucepans, but then, we had an entire set of once Teflon-coated pans to use.

Night-watchmen were another a new experience. Every evening at 6 pm, 'Guard Alert's big green truck would roar along the Golf Course Road, disgorging en route army-surplus-clad night-watchmen at all the houses who employed them. This meant that well-off expatriates and Swazis, embassies and firms paid a large amount of money to the owner of 'Guard Alert' who then paid a very small amount of money to Swazi men in need of a job, so that they would stay up all night, guarding the great and the good.

The rationale of 'guarding' all boiled down to the hope that a burglar might choose to go to a house that did not have a guard to raise the alarm, rather than one that did. The routine was that at about 10 pm, we would go outside and find where the guard was sleeping, wake him up with a sandwich and a thermos of tea (or strong coffee) for the night, wish him well, and then turn a blind eye to wherever he might choose to sleep until dawn. The polite fiction was kept up that he patrolled religiously. If occasionally an outside lounge chair looked a bit flat in the morning we looked the other way.

Our favourite guard was an old man, by Swazi standards, (probably about sixty) – one of thousands of Dlaminis. KJ christened him '*Umdala*', a respectful Swazi term for 'Old Man.' Umdala was a tiny man, and when wrapped up in his oversized khaki greatcoat and balaclava helmet he all but disappeared. His English was minimal, but his smile was broad, and his greatest delight was to catch us out. In the middle of the night there would be a rattle at the door handle, sending our hearts racing with fright; his torch would shine through, and his voice would proclaim: 'Up lightey, Missis!' shorthand for 'The bulb on the outside security light has blown!' while he performed a dance of triumph at having found the Abelungu – the Europeans – wanting again.

One particularly cold night, Umdala was nowhere to be found. We searched everywhere by torchlight and finally spotted a pair of boots sticking out from under the car. KJ leant down and pulled. Attached was a sleepy Umdala, well rugged up for bed. Looking owlishly from under his knitted balaclava he said, in Siswati: 'Boss, Boss, no problem, I was just guarding your car!'

The house, rented from a Swazi member of government, came equipped with staff quarters. Richard, our first gardener, who came from a rural village, elected to stay in town for his job in this 'apartment'. We bought him a small stove, and KJ made him simple cupboards and a wardrobe. Richard mowed the lawn with enthusiasm and grinned as the petrol mower went over stones with the most satisfying bangs. Until, that is, we went away on leave during the rainy season. Richard was overcome by ennui and spent most of his time in bed. When we arrived back, he was barely visible above the fine harvest of grass seeds that had once been our green sward. Thembeni and the neighbours' gardeners were waiting to see what would happen.

They knew Richard had behaved badly. In fact they told us so. Would we show ourselves to be strong or weak employers?

In my first experience of African justice, I listened as KJ quizzed him.

Did he know his duties? Yes, he did.

Did he think he had done them? No, he didn't.

What did he expect to happen? 'I should lose my job.'

And so he did, sadly – but only after he had scythed and mowed the lawn all in one long, wearisome day.

As Richard packed his things and went to town to catch his bus, Thembeni and Velapi – the gardener next door, both nodded approvingly.

Domesticity was all very well, but in time it palled. The cupboards were tidy and most of the boxes were unpacked except for that mysterious pile of objects that somehow defied classification and stayed in an obstinate black pile almost out of sight. Confined to the house, speaking only to Thembeni, Umdala and KJ in the evenings, I longed to find friends. How to go about it?

Not long after we arrived there were rumours that the Mbabane Club was auditioning for a performance of *Iolanthe*. Nervous of this new life as I was, it seemed like one way to make a foray into the European section of the local community at least. I had studied singing in Australia and London and landed the role of Iolanthe herself. What I also landed in, of course, was the world of the Mbabane Club – ex-colonial theatre with all of its small treasons, stratagems and spoils. There is always a resident soprano, who takes a dim view of any newcomer to town, at least one soloist overwhelmed with his or her own pretensions, and a gaggle of people who have been persuaded to come along and sing for a laugh. That's the filling in the sandwich. The good plain bread is the team of hard-working musicians, conductor, scene painters, arrangers and generally pleasant people who make such local creative undertakings memorable – at least for those who take part if not for those who come to watch.

This one was no exception. We had a chorus of fairies, male and female – mostly the well-upholstered wives of temporary technical assistants, and jolly ex-pats who repaired to the bar at every opportunity. In addition (a real coup, this) there were a couple of Swazis among the fairy chorus. I hoped someone was explaining the intricacies of the nineteenth-century British legal system to them – and the many-layered meanings of fairy. We had a tenor with a pleasant voice and impressive acting ability. The resident soprano, Julia, was also the conductress – intelligent, musical and sharp as a razor. 'Phyllis' was a sweet-faced graduate of the Royal Academy of Music, London, and the baritone – ah the baritone! Malcolm had a voice, of that there was no doubt. It was rich, mellifluous and well-trained. He also had an ego and a swagger. He was once heard to ask: 'You will tell me, won't you, if there is anything in my voice which isn't quite perfect.'

And the trouble was that, in general, it *was* perfect.

Rehearsals went well. The director was an ex-Royal Ballet dancer, who by some expatriate mystery had chosen to strand himself in Swaziland. He inveigled me, as Iolanthe, into a make-believe well where I crouched on a box in the dark, waiting to be cranked up for an eerie weed-strewn entrance in romantic gloom. The rugby-playing chorus manhandled their partners into artistic, if perilous, ballet lifts. Male fairies were kitted out in green, and plump female fairies wore concealing robes in pastel colours.

Dress rehearsal came. Disaster struck as disaster can only strike in an amateur production. Phyllis had no voice. So many egos at stake. Julia, ever-resourceful, came up with a solution unknown at most of the world's opera houses. She would sing the leading role herself, while conducting with her back to the audience, and Phyllis, voiceless, would mime. As our conductress was gifted with a true and carrying soprano voice and steely concentration, it worked perfectly. The audience never knew the difference.

On opening night, Phyllis and I waited for our entrances in the downstairs dressing-room, freezing in front of a two-bar fire in that mile-high southern African winter. Malcolm, the pompous baritone, was about to sing his big song with its jingoistic refrain, 'For he is an Englishman!' He had taken to singing it hand on hip, one magisterial foot placed on the fence of the orchestra pit.

The introduction struck up. His fine baritone boomed out: 'When Britain really ruled the waves . . . ' There was a pregnant pause followed by a crash and shrieks of laughter.

'My God, he's fallen in!' said Phyllis, and he had. Right on top of the kettledrums! For the rest of the week the orchestra played in crash helmets.

So far I had met few Swazis. The climate of apartheid in nearby South Africa made real friendship difficult. Then unexpectedly, I was invited into the hearts of the people. One Sunday morning we awoke to the news that the local Catholic bishop, Mandlen-khosi Zwane, had been killed at the Malagwane Hill cross-roads. Young, compassionate, politically aware and a reformer, 'Mandhla' was a bright hope for the future of the church in Southern Africa. He was the first black bishop of Manzini, involved in development work, concerned for the plight of refugees and passionate about the anti-apartheid movement.

Mandhla was a friend of KJ's from previous years and KJ was stricken. We went to a subdued Mater Dolorosa church hoping to find out what had happened and when the funeral might be. Nothing was known of the accident except that it was a head-on crash. And the funeral would be 'announced'.

It was held a week later in the Catholic Cathedral at Manzini, Swaziland's business capital. Clergy had converged from all parts of Southern Africa and further afield. They were resplendent in their gold and lace vestments, and in Episcopal purple. But far more impressive were the crowds of mourning Swazis. Hundreds – thousands, it seemed – thronged the large lofty cathedral. We, the so-called VIPs, sat dressed in black, officially present as envoys of the countries and organisations we represented. Some, like KJ, felt personal grief. But the real mourners were the people. Mandhla had been *their* bishop. He was one of them, a local lad.

The Requiem Mass went on interminably but not too long for the mourners. The choirs sang their hearts out, spontaneously harmonising to the tunes, with Robeson-like bass notes and high, sweet, sharp sopranos improvising descants as they went. Each hymn was repeated, folk style, an unspecified number of times, increasing in intensity as it went, until at some un-detectable signal, it stopped. Speeches were made by dignitaries, by bishops from Rome, Zululand and South Africa. The Zulu Bishop of Eshowe sang his tribute in a rolling baritone voice that could have graced the operatic stage. And finally the time had come for the burial. Slabs had been removed from the floor of the cathedral, so that the body could be lowered into the crypt. Heart-breakingly, Bishop Mandhla's sleeping mat and wooden pillow were placed on the coffin, so that he would have them with him. The coffin was lowered into the crypt.

And then, as if at another imperceptible signal, the thousands of black-clad mourners began to file out of the pews in a procession. They circled round the cavity in the floor, looking down. Almost at a whisper a song began, like a round:

'*Lala Mandla lala, lala ngobuhle . . .* '
'Sleep Mandhla sleep, sleep well . . . '

They were laying their bishop to rest with the softest of loving lullabies. The whole congregation moved forward to join in the procession until the entire cathedral became one circling, eddying, spiralling movement of gentleness. Tears were streaming down faces, Swazi and visitors alike. If Bishop Mandhla had doubted that he was loved by his people, he knew it now. And for the first time I glimpsed what hidden depths of love and emotion lay in the hearts of the Swazi people I saw every day.

RECIPES FROM SWAZILAND

Thembeni's Phuthu

Dry mealie meal – corn meal – eaten like pasta. Delicious!

3 cups boiling water, 2½ cups white mealie meal.

Turn stove to medium heat. Add mealie meal to the water bit by bit, stirring continuously. After 5 minutes lower the heat and allow to simmer, stirring from time to time. Cooking time is about 15 minutes. Serve with curry, or vegetable relish.

Vegetable relish

To be ladled over the phuthu

Four tomatoes, 1 onion (or garlic), some green vegetables or green pepper, brinjal (purple egg-plant). Oil for frying.

Fry the onions, or garlic, and add the brinjal, green pepper and tomatoes. Add the water bit by bit. Turn down the heat and simmer to make a sauce. Can add a pinch of curry powder.

2

'Madam, there is something in the bed!'

There was one thing missing. We were both animal lovers and there were none to share our lives. I had been dropping hints about pets for months, as women do, but to no avail. Then one day at lunchtime KJ suddenly said – as men do: 'We are going to get a cat. Today.'

With huge excitement we drove to the Swaziland Animal Welfare Kennels. We walked through lines of dogs, trying to avoid beseeching eyes, and found the cattery where a dozen cats shared a large shady concrete pen. I was hoping for a Siamese. No luck. There were none. I looked at a little black cat. He wasn't interested. Then a tall teenage tabby cat with white front and paws sat bolt upright and pointedly miaowed.

'Perhaps that one wants to be chosen,' I said.

The young tabby was brought out. He put both paws on my shoulders and kissed all over my face with his nose.

'This is the one,' I said, and carried him out in triumph.

Through the dog kennels and into the office he went, clinging to my shoulders. All the way home, the new little cat curled up in my arms, looking and sniffing curiously at everything we passed. On arrival at the house a strange expression crossed his face, as if it was not quite what he was expecting. I left the little tabby face peering out of a bathroom window as I sped back towards the town, bent on buying every kind of cat-food, cat dish, cat treat and cat toy that Mbabane had to offer.

He was christened Paddycat, because he dribbled balls like a famous Irish footballer. He liked people and soon learned that by judicious twiddling of me around his little paw he could get whatever he wanted.

One thing he did *not* like, however, was thunderstorms, and these Swaziland did in Wagnerian volume. Paddycat predicted storms hours beforehand, by slinking up and down the passageways. He would take refuge on a chair under the table, curled into a tight ball, becoming invisible until the thunder stopped rolling round the mountains, and the hailstones stopped crashing and clattering onto the corrugated iron roof. When Gotterdammerung was over and the birds were singing again, he would unroll himself, give a lick or two to restore his savoir faire, and saunter out from his hiding place with a casual demeanour that said: 'I don't mind thunderstorms, do you? I was just taking a nap under the table.'

Initially, he slept in one of the outhouse rooms, in a cardboard box. Lured there every night with little bits of ham or cheese, he went cheerfully to bed.

Soon after we got him, KJ went away to Botswana. When he came back the conversation went something like this: KJ: 'It's time for Paddycat to go out.'

Pamela: 'Well, er, he sleeps in the kitchen now, it's very cold. I've made him a catbox.'

Two weeks later, KJ returned from Lesotho. Bedtime came: KJ: 'It's time for Paddycat to go to the kitchen.'

Pamela: 'Er, it's *really* cold now, Paddycat sleeps . . . '

KJ: 'Not on the *bed!*'

Pamela (hurriedly): 'Yes, but only at the foot, and only on my side.'

As all cat lovers will know, Paddycat ruled. The bed became the place he slept, in the warmest spots. At bedtime he rounded us up and his bedside saucer of milk had to be in place. Pouring his milk one night KJ looked up and said: 'Here I am, on my knees, begging the cat to drink milk.'

Night-time conversations were punctuated with 'Mind the cat!'

It may not have been the home PC expected to return to, but he created it to suit him, as all cats do. Paddycat was the kingpin of the household. And then, to his disgust, there came *dogs*.

The first Swazi dog was a gentle golden stray who appeared at the far side of the garden, by the barbed-wire fence. She looked thin and hungry, so having the end of a leg of lamb to spare, I ran down to give it to her. This, not surprisingly, gave her courage to come closer to the house and 'Lady' she became, bathed, fed, and given a blanket to sleep on. Lady was part Labrador, grateful for all the good things that life was suddenly offering her. She came in to sit by the fire, curled up in a ball. She grew fatter and stronger, and her tail wagged ever more vigorously. Until, one morning, three weeks later, she convulsed and died on the doorstep. We never knew what had happened. The vet said it was poison. In this country of raw energy and sudden death, we were shocked by the loss and we missed her.

The very next weekend we set off for Durban to find a puppy. The address – 'The Doggie Hotel' – caused us some mirth, but they did have a three-month-old bull terrier puppy. She was inside a secure yard, a chubby dark brindle puppy with a white face and panda eyes. She was playing with a long-coated miniature schnauzer so low to the ground that he seemed to be rolling around on wheels like a clockwork toy. The little bull terrier play-nipped every human part she could reach, then curled up on my lap with a Siamese cat and went to sleep. Obviously the ideal dog. Off we went with her clutched in my arms.

In the days that followed names were considered and discarded. 'Cuddles' was suitable now, but for a thirty-kilo adult bull terrier? Her kennel name was 'Destroya' – tempting fate. 'Tiger'? Just as bad. Finally we had it. 'Panda'. The small cuddly bear would disappear but the Panda eyes would always remain.

Panda lived up to her kennel name 'Destroya'. Her first campaign was to remove a copper pipe protruding from a concrete wall. She persevered for several hours before she fell asleep exhausted. She loved playing with bubbles from a bubble pipe, she loved chewing expensive Italian shoes and she loved KJ. She also loved nipping at ankles and legs so that I did my cooking in the kitchen wearing my green London leather boots for protection. Her love for legs, trousers and shoes extended to the bare legs and sandals of the new gardener, Emmanuel. I looked out of the kitchen door one day to see Emmanuel hopping like a demented frog from one leg to the other, as Panda made determined lunges. The faster he hopped the better fun she found it. As he hopped Emmanuel was chanting, biblically: 'Bite me not, Panda, bite me not!'

She slept in the room which had been Paddy cat's first dormitory, bursting out each morning in a 'Hello World!' explosion of delight. She and Paddycat met – with excitement on one side and watchful suspicion on the other. Paddycat clouted the small soft nose as it bounced up towards him, and proper respect was learnt.

Thembeni and Panda never connected. Thembi did not have the European attitude to animals as pets. For her, animals were strictly utilitarian. She ignored the pets, and they responded in kind, no signals sent or received. But one cold day Thembeni reacted to an animal in the house. She came to me looking very concerned, saying with saucer eyes: 'Madam, there is *something* in the bed!'

We went to look. Thembeni tiptoed nervously, fearful lest a snake had come into the house to get warm. Pretty confident of what it would be, I pulled back the blankets, and there was Paddycat who had inserted himself under the covers to sleep away a cold day.

The cold in southern Africa was a surprise. We had heard about the snow in Lesotho – so severe that little herd boys guarding the family's animals could freeze to death. While it was not as severe in Swaziland there was frost, night-watchmen needed their blankets and balaclavas, and Swazi households huddled around wood fires at night. Houses or huts without a fire would often use kerosene or paraffin heaters which were smelly and easily knocked over. Every winter brought its tragic tale of accidents and small children badly burnt by overturned heaters.

Life was a series of contrasts. Heat and cold, comfort and poverty, socialising and solitude. KJ was away two weeks out of every four. He came back to a hermit wife, who had overdosed on embroidery and fifteen different recipes for croissants, and was all agog for whatever fleshpots Swaziland could provide. After two weeks in plastic hotels KJ hankered after quiet days at home, and the pleasure of week-old 'News at Ten' bulletins every night.

Sometimes there was the diversion of a function at the Royal Palace, or at one of the big hotels. These were invariably attended by a bevy of King Sobhuza's wives. Arriving in a busload, they would descend on the function room, dressed in their orange and red *amahiyas*, and their heavy pleated cowhide skirts, wearing the beaded and braided head-dress that dignified them as married women. Speeches over, food would be served. Trays held above head height to avoid a scrum, waiters would bring in canapés, and chicken legs. To the royal wives, simple country folk who supported themselves on small-holdings, this was the high point of the evening. They would storm the trays and buffet tables, eating chicken legs at a great rate and sometimes even, I regret to say, tossing the bones over their shoulders, so that it could be politic to take shelter behind the nearest pillar. At the end of the evening, the more daring among them could sometimes be seen, going along the table, *amahiyas* outstretched like an apron, sweeping any left-overs into the fabric for a Royal Doggy Bag.

I had a taken a job with the British High Commission as administrator for the British Council Scholarship scheme – the job I had done in London but from the other end. Now I learned sympathy and understanding for those working 'In Post'. Why had I been impatient in London, when people in Africa walked miles to have documents signed by local chiefs? In Africa things take time. I also realised the king's true fatherhood of the nation. Much of the population had the royal name Dlamini and the filing cabinet was bulging with 'D's', all to be filed alphabetically. It was not royal favouritism, just the logical result of a king who, in a polygamous society, had been ruling for almost sixty years. The working environment was a small office in the bowels of the British High Commission. All a bit 'Graham Greene'. Once I received a note instructing me to 'upgrade all politically sensitive files as necessary, using "appropriately coloured labels".'

'What,' I asked myself, 'is the colour appropriate to political sensitivity? If a file becomes politically sensitive does it blush or go pale?' Hard to know.

Back at home, Panda was getting bored. Every day I would buy a large and succulent bone and give it to her before I left for work. After the first two or three she knew what it meant.

'No one to play with all morning!'

She would drop the bone and fix me with two brown bootbutton eyes in a reproachful gaze. Finally she made her point. The Scholarship office was in good order and my minuscule salary barely paid the weekly grocery bill; I wondered why I was doing this and handed in my notice.

Which left us free to look for a companion puppy for Panda. It had to be a male, so they would play together well, and it had to be a bull terrier since anyone smaller would be squashed flat. After extensive phone calls across the Transvaal to Afrikaans dog breeders I had not only found a likely pup, six months old, but had also acquired a vocabulary of bull terrier 'Afrikaaner-isms'.

'Ees a big dog, 'ees got a good 'ead.'

'You 'ave to show 'im now, 'ees a show-dog, mind!'

And 'I cawn't guarantee that 'ee won't bite the burglars, y'know!'

I was intrigued to meet these people. A white pup with the black ears was chosen, and we would meet Frikkie van Vuuren at Wits Petrol Station at ten o'clock the next Saturday.

We were there when Frikkie drove up. A burly white man with a square head and a pleasant face, he leapt out of the car and flung open the back door of his hatchback car. A burly white dog with a square head and a lugubrious expression was sitting there, hunched up and looking sorry for himself. His black ears had not yet stood up and were bolstered with sticking plaster.

I took one look at him and laughed: 'He looks exactly like a Polar Bear!'

And so Polar Bear was named, accidentally but neatly ushering in the era of the Two Bears.

He and Panda played endlessly. Their best game involved chasing each other from one end of the kitchen to the other, cannoning into the dining-room door at one end and into a concrete wall at the other. Two bull terrier puppies were going to be *a lot* more trouble than one. The green leather boots from London became twice as necessary.

The garden of the white house was large – about an acre, fenced only with strands of wire. There was no way that two mischievous bull terrier puppies could be allowed to roam free. We tired of running them on leads, being tripped up and maypoled several times a day. KJ enlisted Emmanuel to help build a 'dog corral' at the side of the house. Once there they could play on their own, we could join in the games, or – fond hope – I could take a book and recline on a sun-lounger there. To screen it from the road, the fence was lined with interlaced branches.

When the fence was finished, KJ and Emmanuel regarded it proudly.

'No one will be able to spy on Madam now, will they, Emmanuel?' said KJ.

'No,' Emmanuel agreed. 'If they do, they will know that they have sinned.'

On the whole, Panda and Polar enjoyed their corral but if they were there for too long, life became boring. One day I came home from town to find a dog-sized hole chewed in the fence, Polar Bear gone, and Panda sitting primly by the hole with a smug expression on her face.

We looked everywhere. We called, we whistled. KJ took the car and drove up and down the forest road looking for flashes of white. Emmanuel reported that Velapi, the gardener from next door, had seen him across the road. KJ went to the house over the road to look.

There he was in the garden, our white bull terrier. He came forward, growling low in his throat. Shocked at this, KJ shouted authoritatively: 'Polar, no! Bad dog! How dare you growl? Come here at once!'

Then he took a closer look. This bull terrier was pure white. He had no black ears. He was not a puppy. And he was not happy.

It was a different dog.

Sheepishly KJ backed out of the garden, making soothing noises as he went and keeping a wary eye on this poor animal who had been guarding his territory so well. He hoped the house owners hadn't seen the apparent attempt at dog-napping. A few moments later, Velapi hove into view, marching Polar Bear firmly by the collar, from down the road where he had been playing happily with a group of doggy friends.

Panda and Polar became well known characters among the office staff, particularly the drivers. The senior driver, Mr Johannes Dlamini, a stout, stocky little man, was sometimes called in to help when the dogs needed to be taken to the vet, since it was impossible for me to drive and fend off two rambunctious young bull terriers at the same time. I would sit in the back seat, between the dogs, holding each one firmly by the collar, while Mr Dlamini drove. The road to Mbabane offered many distractions – cows, goats and stray dogs, which set the dogs jumping from side to side, the better to see and give them a piece of their mind. Most often both wanted to trample across my lap to the other side simultaneously. With all this going on in the back seat, poor Mr Dlamini drove with his already short neck retracted as far as possible into his collar, trying to protect his ears from the bites he felt sure were coming. If at all possible, he would have become invisible and driven the car by remote control.

Mr Dlamini was a Swazi not only of traditional build, but of traditional values. He regarded women and animals as mere possessions – women were always minors in Swaziland law – in fact he remarked to KJ one day: 'Your woman is your dog.'

I am sure this was friendly advice to KJ, but was unclear what it implied in the way of treatment. Possibly better and firmer training, and almost certainly some beating. Fortunately KJ didn't act on it.

KJ's colleague at the Swaziland EEC office was a senior Belgian engineer. He decided to make a survey of the office cars to check on petrol consumption. The next day he went into KJ's office.

'Someone is cooking the books,' he said. 'The mileage and the petrol don't add up. One of the office cars is doing hundreds of miles every month, enough to take it to Capetown and back. It has to be Dlamini. We need to call him in and dismiss him.'

Kieran had spent many years in Africa.

'Well,' he said, 'Johannes has been with us a long time. He's a good driver. He doesn't drink. He is punctual and reliable. He always reports for duty looking immaculate. Would we get someone as good to take his place? Would you allow me to deal with it?'

Calling Mr Dlamini in, he sat him down.

'Dlamini!' he said. 'Can you believe it? Someone is stealing our petrol!'

Mr Dlamini went as ashen as a Swazi can go and his eyes opened wide.

'Yes, I knew you would be surprised,' said KJ. 'It has to be those people at the garage,' he continued.

'I want you to help me check on this. Here's what we are going to do. We are going to change to another garage, and from now on there will be three receipts every time the drivers go to get petrol. One will stay at the garage. One will be in the mileage book, and you will have one to bring back to me at the office.'

Nodding energetically with relief, Mr Dlamini agreed to the scheme.

There were no further discrepancies. Mr Dlamini continued to be the respected elder driver, growing steadily more rotund and dignified over the years.

It was only in 1989, nine years later, when we returned to Swaziland that the topic came up again.

'Ah,' said Mr Dlamini, when he met KJ again. 'That time with the petrol. You really made me a man!'

The two office drivers, Johannes Dlamini and his nephew Sam, were responsible for official driving and I used our caramel-coloured Colt Galant. Driving in Swaziland could be challenging. Speed was not an issue – problems were more likely to occur from ancient *bakkies* belching black fumes as they struggled up the Malagwane Hill. But in the rainy season, storms could blow up, changing a perfect sunny day into blinding rain and turning roads to rivers. The Golf Course Road was surfaced at that time with white clay. This rose in clouds of gritty dust in good weather, and in bad weather transmogrified into a slimy substance like a skating rink made of blancmange. After the rain car after car came to grief and be seen up against the high banks, shipwrecked at disconsolate angles, while the owners trudged for help through the white, sticky mess.

My turn came. In a frightening moment of no control, the car skidded, and with a soft crunch the left bumper and fender were embedded in the bank. The damage was considerable, and she was taken off to the town panel-beater's for repair. It happened not long before we were due to go on leave. After many broken promises it was ready at last, on the very day we caught the plane.

On the morning of D Day I went down to the panel-beater's workshop, and there she was, new, cleaned, shining, and ready. At lunchtime KJ and I went together to collect her, pay and drive her back home. We entered the workshop and my eyes automatically went to where I had seen her two hours before, dentless and pristine. There was the Caramel Colt Galant with its bonnet now dented, buckled and caved in.

A supervisor rushed over to explain. A young apprentice who couldn't drive had taken the car and rammed it up against a milk float. A thousand apologies, it would of course be fixed at no extra charge. Shaken, we left, assured that when re-repaired, it would be safely stored in its original showroom across the road. We went on overseas leave, and human nature being what it is, forgot all about it until we came back. We went to collect it, expecting to find it in a safe and shiny place, well cared for. Instead she was outside in the yard of the car dealers, looking dusty, dirty and sorry for herself with criss-crosses of scratches on her bonnet.

'Oh!' they said, with big smiles, 'The mechanics, they found it a nice place to rest their tools.'

Throughout our years in Swaziland, it was impossible to ignore the shadow of Big Brother South Africa, and the bubbling ferment of southern African affairs. The taint of apartheid infected the area. However colour-blind one might be, once landed at Jan Smuts Airport it was as if a giant pair of invisible apartheid goggles were standard issue, and one was caught in insidious categorisations of fellow human beings as 'Black', 'Coloured', 'White' and 'Indian'. 'Blankes' and 'Nie Blankes' signs were on toilets, café entrances, beaches and even park benches. Every news bulletin on South African radio was followed by its Editorial Comment, spelling out what listeners should think, always heavily critical of liberal United Nations initiatives. Censorship was rife. Woe betide anyone rash enough to engage in a political conversation with an Afrikaaner. Stories were told of copies of Plato's *Republic* being confiscated by suspicious Afrikaaner border guards with the question: 'Who is this chap Plato?'

The new Commission Delegate in Lesotho wanted to bring his parrot from Lesotho. It was agreed – providing the parrot did not say anything against the 'Regime'.

Once a British protectorate and now once more an independent kingdom, Swaziland was a valid political entity. But in the mind of its mightier neighbour South Africa, it was a convenient holiday resort, not far above a 'Bantustan' in dignity and self-determination. South African money had built hotel/casino complexes, an international golf course, and a spa near a hot spring – the 'Cuddle Puddle', where the good burghers of the Transvaal could relax and disport themselves with Swazi maidens. The fact that in Swazi culture it was incorrect for a woman to refuse a request from a man made the girls an easy mark. In the 1960s prostitution was rife, until King Sobhuza made it illegal to approach any young girl wearing the *umcwasho* – a red tasselled sash. The wearing of trousers was a mark of a prostitute, and to this day, trousers are regarded as slightly questionable attire in the kingdom.

Swaziland too was the home of a large and bustling industrial site, in the warm low veldt near the business capital, Manzini. There, under the guise of encouraging Swazi industry and giving employment to Swazis, large South African firms had set up factories so that products could be exported to Britain and Europe free of customs embargos because of the added value of Swazi labour.

There were also sundry 'safe houses' in Swaziland for ANC members on the run. Some escaped, some did not. Big Brother BOSS (Bureau of State Security) kept a wary eye on the kingdom, and many an episode of apartheid-era cops and robbers' drama came to a conclusion – happy or tragic – in these hills and valleys.

In this turbulent time, one of Swaziland's neighbours was becoming a hot topic. Rhodesia, under Ian Smith, was a mysterious country to the north, a country in the grip of civil war, living under a blanket of UDI (Unilateral Declaration of Independence) and sanctions. We had not visited it and knew no one who had. But in December 1979, amid much rejoicing, the Lancaster House Agreement was signed, an agreement between ZAPU (Zimbabwe African People's Union – Joshua Nkomo), and ZANU PF (Zimbabwe African National Union – Robert Mugabe) and the Rhodesian government, represented at that time by Bishop Abel Muzorewa and Ian Smith. It signalled the end of white rule in Rhodesia, soon to be renamed Zimbabwe.

At the conference, £650,000,000 was pledged for recon-struction and development in the new Zimbabwe. European aid money flowed in for the resettlement of refugees, for agricultural development, co-operatives, and education. Salisbury – or Harare, as it would become – was the logical base for a travelling 'Training Advisor'. KJ went to Salisbury for a conference and came back enraptured with the city, its new spirit of hope and optimism, and the possibility of living there.

In 1980 final elections were held, won overwhelmingly by Robert Mugabe's radical Zimbabwe African National Union, or ZANU PF. For Africans this was a foregone conclusion, but pundits from the West who hoped for a ZAPU victory had not factored in tribal ratios or intimidation. Despite misgivings about Mr Mugabe's socialist beliefs, omens seemed good. His rival, big Joshua Nkomo was to be included in government. Europeans were brought into the new administration 'so as to bring about a government that will be reassuring to all people of Zimbabwe'.

After ten years in exile Mugabe returned. His victory was greeted with shouts of joy, and crowds of people thronged the streets, crowing like cockerels – the Party symbol. Ian Smith told the BBC that he expected people to act in a mature, responsible way, and apart from a few acts of vandalism on the part of departing white Rhodesians, they did. Thanks to the enterprising spirit of Zimbabweans, the years of UDI had left the country with the world's only self-sufficient economy. Already known as the 'bread-basket of Southern Africa', all looked set fair for Zimbabwe to become a shining example for independent African nations.

It was decided. The post of EC Training Advisor for southern Africa would move from Swaziland to Zimbabwe. KJ paid another visit to Salisbury, and chose a house, returning even more enthusiastic. We prepared to move.

Moving house is said to be the third most stressful activity that can befall human beings – after the death of a spouse and divorce. Tearing apart a lovingly created home and packing the remnants into boxes, saying goodbye to friends, turning one's back on the fabric of a life laboriously built up over a period of years, sears the soul. It is not only goodbye to a house, but to a whole country and a network of familiar faces, to a culture that is known and loved, and to pathways trodden up and down in that environment, worn to a comfort for living. One loses the sounds of the night, the song of the rainbird, the squeak of the gate, the particular scent of a dry wind in winter. And despite smaller house-moves in the past, this was our first major move to another country in Africa.

KJ made strong travelling kennels for Panda and Polar, putting in enough screws to restrain two lions. We learned about shortages in Zimbabwe. The local wine could be dubious, we were told, tinned fish was unobtainable, medicines might be scarce, and chocolate was of poor quality. We stocked up on these 'essentials', three tenders were put out to packers, and on the day appointed, the chosen ones rolled up in their gigantic van to begin work. Woefully naïve, we imagined that these nice men from Johannesburg would move politely into our home, and pack our goods neatly without us having to do a thing.

They did indeed stream into the house, packing with energy and enthusiasm in every room. Rolls of white newsprint were strewn everywhere, cartons, packing tape, crates – the entire household became a packing factory. The pets were locked away. Boxes were ferried out the door and into the van in a steady stream. When night fell, KJ drove earnestly into Mbabane to the hamburger restaurant and bought the men boxes of hamburgers for their evening meal. The van disappeared and we saw it that night, parked in a lay-by on the edge of Mbabane containing our entire material lives.

The next day the van was locked and driven away. We spent a dismal grey time with Thembeni sweeping up the aftermath of paper shavings and cardboard flotsam that remained, and picking up all the small objects inevitably left behind by packers. It only remained to give the dogs their tranquillisers for the plane.

Their travelling boxes stood open and ready on the back porch. I slipped tranquillisers into little pats of butter and they went down easily. I felt a heel. Polar Bear crawled into his travelling box for a little nap. Panda, on the other hand, wanted to chase lizards. On that hot, humid afternoon she scampered everywhere, refusing like a naughty child to admit that she was tired. She chased, and ch–a–s–ed and cha–a–a . . . until she staggered and went to sleep on the spot.

Their kennels were put onto the back of a small truck. Paddy-cat was posted quickly and protestingly into his smart varnished travelling box. Big green eyes looked out accusingly. We set off for the airport. En route down the mountain there were a hundred and twenty three meows. As we waited, three forlorn little travelling boxes sat alone in the middle of the tarmac. I panicked non-stop until KJ spoke to the Irish Airport manager who promised that he would, with his own hands, place those three precious boxes on the plane. And that was the last we saw of them that day. With leaden stomachs we watched the plane take off, and turned back to Mbabane to begin the long drive to Zimbabwe.

3

Zimbabwe, Living in a Time Warp

The clock stopped in Salisbury on 11th November 1965, with the declaration of UDI.* As we drove into the city in September 1981, we drove backwards in time. Independence had been declared in 1980. Elections had been held. The streets were full of cars from the '60s – shining Morris Minors, Morris Oxfords and Austin panel vans, repaired, repainted and cherished. Ladies in hats and pink make-up drove sedately to coffee mornings, gently weaving from lane to lane. Manners were old-fashioned and courteous. Closed to the world for more than a decade, the 1960s had solidified, and with it the assumption of white superiority.

Young people wearing flared jeans played the guitar on street corners. White ladies dressed up and alighted from their large cars, wearing high heels and pantihose under the hot sun. An evening at the theatre called for pearls, crystal beads, cocktail dresses and even furs. Something bothered me. And then I had it. Fresh as I was from class-ridden Britain, the social signals were askew. These working-class matrons, the wives of post-war settlers with their new money and stiff hairdos were playing the role of the upper-class ladies they had observed back in Britain. A new social group had evolved.

Some local young women came in Amazonian mould; large,

---

* The Rhodesian Front party, led by Ian Smith, opposed the principles of universal suffrage and majority rule, and made a Unilateral Declaration of Independence. The country was cut off and under trade sanctions from 1965 until 1979.

florid and stolid, sporting luxuriant mops of feminine Holly-wood hair, full skirts and stiletto heels. Their ex-army escorts, crop-haired, sunburnt and muscular, wore shorts and long socks pulled up over rugby-players' calves. And sometimes a comb in the socks.

Young Shona girls were tall and slim with hourglass figures and a ready smile.

In the city, restaurants served large plates of elaborate food, stuffed, sauced and garnished They were staffed by legions of polite waiters – always African, and often in the middle of immaculately starched table linen reposed a bottle of vinegar and some tomato sauce in a red tomato-shaped holder.

Shop windows were a 1960s' revelation – console radios with fretwork panels, 'stereograms' with large unwieldy speakers and turntables, furniture upholstered in 1960s' brown tweed checks with huge wagon-wheel armrests. Bars and drinks cabinets abounded in the shape of pirates' galleons and Afrikaaner trek wagons complete with twinkling lights.

Tools were home-made and far sturdier than in Europe. Buckets, wheelbarrows, saucepans and stoves were solid iron and 'made in Zimbabwe', as they had been in 1965. Nothing was imported, and the shops were three-quarters full of soap, cosmetics, perfumes and toothpaste in endearingly home-made wrappers.

There were local fabrics in chintz, there were comfortable shoes and sandals made from local leather, and many efficient shoe repair shops. There were antique and second-hand shops displaying china, old military medals and jewellery – sold to finance the disillusioned 'rat-run' of nervous white Rhodesians who, having fought the 'terrorists', felt that discretion was the better part of valour now that those terrorists had transmogrified into 'freedom fighters'.

Shortages there were, and the local population were used to them. I soon learned, if oil appeared on the shelves, to buy two bottles, not one, and to keep a keen ear to the grocery grapevine so as to join any queues that might form.

Enraged tones rose loudly behind me in the supermarket queue one day, from a pair of fierce matrons, saying: 'There was cheese and I *missed* it!'

Small boys sold intricately wrought wire bicycles, and carvers arranged their wares on the pavements. There was no begging. People politely offered well-made craft work for sale and took no for an answer. African women in headscarves and aprons worked on complex crochet work as they crossed the street, gossiping as they went. Snowy forests of handmade bedspreads hung from trees and embossed macramé hangings dotted the street corners. And then, there was Shona sculpture – green, black and grey stone carvings, in flowing contemporary shapes, representing ancient myths, spiritual truths, emotions and poetry, and sometimes just the essence of a smile or an animal.

In this Rip van Winkle land, it was as if we were moving in some enchantment. There was a fizzy lightness in the air, a bubble of optimism and hope. Far from sensing any darkness from the war or chips on shoulders, there was a prevailing sense of joy and relief that it was over. Shona people in the street politely clapped their hands the correct number of times in traditional greeting. On the TV propaganda messages encouraged co-operation in the new Zimbabwe. We danced the streets, glorying in the smiles around us.

Our first stop on arrival was Philippa's Kennels on the out-skirts of the city. Run by a dynamic Italian couple, to cater for the needs of the European settlers, it housed a breathtaking 1,000 dogs. Each breed was kept in a separate line of runs, fed and exercised by kennel-hands called 'boys' who specialised in one kind of dog – spaniels, great Danes, or, in our case, bull terriers. We asked Ebenezer, their carer, how he liked his job.

'I like dogs better than people,' he replied encouragingly.

The dogs were ecstatic to see us, in a bull terrier sort of way.

Panda spent her time bouncing like a rubber ball to see the dogs next door, and had barked herself into laryngitis. As we left, promising them freedom soon, Polar Bear gazed mournfully through the wire. Paddycat, in the cattery, looked depressed. But it was not as bad as it seemed. As I crouched in his pen, comforting him, I narrowly missed being fed a spoonful of mince cooked in Bovril as the pretty, curly-haired wife of the owner did her afternoon rounds.

We stayed at the old Jameson Hotel until our goods arrived. It was the epitome of 1960s' comfort, with its dark swirly carpets and wood panelling, and its courteous dark-suited staff. In the Sandawana Coffee Shop, local coffee was served in thick local china, and the local light fittings were made in the form of green jewels like the vibrant green of the local Sandawana emeralds.

We spent every evening at the house KJ had chosen to rent in Avondale, north of the city. A large house on King George Road, it was painted lime green, and the high wall enclosed a mature shady garden with plenty of room for the dogs. At one end of the lawn was a blue kidney-shaped swimming pool where a white stone fish gushed water at the flick of a switch. I felt guiltily thrilled at so much luxury, but since pools were almost standard issue in Zimbabwe, it seemed silly to reject the good things that life was offering. Refusing to use the pool would not improve living conditions in the African townships. Employing house staff would. And we would need them. The house was large with acres of golden mustard-coloured carpet, it had a long brick patio shaded by pine trees and a shiny black-tiled kitchen.

One evening after work, after putting up rails in preparation for our wooden-ringed curtains, we decided to visit a Greek restaurant just down the road near the 'Rainbow 7 Arts' cinema and shopping complex. Sitting in the cheerful hubbub, blame-lessly eating our moussaka, we were aware of a rowdy table of gigantic white Rhodesians downing mountainous plates of spare ribs with their beer. A shout went up, as someone came through the door, and we turned to recognise Ian Smith fearlessly coming to join the table. I began to wonder how this much loved and much hated ex-leader of Rhodesia could walk freely in the new Zimbabwe without danger. Imagination conjured up a bullet-spraying assassin coming through the door any minute to take him out. As I ate, my shoulders hunched defensively lower and lower, as I prepared to duck, almost ending the meal with my face in my food bowl.

The household goods arrived. Impatient to be off, the Johannesburg Transport Company's drivers insisted that we sign receipts stating that everything had been received in good order. Faced with an entire container-load of closed boxes this was a difficult attestation to make. New to the game, we agreed and signed. Big mistake.

We unpacked. Our friends, those nice men from Jo'burg had packed on a 'one for us, one for them' basis. The carefully stocked wine had vanished. As had dresses, shoes, tablecloths and suits in bright colours, electrical goods, and – for some reason this rankled – my cooking chocolate. We wrote an aggrieved letter to the forwarding agents in Johannesburg. The letter that arrived in return was the ultimate disclaimer. It put the blame squarely on our shoulders, saying curtly: 'You would not leave liquor and other possessions out in the street in Johannesburg and expect them not to be stolen.'

Evening work continued in the house. One night we returned late to the Jameson, ravenously hungry, too exhausted even to think of going to the Sandawana Coffee Shop for a sandwich. We collapsed on the bed, uncertain whether we were too tired to eat or too hungry to sleep. There was a knock at the door. A discreet bow-tied waiter pushed in a trolley. There under a silver dome were two thick steaks, vegetables, salad, bread rolls, apple pie, cream and coffee. And a bottle of wine. It was like Ratty's picnic in *The Wind in the Willows.* We didn't hesitate. We signed the chit as fast as possible and fell on the food, trusting to Providence to provide a substitute meal for whoever had ordered this food, and not to leave them cross and hungry too long.

Once moved in, we met Jane Nyamararo, our solemn new housekeeper, who had worked for the previous owners of the lime-green house, and who inhabited the staff quarters. She lived with her husband Wyson Dixon (also known as Dixon Wyson) who went once a year to spend time with his 'other wife' in Malawi. A comfortably built lady of middle age, Jane approached us cautiously. Every new set of employers is different and Jane had no idea what we might do. It is easy to forget that local staff too, have issues of adjustment. Expatriates come and go, bringing with them new expectations, new rules, new boundaries and new recipes. Employers were leaving the country after Independence, and jobs were precious. There were queues of fifty hopeful people clutching references at every house where a domestic vacancy had been advertised. Jane valued her position, and we were prepared to value Jane. Asked to choose someone she would like to work with, she brought along Lyson Chingwena to be the gardener. A stunningly handsome and well-built young man with a small scar on his lip, Lyson had an open smile that could have melted snow.

It was time for the pets to arrive. They were delivered to the house in the white van from Philippa's Kennels, painted with pictures of playful puppies and kittens. When the van drew up it was rocking with their enthusiasm, and Panda's white-tipped brindle tail was gaily waving. The dogs gave us a cursory greeting, and disappeared at the gallop, more or less waving their hats, round and round the house and garden.

Jane was *very* dubious. These, after all were bull terriers, known in Zimbabwe as 'The *veryterribledogs*'. She firmly barricaded herself in the kitchen, peeping out over the stable half-door at the veryterribles. Unfortunately she had left her shoes neatly outside the door. They were swooped up, energetically shaken to death and carried off in two different directions. Finally Panda could bear it no longer. There was another lovely person to meet. She took a running jump at the half door, teetered on the top of it, and launched herself into the kitchen straight into Jane's unwilling arms. She did it twice, just to perfect the hurdling technique, and went off to plan future pole-vaulting.

Meantime, Lyson was calmly cleaning the swimming pool with a brush on a very long pole. Panda galloped round the corner and recognised the brush as a deadly enemy. She pounced on it, uttering yodelling growls in an attempt to subdue it. Lyson, alarmed, gave up the job with alacrity, and we walked to the other side of the pool to discuss the garden. Panda wanted to join us. She had never seen a pool before, and naturally assumed that the quickest way to reach us was to walk across. So she set out to walk on the water. Suddenly she was swimming, her front legs flailing up and down, a surprised expression on her upturned little face. We hoisted her out trying to conceal our hilarity. She did a figure-eight shake, and went off, muttering to herself that she'd never do *that* again.

It was a long and exciting day for everyone. Humans appeared and reappeared from strange doors, leaving mystified dogs wondering where to gallop to next. They discovered which were the reddest and muddiest paths from A to B and wore permanent auburn paws. Panda almost caught a bird. Polar frightened himself by executing a splendid backwards bumps-a-daisy in the kitchen with the cat.

After work, KJ came home. We were keen to try out our first ever pool. We put on bathing suits and jumped in. The dogs went frantic with anxiety. What were we doing? Were we drowning? They dashed up and down barking hysterically. In a desperate attempt to save us, Polar Bear jumped in and got the coldest and wettest shock of his life. Even more bravely, since she already knew how awful it was, Panda followed. Spluttering with laughter, we swam them to the steps, got them out, dried them off, and had a serious conversation to explain that this was just something that humans did. They seemed to get the point. From then on, whenever we swam, they just acted cool and left us to get on with it.

Finally, when the fuss had died down we made a cup of tea. After a while, we noticed that Polar Bear was not with us. We called and searched. Panda sat looking smug as if she knew something but just went on enjoying some uninterrupted petting all to herself. After half an hour we found him – or at least his little sturdy legs and hind quarters, tail thumping apologetically. The rest was stuck firmly under the car. With a heave he was free and was extracted, sheepish and oily. As he emerged from the right-hand side, Panda crawled under from the left to see what it was like.

The dog kennels were installed in their traditional place outside the kitchen door. In time, Jane became resigned to them – even fond. Panda developed new tricks. On cold winters' nights the dogs had two rough grey blankets each. On frosty mornings I would find Panda tucked up in all four of them, boot-button eyes peeping out, while poor, slow Polar Bear shivered on the bare boards of his kennel. On sunny days, Panda would drag her two blankets out and spread them on the grass. She would take up her position stretched out in the sunshine, for all the world as if she was sunbathing. Only the sunglasses were lacking.

The proximity of the kennels to the kitchen door had its drawbacks. One morning I was at the sink when Polar Bear stuck his big white head around the door. Seeing him out of the corner of my eye I chirped brightly: 'Hello, Beautiful Boy!'

Unfortunately I had not seen that Lyson was hard on his heels.

'Hello, Madam,' he replied, to my intense embarrassment. Whatever did he think?

As the house took shape, I learned the routine of days in Salisbury. Early in the morning, the symphony of birds began.

There are 650 species in Zimbabwe, and it sounded as if a large percentage were in the front garden. Warblers, thrush, tree creepers, wrens, tiny yellow weaver birds with their hanging nests, and louries – flashing green with scarlet under their wings. People were already astir on the roads, walking to work in canvas shoes with a soft swishing noise. Domestic workers like Jane were used to arriving at 6am to make tea for their European employers. This we did not want, but she liked to come in early to her smart black kitchen, to prepare grapefruit for breakfast, without a single strand of pith – her proudest culinary accomplishment. Jane said she liked to work.

'Madam, I get weak if I am not working,' she told me.

When the time came to discuss when Jane should take her holiday she was undecided: 'Madam, I will go to my house and I will think nice!' she said. Such a useful expression. We find ourselves using it often and always think of Janey when we do.

As the morning wore on a colonial procession of callers came to the iron front gate and rang the big brass bell. At 7.30am 'The Milk Boy' arrived on his bicycle, selling milk from a coolbox. He was followed by 'The Bread Boy' with fresh bread and cakes, 'The Butcher's Boy' with his meat delivery, and 'The Post Boy', bringing the first post of the day, all wearing smart uniforms and caps, and ringing loud bicycle bells.

In the house I was introduced to the concept of 'Rations'. This, Jane explained, was the custom of paying staff partly in kind. Tea, sugar, flour, oil, tinned pilchards, meat and toilet paper must be made up into plastic bags and issued each week from the larder. It meant that price rises in basic foods were absorbed by the employer. Things would change, edicts would be issued so that domestic employees would be paid more, and the paternalistic ration system would cease. Salaries would rise, but so would prices.

Jane was pleased when she was made custodian of the larder

and given all the keys. She was even happier when I found an advertisement for a cookery school called 'Dom Cook' (Domestic Cook) and eagerly accepted the offer to be enrolled at the classes. Off she went every week and came back glowing with excitement at what she had learned. During the week we were regaled with delicacies of ever-increasing difficulty. From 'eggs, poached, boiled, scrambled and fried,' we progressed to 'fruit cake', 'poor man's turkey', 'corn patties', 'scones' and Jane's rock buns. Always fondly pronounced 'lock buns', these were infallibly good and requested for every possible occasion. Jane loved to watch them cooking through the glass door of the oven, exclaiming: 'Madam, my cakes, they are growing up!'

With all this cooking, I needed to come to terms with the living-in-the-moment immediacy of southern African philosophy. In the beginning I could be caught out. I would ask, as I went out the door: 'Jane, do we need any flour or sugar today?'

'No, Madam.' Jane would reply, and off I would go to the shop.

On my return, Jane would be waiting with the empty sugar bowl in her hand.

'Madam, there is no sugar!'

'But Jane,' I would say, 'I asked you this morning if we had any sugar!'

'Ah Madam,' would come the reply, 'But this morning there *was* sugar!'

Even worse, of course was the response if I should be so silly as to say: 'Jane, haven't you got any sugar?' which would bring the reply: 'Yes!' and I would retire from the kitchen wondering if it was a 'Yes, I have' or a 'Yes I haven't'.

Janey firmly spoke her own brand of English, infinitely better than my Shona. Flour became 'frow', bacon became 'bocon' and one day when it was 'fleezing', poor Jane was 'rocked' out of the kitchen. The letter 'r' does not exist in the Shona alphabet.

She delighted me one day by saying, as she sniffed by the dustbin: 'Madame, I hear a horrible smell!'*

There were other signs too that English in Zimbabwe was different from elsewhere. In the local supermarket a lavish display of cakes was labelled in best French: 'Gatox!' At the Health Food Shop, they sold 'Hole Meal Flour'. At the Lake MacIlwaine Game Park a sign pointed to 'R. Boretum', and the Chinese restaurant down the road advertised 'Heavenly Fried Rice'. At a small vegetable shop I bought a selection of vegetables from a slim young Moslem woman in a hijab – tomatoes, onions, garlic, green pepper and courgettes. As she totted up the list, her face broke into a delighted smile.

'I know what you're going to make!' she said. 'You're going to make Ratta-Tootle!'

Lyson's language, on the other hand, was influenced by both his sincere church-going, and his studies of English. Whenever possible he liked to use rounded sentences and long words. One day, when the weather looked uncertain, it occurred to me that Lyson, being Zimbabwe-born, might be a 'fundi'† on the weather.

'Lyson,' I asked, 'is it going to rain?'

He leant on his rake in the middle of the lawn, and looked up at the sky. After a longish pause he said, in an oracular voice: 'Otherwise . . . sometimes!'

From time to time the staff went on an outing. We knew this was in the offing when Lyson's best pin-striped dark suit was energetically washed and hung upside down and inside out on the clothes-line.

One weekend Lyson, Jane and Jane's husband all went together to the races. On their return, late in the afternoon, I caught Lyson as he went past the kitchen window.

---

* Bantu languages have a concept meaning to 'sense' or 'perceive', so that the real translation would be 'I sense a horrible smell.'

† 'Fundi' – one who is an expert – from 'funda' – to learn.

'Lyson, how did Janey enjoy the races?' I asked.

Once more, Lyson drew himself up to his full height, as he pronounced: 'Jane rejoiced greatly at the running of the horses!'

Sometimes I needed to stop and think about how my requests must appear to the staff. Why, for instance, would we want several different knives and forks on the table, in a particular order? Who could know what these mad Europeans might want next?

One day Polar Bear was on the rampage. He killed a bath sponge and an oven glove and severely frightened a furry hot water bottle. The latter was brought in from the garden by Lyson with a faintly querying expression on his face. For all he knew these weird people might actually want to keep it in the garden!

Outside the house in the new Zimbabwe life was hopeful. Robert Mugabe had taken heed of advice from Samora Machel in Mozambique, and had offered European public servants a pension incentive to stay in the country for five years, while replacements were trained. The television was awash with news of aid projects. Agritek farming projects and co-operative schemes were under way in the rural areas. There was talk of a new veterinary faculty at the university, water projects, rural dams and new schools. People were hopeful that *this* time, *this* African country, with all its advantages and its positive balance of payments, would be a success and an inspiration to the rest of the continent. After all, it was known as the 'food bowl of southern Africa', and fed millions of people outside its borders. What could possibly go wrong? How could we see the future?

October brought the jacaranda season. Double avenues of these gorgeous trees were hung with purple bells and after a shower of rain, the roads were carpeted with blue. The streets were a procession of colour, lined with spreading red flamboyants and poncianas or pink bauhinias with their camel's foot shaped leaves. Luxuriant red, pink and orange bougainvillea and purple petrea gushed and foamed over garden walls, and in the garden, 'Yesterday, today and tomorrow' bushes bloomed starry with purple, pale blue and white flowers all at once.

Change was afoot at the office. KJ's jovial tennis-playing boss departed with his chic wife. The new Head of Mission would arrive at midnight. As usual on such occasions, office personnel were on parade at the airport to greet him, lining the red carpet, all decked out in best saluting gear. After the respectful greetings the new Delegate, a strong-disciplined German, and his wife, a statuesque blonde, disappeared to the cargo section of the airport, and reappeared pulled by Nira and Gongo, their German shepherd dogs. KJ was good with all dogs, not only bull terriers, so he offered to help. This meant accompanying new German Delegate and German shepherd dogs to the Kennels at midnight, waking up the night-watchman and explaining in Zulu that these dogs *must* live together in the same run. The new Delegate watched with interest. After it was over and the dogs were settled in he asked: 'What language was that?'

'Zulu,' KJ replied. 'Sindebele, a form of old Zulu is spoken in the south of the country.'

'Ah so!' was the response. 'So you will be a useful member of staff then!'

Not only was KJ henceforth to be Delegation Dog Man it seemed, but also a consultant on all things linguistic and southern African. Perhaps it would stand him in good stead.

Christmas in Salisbury was celebrated in traditional English style. Sweating choirs in every church sang Christmas carols about snow, the shops were full of holly and Santa Claus, and large, hot meals, devised for a northern winter, were cooked and served. Christmas presents or 'bonselas' were given to staff. Churches, big and small, went into top gear. Local church groups in their white robes, trimmed with blue, red or green, marched to services. Zionist bishops paraded in the multi-coloured robes and bright mitres revealed to them in dreams.

The cheerful butcher on Second Street Extension who had trained in Smithfield, London, advertised his 'Luxury Stuff.' This proved to be apricots, inside a chicken, inside a duck, inside a turkey. Jolly and joking in his striped blue and white apron, he was set off when I rashly asked him: 'Do you have a liver?'

'I hope so!' he replied and promptly told the story of a little boy who phoned him every Christmas, saying: 'Is that the butcher?'

'Yes.'

'Do you have a pig's head?'

'Yes.'

'You must look very funny! Ha ha ha!'

The dear man concluded: 'I'll be so disappointed if one year he doesn't phone. I'll know he's grown up.'

We invited the new Delegate, Mr D, and his wife Reinhild for Christmas dinner together with our Zimbabwean friend May Davey, her husband Chris, like a young and handsome Henry VIII, and their minute and dainty daughter Lorna. Mr D was delighted with the chance to grill some real live Zimbabweans about the political situation. One day KJ would realise how valuable such contacts could be when testing the water of a new posting. I cooked a 'Luxury Stuff' which was carved with ceremony and served on our earthenware plates. It went well, though Paddycat sat on the boss's lap and activated his hay-fever. Then in return we were invited to the Delegate's residence. Dazzled by the official white linen, the crystal and silver, I was covered with embarrassment at my earthenware efforts and didn't dare invite them again. Reinhild, an artist who loved simplicity, never understood why. Neither did I, until years later when I too was puzzled by the lack of invitations from junior staff. Only then did I realise how lonely the job at the top could be.

There was a chance to enrol for a BSc in Psychology at the University of Zimbabwe, something I had always wanted to do. Set north of the city, the modern campus was abuzz with new students. Standards were high and the staff list read like an international academic conference. Until Independence, examinations had been marked by external examiners from the University of London. Now the air was full of new courses and ideas for the new Zimbabwe. As in the city outside, there was excitement in the air. It was going to be fun.

In early 1982, just as the university term was due to begin, the Beira pipeline was blown up by the ANC near Mozambique, despite being guarded by the Zimbabwean army and South African troops. Since this was the source of Zimbabwe's fuel, it was the signal for panic, petrol rationing and queues. We were in London at the time. May phoned to say, 'Bring bikes. There is going to be a petrol shortage!' We chose two strong green three-geared jobs from a bicycle shop in Notting Hill, and stowed the huge cartons in a London taxi. The trolley at the airport was a sight, as were the porters' faces, but we talked our way onto the British Airways plane.

Once assembled and in operation they were a joy. In the midst of the fuel crisis cars had to be registered with a garage to buy any petrol at all, and queues stretched three times around the block. As most garages only had enough petrol to sell for two hours once a week, drivers would leave their cars in the queue on Friday or Saturday, ready for the Monday morning opening time, sometimes paying domestic staff to stay there in their stead. As I wrote at the time: 'The Government is doing something about the petrol supply, though no one seems quite sure what. Objectors seem more concerned with the principle of *not* approaching South Africa for help, than with getting anything positive done. No doubt the Beira pipeline is being repaired, but equally likely, it will be blown up again the following week!'

All Zimbabweans who could, took to their bikes. Second-hand machines were unobtainable, and new ones very rare. Even basic models were far beyond most local budgets. Poorer people, as always, suffered from the decreased numbers of buses on the roads, and the trudge to work in the early morning light began even earlier. On the outskirts of the city, before dawn, the rhythmic swish and tramp of feet could be heard in even larger numbers.

Despite the seriousness of the situation there was a feeling of mild eccentricity about it all. A bike is such a happy thing. Wind through the hair! I really felt that I should wear a bicycling hat with a feather in it, and sing a special bike-riding song. It always put me in a good mood – something to do with recapturing schooldays. 'Didn't we have a loverly day the day we went to Bangor!' and 'Daisy Daisy . . . !' gave way on really tough hills, to a grim repetition of 'Shapely legs, shapely legs, shapely legs!'

Pedalling along with three-speed gears, on the city-wide bicycle paths, I learned cycle path protocol. Whenever I rang my bell, to warn pedestrians that I was coming, they panicked, scattered and fell about under the wheels in terror. Much better to creep up behind them unheralded since at least then, they continued in a straight line and there was a chance of avoiding them.

Bicycle riding had other dangers for Shona speakers too. Respectful greetings in the Shona culture involve a series of formal hand claps. One day Wyson Dixon – Jane's husband – arrived at the front gate at the same moment as I did. With innate courtesy he began the Shona greeting, took both hands off the handlebars to clap – and promptly fell off his bike!

One solution to the fuel shortage was to add large quantities of ethanol. The question of whether this was a potentially explosive mixture much exercised letter-writers to the *Herald*. After a speedy run the ethanol-spiked fuel had a nasty habit of vaporising in the carburettor. Until all this happened I had never to my knowledge seen a carburettor, like Gwendolyn in *The Importance of Being Ernest*, who was thankful that she had never seen a spade. Now when the car choked up I had to start the engine, keep the accelerator pedal pressed down *and prime the carburettor* from a gin bottle kept in the boot. All at the same time. Sometimes it worked. If it didn't, I resorted to looking blonde and helpless. And if that failed, the only option was to start walking. This was not such a bad idea. It was so unusual to see a relatively well-dressed young European woman walking along a main road that almost immediately a car would draw up and offer a lift. And such was the feeling of trust and mutual help in those post-Independence days that I had no hesitation in accepting.

We grew used to the vagaries of ethanol fuel. As the year progressed, there were some important markers. In March 1982, two years after Independence, Salisbury was officially renamed Harare, a Shona word meaning 'the one who does not sleep', to great rejoicing in some quarters, and muttered discontent among the diehards. The main street in the city was renamed 'Samora Machel Avenue' after the President of Mozambique, and the first rumours of State-inspired violence in the south and west of the country began to filter through to Harare.

KJ was deeply disturbed about these rumours when first he heard them. He rushed to his boss, Mr D, international lawyer and Delegate of the Old School. He listened to KJ's impassioned pleas that a report should be written and heard him out. Then he thought deeply, took a puff on his pipe, and delivered a lesson in conservative 'wait and see' diplomacy: 'Where did this happen?'

'Did you go there?'

'How many people were killed?'

'Have you counted the bodies, Mr O'Cuneen?'

What could KJ say? Reports were eventually written by many

people. As we now know only too well the killings were a chilling sign of things to come. It has been alleged that up to 20,000 Amandebele were killed at that time.

But for most people, life still went on as normal. We had become used to the idea that we were living in a land where there would be a hot wet summer and a cool, even cold, dry winter, when lawns dried up and aloes bloomed. Summer rains usually poured down at 1pm, as workers were coming out of their offices. This year it didn't happen. Zimbabwe was heading for a drought. Water became headline news in newspapers and on the TV. In the rural areas people carried buckets for miles. In the cities the preoccupation was wastage. Articles were written on the iniquity of running taps. Teeth were to be cleaned in a cup of water and babies bathed in a small dish. Each house had a 'water ration'. We assiduously read the water meter at the end of each day, and kept a graph of consumption. Sometimes we saved so much that we could give a treat to a favourite tree or plant before the official civic meter reader came at the end of the month. Any household that went over the top was severely fined. Do it twice and the water would be cut off. Public taps left on were 'named and shamed' in the press. Shower water was kept, and used for washing, then for flushing the toilets or to water the vegetables and a few precious plants. Swimming pools became unusable chlorinated reservoirs, and evaporated slowly in the heat. Tales were told of ambassadorial and presidential receptions where long lines of VIPs queued up at the men's toilets, faced with stern warnings against flushing pasted on the august toilet doors. Rhymes began to be bandied about: 'If it's yellow, let it mellow; if it's brown, flush it down.' No one was exempt.

In time parsimony with water became a habit which was just as well, since the drought lasted for three years. Lawns and gardens dried up and the Botanical Gardens were brown. In rural areas crops were failing, and food aid was needed from the

National Maize Reserve. Jane was less than happy when white mealie meal ran out and she had to make do with yellow. Thin cattle bonily cropped at dry twigs and thorn bushes. Lake MacIlwaine, the town's water reserve, was a dry and cracked lake where people could walk out for hundreds of yards, and pull stranded floundering fish from the stagnant puddles by hand.

Finally, in the summer of 1984 rain began to fall. There seemed to be no sun at all, just rain, light or heavy, day and night. To those who had lived through the years of dying animals, crops and gardens, every drop that fell was a benison. Never mind that the clogged gutters caused the roof to leak and buckets of water were pouring through the light fittings. Trees and gardens were drinking in moisture. Children were out splashing in the puddles. People walked in the rain, so glad to see it that they didn't bother to wear dustbin liner raincoats, or plastic bags on their heads. Every day the newspaper and TV were filled with speculation as to whether the MacIlwaine dam would overflow.

Early in February 1985 it happened. One Sunday morning we went, together with half of Harare, to see the water flow over. The lake where people had pulled fish out by hand was now full. Treetops showed above the water and the jetty was barely visible. Near the spillway hundreds of people were picnicking, groups singing, ululating, dancing, shouting or drinking champagne. Leaning over, we could see large fish tobogganing down with the overflowing water, sparkling silver in the sun. We felt that we truly belonged. At least a bit of the rejoicing had to be due to our bricks in the toilet and miserly counting of water units. We had done our bit!

Jane's Famous Rock Buns

450 g (1 lb) plain or cake flour, 230g (8oz) sugar, 3 tspn baking powder, 3 eggs, 230g (8oz) margarine, ½ tspn mixed spice, 450g (1lb) mixed fruit, milk, ½ tspn cinnamon, ½ tspn salt.

Rub margarine into sieved flour and baking powder. Add sugar and then fruit. Mix well and add cinnamon, mixed spice and salt. Add beaten eggs and enough milk to make mixture moist (may not need any). Using a teaspoon and a fork, place mixture in rocky heaps on a greased baking tray and bake in a hot oven at 450°F(230°C) for 10–15 minute. They will be slightly soft when you take them out but will harden as they cool.

Poor Man's Turkey

450g (1lb) beef mince, minced chicken or corned beef, 1 large onion, 1 egg, 2 slices of bread, salt, pepper and herbs to taste.

Mince the meat, onion and bread together. Add salt, pepper, herbs and egg to bind. Place on a baking tray and shape into a loaf. Put 3 slices of bacon on top. Roast with potatoes in cooking oil, basting well until cooked. Cook at 200°C for 30 minutes.

Banana Fritters

110g (4oz) plain flour, ½ tspn salt, 1 egg, 2 tspn baking powder, caster sugar, cooking oil, approximately 140ml (½ pt) milk, bananas.

Sieve flour and salt. Add egg and mix well until smooth. Add the milk and beat for 10 minutes. When it is thick enough to coat the back of a wooden spoon, coat bananas in batter. Fry in hot oil. Drain on a crumpled paper. Dust liberally with sugar and serve hot with ice cream or cream.

4

Learning to be a Diplomatic Lady

For two weeks out of every four KJ worked in Botswana, Lesotho, Swaziland, Zambia or Malawi. While he was away my companions had been Jane, Lyson, Paddycat and the dogs. Now, enrolled at the university I could pull a switch into 'single-girl' mode and bicycle off to lectures on white rats or statistics. Perhaps it was partly a form of escapism, but unknown to me at the time, the course would, in the end, deepen my understanding of the ex-pat and diplomatic life.

We were a mixed lot at the university. The class contained bright young Zimbabwean nationals, including the star student, Tsitsi Dangarembga, later a well-known novelist and filmmaker. There were a few young European students, and half a dozen mature women including my friends May Davey and the glamorous Ruth Steiner. We, the older students, all had a life beyond lectures and a keen sense of the ridiculous. We read widely and wrote surreptitious shopping lists in the margins of our notes. Having seen a bit more of life we often annoyed lecturers by asking awkward 'global' questions. But regurgitation of the lectures was required, not Socratic debate.

Skinnerian conditioning was the vogue – positive and negative reinforcement could solve all of the world's evils. Animals could be conditioned, schoolchildren could be conditioned, criminal offenders could be conditioned, societies could be conditioned. But we did raise an eyebrow when told by one lecturer that she could potty train a toddler in a day, with nothing more than a toilet, a bag of sweets, and innumerable jugs of water.

Social Psychology was taught by a small man with reflective

spectacles and a toothbrush moustache. It involved research done with American College students in the 1960s, with premises like 'men are stronger than women' and elaborate experiments to prove it. Researchers called 'Zimbardo et al' did experiments like persuading students to eat grasshoppers, to prove that when people realise they have done something very silly, they pretend it was terribly clever and important, and that they wanted to do it all along. We had to wonder what relevance these studies might have to people born in rural Zimbabwe, where grasshoppers in any case were regarded as a delicacy, and many long and passionate discussions were held about the need to make psychology cross-culturally relevant.

But psychology student or not, I needed to remind myself that I had a new role to learn. The reason for being in Zimbabwe was that KJ was now a diplomat. We did some entertaining when he was in town. It also meant taking part in 'The Diplomatic Wives Association'. Among other things the wives from all of the embassies and high commissions met periodically for 'Big Teas'. Every month some unfortunate ambassador's wife was the hostess for a Big Tea, for 200 or so women. She and her helpers were expected to produce delicious cakes and sandwiches on which the reputation of their country depended, to organise speakers, and raffles for charity, and to clean up the ravages made by 400 stiletto heels on carpet, parquet and lawn. Not to mention the washing up. Every embassy dreaded this event – much though it may have been enjoyed by participants. Finding new and original entertainment for the afternoons was a challenge – once I was roped in to play the harp and sing Celtic folksongs to the throng, balanced precariously on the edge of the Austrian Embassy swimming pool.

Then someone had the bright idea of holding a Diplomatic Bazaar to support Zimbabwean charities. It was planned for months. Diplomatic representations were made to government and customs departments who wanted to tax all the goods imported for sale into the country, and then tax the proceeds again – even though the profits were destined for local charities. In the European Union camp, we met at Reinhild's house to make sundry articles of art and craft. Reinhild brought back from Bavaria a selection of exquisite cuckoo clocks to sell. I coveted one, except that a cat or bull terrier would be sure to bite off their swinging weights when no one was looking.

An International Incident loomed. The Americans offered the services of the marines to man the hot-dog stall, whereupon the Eastern Bloc countries staged a walk-out. It was suggested by peacemakers that the KGB might come along as well to keep an eye on them and take part too. Sell caviar perhaps? Run a fingerprint stall? Sell portable spy kits?

The day of the bazaar was hot and sticky. Well before opening time the gate queue stretched round the block. The noise level was eardrum-rattling. So soon after UDI, it was a novel experience and crowds flocked in. The words 'Imported Goods' acted like an aphrodisiac for people cut off from the world for fifteen years. Ridiculously priced items were snapped up – we could have sold our husbands as 'foreign imports'. The French sold wines, the Germans sold sausages, the British sold Earl Grey tea, footballs and anything with a Union Jack on it. The Australians sold furry kangaroos and koalas, and the Dutch, dressed in orange of course, sold wooden tulips of no discernible use to anyone. The event went on until there was nothing left to sell. Even the wooden tulips had gone and the recreation ground looked like the aftermath of an earthquake. We staggered home, to await the counting of the money, destined to provide wheelchairs, school equipment and scholarships for needy children.

Late that evening the phone rang at the home of Reinhild and Mr D. A reproachful Middle Eastern voice was at the other end. It said: 'Sir, His Excellency my Ambassador today bought a cuckoo clock at the European stall of the Diplomatic Bazaar.

Now His Excellency has to state that the European cuckoo is not working correctly. His Excellency feels that the Honourable Delegate of the European Commission should know that the bird regrettably does not come out of the clock when it is time to do so . . . '

The formal Diplomatic complaint droned on about the tardy cuckoo until Reinhild, stifling her giggles said: 'His Excellency should knock on the roof of the clock. If the cuckoo still does not wake up the Embassy should return it to avoid a Diplomatic Incident.'

After the phone was hung up, the Representatives of Europe exploded with laughter.

Diplomatic life abroad also involved periodic upheavals known as 'Visits from Headquarters'. Planning went back and forth between Post and HQ for months, as to which projects should be visited, which government ministers met, which receptions and functions held. This was all new to me but fortunately for 'junior wives' the brunt of the work fell on Reinhild. Longing to spend time in her art studio, she was obliged to organise formal gourmet dinners, plan cocktail parties for hundreds of people, solve background problems, look cool and glamorous, and probably put up guests in the house as well. Very occasionally she would roll her eyes to heaven and say: 'My life!'

If I had thought of diplomats at all I had assumed that their sole occupation was attending endless parties, sipping champagne from long-stemmed glasses. Once I had spent a 'function day' helping Reinhild I knew better. We prepared trays of canapés, stuffed hundreds of curried eggs, fried a million prawns in batter, buttered mini rolls to absorb the alcohol consumed by hungry guests, and arranged umpteen trays of cold meats. Someone does the planning and the work, thinks of the logistics, and keeps an eagle eye on the food, the drink, the happiness and sobriety of guests, whether they number a dozen or several hundred. And that someone, the unpaid central co-ordinator, is the wife of the Head of Mission, who, while looking stunning in her little black dress, appears to be making mere social chit-chat.

'Missions from Headquarters' could involve extraordinary sunrise trips to the back of beyond, to inspect crops or dams, herds of cattle or rows of latrines. One morning KJ came home for lunch feeling elated, after a 6.30am 'promenade touristique' with the highest VIP of the visit, the Commissioner Himself, accompanied by a posse of henchmen. The commissioner was tall and intellectual with a white goatee beard. He looked distinguished, and charismatic. At a certain point, he clicked his fingers and the henchmen disappeared. Seating himself on a balancing rock, he said to KJ: *'Parlez-moi de pedagogie!'* ('Speak to me of pedagogy!')

I don't know what KJ replied, but I'm thankful no one ever said that to me at 6.30am, let alone on a balancing rock.

That week was a procession of meetings, visits and star-studded functions. When lunch was scheduled at our house, I cooked my best, and drinks were served by the pool, fish fountain gushing the while. The Delegate from Botswana, an aristocratic Frenchman, seemed to regard his overseas posting as a chance to indulge in the ancient and noble pursuit of hunting. While expounding on this passion, at one point Polar Bear ambled into view at the other end of the garden. The delegate's oration stopped.

'Est-ce un chien?' ('Is that a dog?') he asked.

Now English bull terriers may be unusual dogs, but they are indubitably dogs. Their little hind quarters may be slightly piggy when young, and if their roman noses were about a foot longer they could be taken for a tapir. But such uncertainty on the part of so great a hunter cast doubt on either his eyesight or his hunting exploits, and I resolved to keep my animals safely locked away for the rest of his visit.

Once the VIP invasion was over KJ set off once more on his

trips around the region, and, left to myself, I got back to studying. Winter weather in Harare is idyllic. Sunny, frosty mornings, flowed into sunny, warm days, perfect for solitary reading or studying in the sun, and the nights are cold enough for roaring fires.

It was on one of these cold winter nights that Paddycat came in through the bedroom window with a large brown mouse. It escaped. There were scampers in the room, then silence. At 3am, there was a tap on the shoulder from Paddycat with a plaintive expression on his face.

'Excuse me, I've lost my mouse.'

Sighing with resignation I got up and moved the furniture. The only other place the mouse could have been was in the wardrobe among my Imelda Marcos collection of shoes. That search was not going to happen at 3am. The door was firmly closed. PC did guard duty for a while, and then gave it up as a bad job.

Next morning, as I put a slice of bread in the toaster, the toast rose up in protest, then scurried down the sideboard and across the room. Mousie's refuge had been blown. He exited out of the dining-room window and has probably been dining out on the story ever since.

Some august committee must have declared 'Rodent Week' because the very next night, there was a commotion outside. I peered through the small dressing-room window. There was scuffling in the dog department. By morning, there in the dewy grass was a rat. But what a rat! It was a cane rat, a foot long and six inches wide, and with the tail must have measured two feet. Panda was told she was a 'Good dog,' and preened herself. She guarded her catch until she was enticed into the kitchen for a treat, so that Lyson could bury the body with honour. It had been a brave fighter.

'That is a *veryterrible* rat!' Jane pronounced.

That evening KJ returned home from one of his trips and we

took tea into the garden. As we sat, Paddycat focused on something twenty metres across the garden. He crouched on the starting blocks, hind quarters flexing, then sprang across the lawn, returning with a very small grey mouse. He was pleased with himself and although we were sorry for the mouse, he in turn was told he was a 'Good cat!'

After tea Polar Bear disappeared. We wondered. And then he came into view, with a wide bull terrier grin on his face, trotting with his best nautical roll and carrying something in his mouth. He laid it at our feet. He had been to fetch the oldest and most mummified dead frog in Harare. Not the brightest of chaps, he must have *very* much wanted to join the ranks of the other two hunters so he could be a 'Good dog' too.

To cap it all off, at the end of the week, one lunchtime when I arrived back at the house, I was greeted excitedly by Jane. Lyson had been asked to move a pile of firewood from the front drive. While he was doing it, Panda smelt a rat, quite literally, and watched, with prick-eared attention as each log was shifted.

'Madam,' said Jane, 'Panda she catching rats 1–2–3–4–5–6–! Polar he not catching, he just looking! Panda she is a *veryterribledog*!'

In this life of alternate company and solitude, I still missed life in London and above all, girlfriends. Letters flew back and forth, but it wasn't quite the same. Then mid-year we received word that our long-time Canadian friend Mary Dwyer would come from London for a visit. Mary arrived, dressed immaculately for the tropics and Polar Bear fell in love with her as he often did with attractive young women. This involved gazing adoringly at her and sitting very close, and I regret to say, sometimes goosing her from behind, so that she would suddenly lurch forward, mid-conversation, to her own and everyone else's astonishment.

We went to downtown Harare, explored the antique jewellery shops, and had tea and impossibly high and fluffy scones on

Barbour's rooftop terrace. We visited the Lion Park, south of the city, with its pride of purring lions, and its two sad, chained elephants. We drove to the cool mountainous region of Inyanga, and stayed at the Olde Englishe Troutbeck Inn with its ever-lasting flame. Becoming more adventurous, we planned a longer journey to the Chimanimani mountains on the border between Zimbabwe and Mozambique. It was said to be spectacularly beautiful and, even better, so far from Harare that it was not much visited by tourists except for hikers, scouts and orienteers. Perhaps that should have been a warning to us that Africa was about to show its darker side, ever ready to pounce from the shadows.

The old-fashioned Chimanimani Hotel was cosy and cluttered, with brown carpets, fat brown chairs, brown tables and bureaux and piles of brown cushions. Tea and biscuits were offered on arrival and at frequent intervals during the day. Every time the cosy proprietress saw us she put the kettle on.

We went exploring, and followed the Bridal Veil trail into the forest, past an old training centre, abandoned during the guerrilla war. The decrepit noticeboard claimed that the centre had been used for 'Outward Bound' courses but now it was dismal and menacing. Further along the track were the 'Bridal Veil Falls' and 'The Maiden's Pool', a natural pool, fed by a lacy waterfall, overhung with ferns and a rope swing. KJ and I were enchanted and wanted a dip in this magical place. Practical Mary on the other hand, was unimpressed. A feisty young woman who preferred her own agenda, she took herself back to the car to wait.

We luxuriated in the cool green waters, then, feeling un-comfortable at not taking better care of our guest, we dressed hurriedly and went back to the parking ground. She was not there. We went up the path, calling for her, then went back to the pool to see if there was another path, then back to the car to see if there was a note. Had she decided to take a walk? The mystery deepened. Enlisting the aid of a young Israeli couple who arrived at the car park, we combed the area, shouting, whistling, and making the good Australian 'Coo-ee' noises famed for carrying in the bush. We shouted and searched, until we were hoarse. There was a forest rangers' hut near the Outward Bound centre. We took the car and found a ranger. Hearing that someone was lost he immediately radioed for a senior member of the Park staff. The two men in their jungle green uniforms were serious as they quizzed us as to how our friend had disappeared. How long had we been in the pool? How long had we been searching? Did we see her leave? Which way did she go?

Hearing the answers, they were instantly galvanised and radios crackled to the town of Chimanimani. In the last few months, three people had disappeared, either taken by leopards or kidnapped by Frelimo Freedom fighters from Mozambique. One had been ransomed. Two had never been found. Was Mary to be the fourth disappearance?

Three hours had passed. It was dark and eerie. A thick mist was rising. We stood shivering. The only lights were near the rangers' hut and we were loaned large torches. One of the rangers disappeared in his Land Rover to cover more ground, even while explaining that it was probably useless to search the open spaces. The senior ranger was in contact with the town and by a lucky chance a contingent of the British army was on manoeuvres that week. The troops were summoned by radio to take part in a massive organised rescue search.

We were relieved. We knew that if necessary the army would search all night. At the same time my stomach was in a knot. What would they find? I visualised a pine coffin, wondering how I could organise to have the body transported back to Harare, and then back to Mary's home in Canada. Would there even *be* a body? What would I say to her elderly mother when I telephoned? And I didn't even have the number! There was an air of chill unspoken dread. No one dared voice their fears. But we all knew too well the likely outcome. The Chimanimani mountains cover an area of fifty kilometres of rough, mountainous terrain. How could she ever be found?

We waited. A long period of silence. It was dark now. Misty rain was falling. She had been missing for four hours and we had run out of both words and optimism.

There was a distant shout from the young couple who had joined the search. The young woman, Leah, was running along the road towards us, from the direction of the Outward Bound Centre.

Waving excitedly, she shouted: 'Mary's found, we've found her!'

And there was Mary, walking calmly down the road, with a smile on her face. Calm and unperturbed, she described how she thought she had taken the path to the car park. Realising it was taking too long, she had continued walking in a huge circle – a common and often fatal mistake of people who are lost in the bush, but in this case she was lucky. Following a glimmer of light, she eventually found the Outward Bound centre again. Unaware of our panic or that the troops had been called in, she seemed oblivious to her own peril. She had seen one small deer among the trees. She had no idea that there were leopards in the forest – or freedom fighters.

It is hard to describe our feelings. Shared relief. Intense warmth towards this friend so nearly lost. Not daring to express all that we feared, we thanked everyone over and over again. The British army contingent was called off. We returned to the hotel and were fed hot soup and stew to restore the soul. Never did life seem more precious. I went to bed knowing a new level of gratitude.

Our guest left, replete with souvenirs of beadwork and sculpture tucked into her luggage, still apparently unfazed by her adventure. We were thankful that she left alive.

After her departure, local life resumed. Out of the blue 'The Championship Show of the Zimbabwe Bull Terrier Club' was announced, another example of the way colonialists in all African countries carried on their lives as though living in another time and place. English place names, fish and chips, and a dog show modelled on Crufts. All ways of dealing with the more threatening side of Africa and controlling unknown or apparently sinister surroundings.

Panda and Polar Bear were entered in the show, and there were long telephone conversations with bull terrier people to find out what to do. What scrubbing and washing ensued, what covering with powder and shining with baby oil, what brushing of coats and clipping of whiskers. Both dogs were dosed with dog vitamins for weeks, and Polar Bear was on half rations for a fortnight to trim his waist. We bought heavy chains to secure them to their show stalls, and special white show leads.

In the event, the dog show was fun. About fifty dogs were entered, all more or less well behaved, though one or two excited youngsters did huge leaps to the ends of their leashes and turned somersaults in the air. Some of the owners were also a bit overexcited, and worked frenetically with squeaky toys and dog treats to liven up their charges. A bearded chap with a hat marched about bellowing: 'Show your dogs!' whereupon the experts held up tails and adjusted ears and squeaked their squeaky toys, and KJ and I tried to look very knowing. Polar Bear behaved in an exemplary manner, happily trotting round the ring as if he was born to it – as indeed he was. After all he was purchased with the proviso: 'Ees a show dog you know. You must show 'im!'

He even behaved impeccably when a nervous dog broke its lead and flew at him, biting him on the nose. He won the prize for Best South African dog, and fifth best animal in show – a bit low down the ranks, we thought. We came home laden with cups, a rosette for his collar, a certificate saying he was of champion quality and enough packages of vitamins and flea powder to set up a small shop.

Panda, however, stood scowling with ears down and tail clamped, apparently sworn like a canine Germaine Greer to sabotage all beauty pageants. Her sulks reduced the judge to such helpless laughter that he gave her a prize anyway.

Impelled by their curiosity to see another African country my parents arrived for a second visit. They loved Zimbabwe. They loved Jane and Lyson, and remarked how happy everyone seemed to be. They loved the lime-green house in Avondale, and they loved Harare town with its crowds and craft markets. Mother, an artist, enjoyed watching craftsmen at work in small factories as they created jewellery and tiny boxes out of certified ivory with tiny fret saws and chisels.

The parents loved the old colonial Victoria Falls Hotel where the Marimba Band played in the courtyard, upper notes belling out over the buffet noises, huge bass gourds resonating in our bones. They loved the West African masked dancing. They loved breakfast on the terrace, watching the clouds of spray rising from 'Mosi oa tunya' – 'The Smoke that Thunders'. They loved the baboons, especially the one who sat on the car and made faces.

At the Victoria Falls, standing beneath the large statue of Livingstone that overlooks the torrent, Mother said, in wonderment, as much to herself as to anyone else: 'Victoria Falls! I'm in Victoria Falls!'

I knew what she meant. We Australians, when we travel, are particularly prone to wide-eyed wonder, since we ache for so long to visit the worlds we have only met in books. And when we see these places, they are illuminated with the radiance of our longing and the poetry of our long desire.

Dad gently enjoyed everything with a quizzical eye, and made the occasional laconic joke – Australian style – with a deadpan face. Mother however, a passionate traveller, was open-eyed and curious. She talked to everyone and was willing to ask any question that occurred to her. And there was one thing in particular that puzzled her greatly.

Born in the early 1900s when the sun had not set on the British Empire and the world map was splodged with red, Mother was a small-town girl from the north-west of Western Australia. She, like many of her generation, felt insecure as twentieth-century changes accelerated and compensated by clinging to what she had learned in her youth. When she was young political correctness had not been invented. From her history books at school she had learned about the 'Kaffir Wars' and Mother could not now see why this adjective was now offensive. Derived from the Arabic 'Kāfir' meaning 'infidel' – one who is not a Muslim – cruel use of the word in Colonial times put it far beyond the pale. KJ, new to the fray, tried to explain and educate. He thought he had made headway, and that the dread word had been eliminated from the vocabulary.

The test came at dinner one night. Among the guests was a government Under Secretary, with whom KJ worked. Like many in the new Zimbabwe Sipho had studied in the USA during the years of UDI. He had returned after Independence with a beautiful American wife and a long American car. He was a sophisticated and witty conversationalist and the evening was going well. Then Mother had an idea. Leaning forward in her best silk dress and pearls, she fixed Sipho with her large blue eyes and said: 'I want to ask you something.'

'Yes?' said the unwary Sipho.

'Tell me,' said Mother, 'You don't mind being called a Kaffir, do you?'

KJ froze and prayed for an invisibility cloak. I hoped the rest of the table had not heard the words too clearly.

Catching our pleading eyes, Sipho fortunately saw the funny side of it. Winking at us he replied: 'No, of course not, Madam!' and the crisis was averted.

But Sipho's urbane reaction meant that KJ's chances of changing Mother's viewpoint on the matter had dwindled forever to zero.

That visit safely negotiated, university term began again. It was time to think about a topic for the final dissertation. Despite the pleasure of new places and experiences, this travelling life was stressful. I knew that when the time came to pack up my house I suffered sleepless nights. It tore at the heart to say goodbye to friends, to the home I had created, to beloved plants and to the familiarity of it all. This would happen every four years. How could I bear it? How did others bear it? And on arrival at a new place, however exciting, I would stand dismayed, wondering where to start, how to cope and how to recreate myself to fit. Was it just me or did others suffer? I set myself to find out, and wrote up a proposal for the Psychology Department. Suddenly I saw that here was a way to mould together those conflicting roles of student, person and 'trailing spouse'.

In the 1960s, many Peace Corps Volunteers went home, suffering from a mysterious bundle of symptoms. Since then, 'Culture Shock' has been found in the majority of people up-rooted from their homes. Even when the change is chosen, a grief process takes place. We suffer loss of identity, of friends, of familiar places, of jobs, of home and family connections. Our very sense of self is threatened. We can suffer alienation, anxiety and sleeplessness, depression and minor illnesses. We can become paranoid about cleanliness and health. Why then, I thought, do families who move often, not live in permanent culture shock, unable to cope with the demands of normal life? Somehow we seem to manage. So how do we do it?

I interviewed a large number of wives in the Diplomatic Corps. In the 1980s common law partners and male spouses and same-sex partnerships were practically unknown. Efficiency studies had been carried out by international companies on male employees, but most of them had concluded that a great deal depended on the support of the spouse.

'So what about the spouse?' I thought.

Male employees go from one identikit office to another, speaking their own language, supported by personal assistants, translators, administrative assistants, drivers and general Mr Fix-its. Trailing spouses, on the other hand, must deal with domestic staff head-on, go to markets, and generally trip over local customs without the benefit of any of their husbands' orientation programmes, secretaries or language training.

A series of questionnaires was designed to measure satisfaction with life, friendships, participation in local life, sense of home, happiness in the family – whatever might reveal how satisfied these diplomatic gypsies might be with life, what they saw as their main problems, and how they coped – or didn't.

'I cry for two months every time we move,' said one.

'I spend all day writing letters to everyone I know,' said another.

'I have to put on an act for the sake of the children,' said a third, 'but in the beginning, the days are *so* lonely.'

'I've made and lost too many friends,' said a middle-aged American woman, who had chosen to live like a recluse. 'Now I only want to talk to my husband. I just stay at home and do my embroidery.'

Women with children were forced out into the community to find schools, and quickly met other parents. Some women, as soon as they arrived, talked to everyone they met, in a desperate effort to find friends. Sometimes they wished they hadn't. Others were more cautious, and observed for months before venturing out. The major issue was friendship – losing friends from home and from each new posting, children's distress at losing peer groups, making new friends each time while knowing that goodbyes would be inevitable.

People were unsure where they belonged. I asked the question: 'Where is home?'

'I don't know, I no longer use the word,' said an Australian woman.

Sometimes every member of the family gave a different answer. Children, asked to sing the National Anthem, might proudly sing the anthem of the country where they had been happiest, rather than the country of their parents.

One German woman confided that she and her husband would not retire in Germany, since they no longer felt at ease there. Another said that her small daughter had staged a tantrum, saying: 'Mummy, I am not coming with you again! I am staying with my friends. I am a little girl, I am not a dog!'

That daughter elected to stay for the rest of her life in Germany. A second child opted to become an air hostess so that she could go on travelling forever.

A British woman cancelled the interview because her eight-year-old son had just left for boarding school and she could not bear to speak about it. And in another Foreign Service a rash of teenage suicides suggested that children left behind in boarding schools suffered even more traumatic alienation than their parents.

It made little difference how long or short the diplomatic career had been. Younger wives might be more outwardly upset, but older women confided that however good they became at packing and organising, their own hidden distress was no less sharp each time.

There were women who learned the language and joined local choirs, women who brought suitcases of hobbies to occupy themselves, or threw themselves into charity work. One senior British woman was writing a book on Zimbabwean cave painting. Most managed, by the end of their stays, to create a life – until the day came when the next postings were announced, the packing cases were pulled out and that life had to be dismantled yet again.

Those sent home on alternate postings fared better, although they often then felt like strangers at home. They learned not to bore people with tales of exotic places. Relatives and friends were much more interested in who had won the prize for the biggest pumpkin at the local village show than in tales of foreign parts.

Under a quirk of the Vienna Convention, the wives of diplomats were not allowed to work, leaving women with advanced qualifications frustrated, knowing that they would not easily be able to resume careers as lawyers, executives or economists. An Australian ambassador's wife who was a surgeon was refused a work permit and found solace in organising the Zimbabwe Boy Scouts. They camped in the embassy garden, burying half the diplomatic silver cutlery in the process. The choice was between working in another embassy or volunteering in a local charity.

Least content were those with the highest levels of education and training. A Canadian woman with a PhD in French chafed at the impossibility of establishing a translation bureau in post-Independence Zimbabwe.

By far the happiest were women who had not had careers themselves, who loved entertaining, and were convinced that their efforts were of immense help to their husbands, thus fitting neatly into the nineteenth-century model of the diplomatic wife.

But we were not nineteenth-century diplomatic wives. We were women living in the mid-1980s, trained, university educated, but of a generation still on the cusp of single-minded pursuit of a career. Our mothers had, for the most part, dedicated their lives and talents to husbands and families. Our daughters, if we had them, would be career women who would want to 'have it all'. These women were somewhere in the middle, struggling to create homes and families in the midst of constantly changing countries, sometimes in uncomfortable or dangerous conditions. Careers and aspirations were in headlong conflict with their sense of duty. We had few role models. There was no magic bullet, no answer or cure-all. The best outcome I could hope for was a bundle of helpful ideas on how to cope. And so it has proved, since I still give talks to young men and women struggling with the same tensions and anxieties that all human beings feel when, ousted from their natural habitat, they go into the unknown.

We all hope life will be different if we go somewhere new, get a new job, a new nose, a new husband or a new country. One change, and life will be transformed; we will leave ourselves behind and be fulfilled forever. But we take the same person with us. We have the same capacity to be irritated, disillusioned, depressed and bored, as well as to be excited, stimulated and delighted, wherever we are. The process of successfully adapting to a new country is one of crossing over from a state of negativity to one of enjoyment, humour, ease and delight in what is, and that takes time. The Rubicon that we must cross is within ourselves. Its sign is the re-appearance of our sense of humour as we begin once more to live in the present moment in our new environment.

Meantime, in our environment of 1980s' Zimbabwe, exams and work were done, results came out, and graduation loomed. We excitedly ordered gowns and hoods – purple with a gold edging on the Oxbridge model, as the academic traditions of ancient Europe prepared to parade in the hot African sun. Staff peacocked in full regalia, scarlet PhD robes and feathered hats to the fore. President Canaan Banana was installed as Chancellor of the University, wearing an appropriate robe with yellow stripes.

The ceremony was long and colourful with loud singing and ecstatic dancing. The rejoicing of parents whose children were graduating was touching in the extreme. Proud mothers and fathers leapt from their seats in ecstasy. Every new graduate, shining with pride, was greeted with wild shouts and ululations, and walked back with shyness or bravado through the forward rush of rejoicing parents.

So what do you do after you've got the degree? I was musing over the possibility of postgraduate studies. May and Chris Davey were renting out their house and leaving for a stint in Ethiopia. Ruth Steiner was giving talks on child-care and clearing out her house to move to Johannesburg. I visited them in their states of distraught chaos. We went back to England on leave and KJ went 'en mission' to HQ with strict instructions not to rock the boat. We had just bought an apartment in an old mansion in the wilds of Kent and were excited about it. Life in Zimbabwe was good; we wanted it to go on a little longer.

KJ came back from Brussels in a high state of excitement. He bounded enthusiastically out of a larger than usual hired car.

'I've been promoted!' he said. 'I've made it to Head of Mission. We're going to Angola!'

'Angola!' I thought. 'Where's that? Somewhere bottom left-hand corner of Africa?'

What I said was: 'I thought you were going to keep your head down and not rock the boat!'

Apparently this was a posting I should be excited about. But sang froid was in the genes. In Australia tall poppies have their heads lopped off and it isn't done to be puffed up. I refused to be too impressed. After all, it would be much the same. I would still have music, art, books, letters, dogs and cats, still live a quiet life, only in another country. Pity about Zimbabwe, though, but it would be only a short flight away.

The first indication I had that life might change came when Reinhild arrived at the door, highly excited at the news. Smiling broadly she thrust a bouquet of flowers into my hands with the words: *'Felicitations, Madame la Deleguée!'* ('Congratulations, Madame Delegate!')

She must have been deeply disappointed at my underwhelmed response. Which was something like: 'Oh, is that good then?'

She followed up a few days later with the offer of a coffee morning to 'pass on some informations' about the new job.

She felt there were things I might need to know. How right she was.

Reinhild produced an elegant silver tray of coffee and petits fours and a series of lists. The coffee mornings extended from one to three, on succeeding weeks. Each session left sleepless nights in its wake. There were pages of notes. Apart from her own considerable experience she had somehow acquired the complete guide of the Swiss Diplomatic Service – surely the acme of correctness! There were notes on every aspect of protocol. Notes on the correct setting of tables. Notes on organising and running a cocktail party for up to 400 people. Notes on the seating of dignitaries and how to take care of 'honoured guests'. Notes on the correct place to sit in the official car in all of its permutations – the position varied like chess moves, depending on whether one's companion was king, knight or pawn. There were notes on welcoming guests, controlling bar staff (particularly those prone to drinking the dregs from guests' glasses), accepting presents (never) and how to reply if a dignitary's wife wants the gift of a dress watch. How much and what kind of charitable work to undertake. How, where and to whom to pay official visits and for how long, how to receive an official visit and what to do if someone who ought to pay a visit, doesn't. Notes on the food that could be served to different nationalities (only chicken could be guaranteed not to offend) and how to unobtrusively eject an inebriated VIP from a function.

There were notes on what to wear. A diplomat should never be seen in a brown suit or a checked shirt, it seemed, and for some completely unfathomable reason, now disappeared into the distant past, white shoes should not be worn by ladies. I have never found out why, apart from the fact that white shoes invariably make feet look five sizes larger – like Minnie Mouse – but it has remained amusedly engraved on my memory. There were notes on when to express a political opinion or take part in gossip. (Absolutely never – you never know what hornets' nests you might stir.)

And then there was the equipment. At that time the commission did not provide cutlery or tableware for the Head of Mission but still expected formal entertaining of professional standard. There was therefore a king's ransom to be spent on table settings for fourteen people, twelve more plates for buffets, equivalent cutlery and glassware plus 200 cheap glasses for cocktails. We would need table linen to seat fourteen, huge saucepans, fish kettles, flower vases, silver tea and coffee services, candelabra – the list went on, enumerating objects I had never had the least desire to own and some I had barely heard of. I was shown inside Reinhild's cupboards, which contained an astounding amount of equipment, and we pored over menus and lists of cocktail fare. I learned the mysteries of planning a cocktail and the magic number of the six pieces of food likely to be consumed – eight large pieces if the guests were mainly men. I learned the subterfuges to use in order to ascertain the religion or food taboos of invited guests, and the importance of reminding African guests on the morning of a dinner party, lest more important family events might have occurred meantime. I heard about the necessity of being prepared for guests to arrive minus wives, with two, not at all, or perhaps with four or five friends who happened to be visiting at the time.

This promotion would come at a price. I learned the importance of humility before almost everyone, other diplomats and their wives, local dignitaries, and visitors from HQ, and the wisdom of always taking the last place even at one's own National Day. In short I discovered that my role was henceforth to be that of caterer, purveyor of endless repasts of professional standard, unobtrusive smoother of ways, beautifully dressed and acquiescent shadow of my husband at all times and echoer of his political position. I would also be a consummate interior decorator, arranger of flowers, purveyor of little gifts, and soother of male egos *nunc et in aeternum*. It promised a whole new lifestyle; one I had never aspired to, and quite frankly I was terrified!

There were other signs that things might be different henceforth. Mr D, ramrod straight, gave KJ formal permission to call him by his Christian name, as a sign that they were now of Equal Rank. When KJ was away I found myself subtly invited to formal dinners and functions at the official residence. Since Reinhild had advised me to observe how things were done whenever I went to a function, this was her kind way of offering practical demonstrations. Without such freely given mentoring, life in the future would have been an embarrassing nightmare. Her guidance would steer us through the treacherous and sometimes apparently illogical waters of diplomatic protocol for the next sixteen years.

Apart from this bombshell, life went on as normal for a few months, until KJ was called to Brussels for preparatory briefings. Since he would not be working in Zimbabwe any longer I no longer had the right to live in the lime-green house in Avondale. His successor was on the way. There were phone calls from KJ in Brussels. He was going to Angola on mission – and then he was not – five times. His successor was coming in December, November, January and not at all. The office wanted me out of the house immediately to repaint it – then not. I must return my diplomatic number plate immediately. I filled in the forms and nothing happened. In the end I just hooted with laughter when another 'urgent' phone call came but there was obviously a need to find somewhere else to live. It might be up to six months before we could actually go to Angola, and I, the dogs and Paddycat needed a home. I began to scour house agents and property advertisements.

'Wanted for six months. A small two-bedroomed house, with wall and secure garden.'

House agents laughed at the request. Friends thought about

their granny flats, but invariably had a pair of bull mastiffs ranging the garden. One likely house of Swiss design had a yodelling balcony and a great Dane. What to do? Then one morning I saw it. A small advertisement for a two-bedroomed house. I telephoned at 8am for fear it might be snatched and the agent apologised that it was for only six months rental. Exactly what I wanted. I could have hugged her. It was perfect. Miniature house in a quiet suburb, high walls, iron gate, with a tiny straw gazebo in the little garden. The garden consisted of a flower bed in each corner and a few roses in square holes, but it was a garden. It was furnished in old Zimbabwe style in solid imbuia wood and had bright orange curtains. The owners were studying overseas, their only proviso that their maid should continue to live in the staff quarters and take care of the house. And when I opened the drawer of the old-fashioned dressing table in the bedroom a tract fell out saying 'This is a place of peace!' Omens were good.

KJ returned to say his farewells. He phoned from the office to say that movers would be at the house in two days' time, ready or not. The packers this time were an old family firm. Apart from one small hiccup involving a bottle of whisky, they went through the house like a dose of salts, clearing everything in their path. A half-eaten tub of yoghurt was packed with the spoon still in it, a pile of glossy magazines, all of KJ's socks, and my harp key. Anything that stood still was wrapped and boxed. We took care to keep moving.

When they had gone the house was the same, and not the same. It was our house and yet the heart had been ripped out, leaving behind pale ghosts of happiness blowing like shreds of paper, and the soft echo of laughter. I ferried carloads of 'essential' possessions to the new little house. Clothes and shoes, cushions and pictures, a desk, a bookcase, books and papers, a few kitchen goods, and the hired piano came along. Finally the dogs arrived, with their usual boisterous delight in anything new. Paddycat was installed, in a state of passive resistance, and we spent the first night there. Number 151 Meath Road felt right. I sat on the brown leather settee sensing a welcome from the house, a feeling that it was a place where good things would happen.

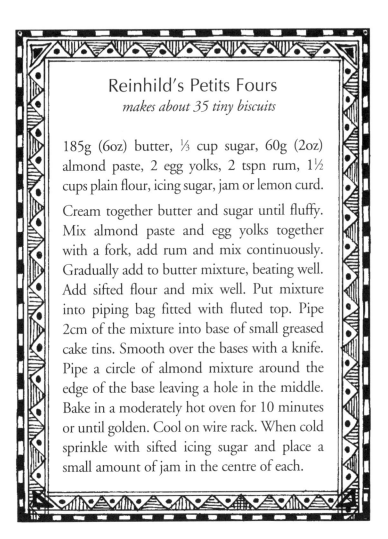

Reinhild's Petits Fours
makes about 35 tiny biscuits

185g (6oz) butter, ⅓ cup sugar, 60g (2oz) almond paste, 2 egg yolks, 2 tspn rum, 1½ cups plain flour, icing sugar, jam or lemon curd.

Cream together butter and sugar until fluffy. Mix almond paste and egg yolks together with a fork, add rum and mix continuously. Gradually add to butter mixture, beating well. Add sifted flour and mix well. Put mixture into piping bag fitted with fluted top. Pipe 2cm of the mixture into base of small greased cake tins. Smooth over the bases with a knife. Pipe a circle of almond mixture around the edge of the base leaving a hole in the middle. Bake in a moderately hot oven for 10 minutes or until golden. Cool on wire rack. When cold sprinkle with sifted icing sugar and place a small amount of jam in the centre of each.

5

Waiting for Angola

Another Christmas over, KJ went back to Brussels to wait for news of the Angola posting. I awoke in the little rented house in Meath Road, to the sound of crowing roosters and hens gently fussing in the garden next door. Janet, the landlord's maid, was crashing brooms in the tiny kitchen. Janet was a very small lady with a very large bosom. She was fiercely loyal to her employers, and took seriously her duty to protect the house from mere tenants. She had a passion for cleaning, which she did with noisy ferocity, arms and legs shooting out at awkward angles. Outside the bedroom window a colony of yellow weaver birds chirped as they flew in and out of their cunningly woven nests, which dangled from the branches of an acacia tree. Paddycat was loudly demanding breakfast. The dogs were busy looking through the iron gate for anything that might be barkable.

I realised that I was a transient wife, without a partner. I felt lost and vulnerable. The wolf tongue of depression was licking around the edges of life. Action was needed. Perhaps I had better do something to prepare for the new role.

Cookery classes with Mrs Bakewell were held every Wednesday in the crypt of the Anglican Cathedral. Mrs Bakewell was a short, stout Swiss-French lady of a certain age whose speech was peppered with exclamation marks. The roundness of her figure promised well for her cooking. Her *cordon bleu* credentials were impeccable, she informed us. She had done the full five-year course in Paris. She had a certain grim sense of humour, particularly where English cooking was concerned. We were regaled with stories of past triumphs, and a few disasters, all replayed with Anglophobia obligato.

We heard, en passant, tales of Mrs B's several husbands and their various demises, including the noble Chinese fiancé who was sent packing when his family served dog stew at a formal banquet. ('I tell you I will not go to 'eaven unless there are dogs there!') We heard of the society hostess (English, of course) whose husband, carving a turkey, managed to launch the entire bird, grease and all, over Mrs B's Parisian evening dress. We heard of Mrs Bakewell's catering for the Malawian Independence banquets, for which she travelled to Malawi with a retinue of fifty chefs. And, too, she told us with some pride of her constant vigilance in Harare restaurants and hotels, where she was the bane of local chefs. Dining at Meikle's Hotel, for instance, she was wont to call her ex-student – be it Ebenezer or Elias or Thomas – from the kitchen where he was now head chef. She would point to her plate and in ringing tones, proclaim to the entire dining-room: 'Ebenezer! I ordered duck à l'orange! This is not duck à l'orange! This is not what I taught you! Where are the orange slices? What have you done?'

Mrs Bakewell believed in establishing basic principles in the early lessons. Eggs were initially to be beaten with two forks tied together. This suited me fine since all my kitchen equipment was packed and stored.

She worked with smooth TV-presenter professionalism, aided by her amanuensis and general factotum, Samuel. Samuel was a grave, greying, middle-aged African gentleman, trained by Mrs B from a boy. We suspected that he could by now cook at least as well as she did. Samuel it was who produced 'the one I made earlier' with a flourish, when called upon, and his apfel strudel demonstration brought gasps of admiration as he whipped the pastry around in a cloth in a theatrical feat of legerdemain. As the class progressed we moved through the correct methods for stock, French dressing and white sauce, to crème Crécy soup,

Escoffier soufflé, and délicieuses de fromage. Each week we took home samples for our putative families to try, and did our 'homework' which Mrs Bakewell inspected. Any signs of 'Englishness' in the cooking was met with a curl of the Bakewellian lip and an acid aside ('Zis has ze English heaviness. Zey are lazy. Zey do not know how to beat!')

But one thing never varied. Throughout the entire ten-week course, during the two-hour lessons, Mrs Bakewell would call upon Samuel. At regular intervals of approximately seven minutes, the cry would go up: 'Samwell, Samwell!'

And every single time, despite myself, I fully expected him to answer: 'Speak, Lord, Thy Servant heareth!'

During this time Harare was in a crescendo of excitement. The Non-Aligned Conference was coming to Zimbabwe. For months, advertisements in the *Herald* had offered princely rental sums for princely accommodation. Zimbabweans with large houses planned visits to friends in South Africa or England, vacating their houses in order to earn up to $Z2,000 in priceless foreign exchange. The sudden building of the multi-million Sheraton Hotel with its international conference facilities now made sense.

Fidel Castro was expected, Jesse Jackson, Rajiv Gandhi and Coretta King, along with leaders from the other seventy-two non-aligned nations of the world. Colonel Gaddaffi arrived with a full panoply of courtiers but no camels. Refusing to sleep in the mansion provided, he pitched a palatial nomad's tent in the garden and held court there instead.

Shiny black Mercedes limousines had been imported for the motorcades, and teams of motorcycle escorts were requisitioned from Zambia and other neighbouring countries. Day and night the city was a network of road blocks and ever-changing detours as cars and motorbikes, their howlers wailing, escorted dignitaries to and fro.

Police and armed guards stood everywhere, looking important, while we ordinary citizens tried to go about our normal lives, dodging trouble. Second Street, one of the main south to north arteries, was decorated at every corner by enormously fat female police officers, so well upholstered that the hems of their skirts were at a foot higher at the back than in front. They wielded stout batons, but their orders must surely have been to sit on any malefactor, since they could hardly have chased and caught one.

Stories were told of how one night, at the height of the conference, two motorcycle escort teams met at an intersection. Each team had strict instructions not to stop on any pretext for fear of assassination attempts on the lives of world Leaders. They obeyed orders and forged ahead with spectacular results. 'Into the valley of death rode the six hundred.' Onlookers spoke of motorbikes describing arcs in the air as they collided. Five bikes were written off. Miraculously no lives were lost. Sometimes it doesn't pay to be slavishly obedient.

One aspect of the diplomatic life that goes largely unnoticed is the waiting time. It's not all about champagne, white gloves and chocolates. There can be long intervals between posting when one is between identities, just coping with the minutiae of living.

During this period of waiting, the pets settled into the small house. It was well barred and gated. Paddycat knew his territory, and rarely ventured outside the wall, except for an occasional foray when he sat on the very edge of the property boundary, glaring at the cat next door. Sometimes said cat came into the garden at night and there was a flurry of cat-fight but Panda would come to the rescue, chasing away the stranger with a growling rush.

But coping alone with two lively bull terriers was a handful, especially when taking them to the vet. They loved going – that was not the problem. They would pull to get in the surgery door, wide grins on their faces, leads taut, panting with excitement like two steam engines. The vet wanted a video of them to show to nervous dogs. The problem was getting them there – two dogs, one car and one pair of hands. Panda did her 'good girl' act sitting primly on the back seat. But Polar Bear thought he was my special dog and would squeeze his sturdy form between the seats to sit proudly on the passenger's seat with an air of achievement. However many elbow-jabs I employed to keep him in the back it never worked and the battle only caused the car to swerve. So in the end he sat in his precious front seat, anchored by the seat belt, worn proudly across his chest like a royal decoration.

As the six-month lease on Meath Road drew to a close, there was still no sign of moving to Angola. KJ was waiting in Brussels for his Agrément – the Agreement for a new Head of Mission or Ambassador to take up his post. In Angola the Marxist government was split on the question of whether they wanted Western Europe there at all. Each time the Agrément seemed close, and air tickets were booked, yet another fax would come from the Angolan Department of Foreign Affairs saying, like Jeremiah, '*Lamentamos . . . . . . !*' ('We regret . . . . . . !')

Post reports began to filter through, and my heart sank into my sandals. Heat, mosquitoes, cholera, typhoid, malaria. There were 55,000 Cuban troops in the country, fighting for the MPLA against UNITA. Cuban troops were also protecting American oil crews and oil wells in Cabinda, against Jonas Savimbi (UNITA), who was funded . . . by the USA! The city of Luanda was cordoned off, there was a curfew at night, and gunfire in the streets after dark. Minimal goods were available. This city built for half a million inhabitants now housed 1.5 million. There were frequent power and water cuts and no rubbish collections. There were few doctors, and empty pharmacies. Housing was unavailable except to party members and their relatives. I quailed.

I went to the Harare Parireynatwa Hospital to enquire about vaccinations. A tough sunburnt nurse was sergeant-majoring patients into lines: 'Over there for typhoid and yellow fever,' she bellowed. 'And stand here for the cholera injection if you want it, but you might as well skip it and just get the form filled in – 5 per cent immunity is no bloody good!'

And there was the language. Angola was an ex-Portuguese colony and no English was spoken. KJ had been given the new job on the understanding that he could operate in Portuguese. That was a bit exaggerated. He *had* been in Brazil fifteen years previously. But he spoke five languages already, and had the chutzpah to think he would crack it in no time. Out he went to buy a language-learning book and tapes. The next thing I knew, he had negotiated a three-week intensive language course in Lisbon. In those days, wives were not considered important by HQ, but knowing that both of us would have to communicate, I went along anyway.

We stayed in the Hotel Da Gama, where everything was covered in bright orange swirly patterns, tiled mosaic or both. It was in the cheap quarter of Lisbon, recommended by Professor Annan, linguistics professor at the University of Zimbabwe. The professor was something of an expert, since he went to Lisbon every year to listen to Portuguese and record it. He had a theory that it was the only language in the world that could *not* be captured by the International Phonetic Alphabet. This was not reassuring.

On our first night in the little orange room, it was extra-ordinarily noisy. All of the house facades were covered in 'azuleijos', or ceramic tiles, which made a perfect amplifier for the noisy street, funnelling every grinding gear, crash and shout straight upward. A dismal dog howled and the howling broke off in horribly sinister fashion. A cacophony of squawks and squeaks broke out from the bottom of the street. Could it be . . . ? It was. Bagpipes, of the most virulent variety. There was an election campaign going on. Rival political parties had hired rival bands of bagpipers and the competition went on all night.

We had enrolled in the 'CIAL' language school on the other side of Lisbon. This meant a tram journey each day, listening to the conversation around us, and occasionally making out a word – usually 'Pois' or sometimes 'Pois pois!' This interjection seemed to mean 'Yes', 'Well, well!', 'Really?', 'You don't say!' or any other sympathetic noise to encourage the speaker to continue. Not that they needed much encouragement. There was a constant stream of banter in the trams, and everyone joined in as they hopped on and off. I loved being among the people of Lisbon. Polite and humorous, they worked hard for low wages, but always seemed warm, vivacious and human, even if we didn't yet understand much more than 'Pois'.

The language school was in an ancient part of town, an area of steep, narrow streets. Tiny dark shops were piled with higgledy-piggledy displays, smelling of fresh bread, and cakes, toasted coconut and coffee and old cheese. At the school we passed through a carved and studded wooden door into dark shuttered rooms with heavy black furniture that Vasco da Gama himself might have used.

We were in different classes. I cheerfully admitted to knowing nothing, whereas KJ's work on his taped course put him ahead, although it emerged, after an initial test, that he spoke a confident brand of Portuguese without verbs (*'Portugues cem verbas'*) or with very few of them. He had thought he'd catch up with them later. Since Portuguese boasts the largest number of ferociously irregular verbs of any Western language, this catching up was about to happen very fast.

We set to work, one to one with our tutors for eight hours per day, resolving to absorb as much as human beings could in the three weeks ahead. One-to-one language classes are no fun. There's nowhere to hide, questions can't be dodged, and there is not a moment to slacken off. We ate lunch sitting on a gravestone in a nearby cemetery. Shopping was a chance to try out phrases as we bought a bread roll, a 'paozinho', stuffed with cheese or sausage, or one of the delicious 'pasteis de nata', of which the humble custard tart is only the poorest and most distant relation. The Portuguese, as a race, seemed devoted to nursery puddings and little cakes, and the ubiquitous Pudim flan or crême caramel was consumed in industrial quantities. I was entranced to see a muscular, overalled workman eating a dainty dish of 'Arroz Doce'(rice pudding) for his lunch with a tiny teaspoon. Despite lunch on the gravestones, and cooling off in a gilt bedecked baroque church nearby, we ended each day with pounding headaches and shoulders that were stiff and painful from the hours of concentration.

Every evening we dragged ourselves up the Rua 22^e Dezembro, to our bright orange hotel and collapsed on the hard orange beds. Then we would set out again, in search of a small local fish restaurant. There were many of these *Grelhados* in the area, barbequing freshly caught sardines over hot coals. The hot, sweet fish were served with boiled potatoes and a few herbs at a ridiculously low price. Sometimes we treated ourselves to *Gambas* – prawns, grilled and hanging from a wire frame, a mini chandelier from which the crustaceans dangled like Dali-esque pink jewels.

One night, in search of a new place to try, we ventured further than usual. Down some stone steps, past a disused fountain and under the arch of a bridge, we found Pedro's, a tiny brightly lit restaurant. We peeped in. The lights were on, the few small tables neatly set with red checked cloths, but there were no other customers. Senhor, mustachioed rosy, and rotund, jumped up in surprise from the TV when we came in, rubbing his hands together. We were ushered with ceremony into a private room. This contained a tall dresser at one end, stacked with a variety of wines, prints of horses, pet dogs and some framed wrapping paper. On the walls was a ship made of shells, a leather belt and a variety of objects, including, I swear, the ball from a lavatory cistern. The room also contained an immense chest freezer. The menu was brought. Senhor hovered over us with embarrassing unctuousness. There wasn't much that we recognised on the menu. KJ settled for a *Caldeirada* or seafood stew, and my eye alighted on the word *lulas*. Surely I remembered that from somewhere? And it was *grelhado* (grilled). That couldn't be bad.

Senhor sprang into action – literally. He flung open the lid of the giant freezer and launched himself into it. Since he was so short and the freezer so deep, only his legs and feet were visible as he groped. He emerged bearing several packages in triumph and disappeared towards the kitchen. There was a clattering of pots and a babble of voices and it seemed as if all the neighbours had been called in to help prepare the feast. We listened, buttering bread rolls, for a very long time. The battle of the pots and pans raged off-stage. Finally Senhor appeared with two large white plates. One of them did not meet his standards so he blew on it and polished it on his sleeve.

The plates were placed before us with a flourish. KJ's *Caldeirada* arrived, in a huge pottery container. Senhor scurried in with it, and with two-spoon dexterity, turned it all round and over, ladled it out, and rolled the plate around to settle it nicely. And the *lulas*. Ah! The *lulas*. Two large, fat, repellent creatures like sea slugs stared up at me challengingly. In despair I looked around for a handy pot plant or jardiniére – anything – to get rid of the things. But it was no use. Senhor Pedro stood, napkin over one arm determined to watch these grand people who had come into his restaurant as they savoured every bite. Reader, I ate them.

The entire meal for two – main course, drinks, bread and butter and fruit – cost a princely $6, entertainment included – and the little proprietor backed out before us, hoping that '*Vossas Excelencias*' were satisfied.

Sunday afternoons were spent in the *Estufa Fria* (the Cold Hot-house), giant tropical greenhouses in the centre of Lisbon, where we recited verbs to the pink flamingos. We ended the three weeks feeling that we had done our best, not necessarily that we could now speak Portuguese. How many months would it be before we would actually be in Angola, using it?

KJ returned to HQ to wait for his summons. Months went by. Finally the call came. In great excitement he left Brussels for the first appointment as Head of Mission, together with his trusty team – Roland, a slim elegant French economist, Bernard, a small pragmatic administrative officer from Belgium, and an even smaller, nuggety Italian agriculturalist, nicknamed 'The Teddy Baar'. Later would come Luciano, engineering advisor and lothario extraordinaire among the local ladies.

After they arrived I had a phone call from Luanda. It had taken five hours of dialling into crackling ether peppered with ghostly voices. KJ had been out to the airport, he said, every hour since 3am, trying to get an official from HQ onto the plane. Seven hours later, at 10am, he succeeded, except that by then, the only plane available was going to Zaire, which was not where the official wanted to go. The key to the official's room went with him to the airport, as it was booked for a second visitor. But by the time the second VIP arrived his room had been given away. After pressure from protocol, another room was found, sadly this time with no key. First a key without a room, then a room without a key. So far, they had had two days without water, and two days without electricity. Turning on a tap or light switch was an hourly guessing game, hoping for the moment when both might be on together.

For his first formal banquet, KJ was nervous. He had to entertain VIPs, officials from Brussels and members of the Diplomatic Corps at the only functioning hotel in Luanda. Without Reinhild's coaching he was hazy about some points of protocol but hoped for the best. Dressed in his best 'going-to-the-President' dark suit he set off for the banquet. A colourful red soup was already set out as the company took their seats. KJ pulled out his chair and slipped into his seat, and at the same moment, with a fluid movement, his silk tie slipped ribbon-like into the soup. What do you do? Being an Irishman, he laughed, retrieved the dripping object, wrung it out, removed it from his neck, and tieless, hosted his first official dinner.

The team set up their offices in the Meridien Hotel. Not because it was French and grand, but because it was the only hotel in town. There were rumours that another one was being refurbished but so far it had no plumbing.

The hunt for housing was on. It was not easy. There *were* houses available. Thousands of Portuguese citizens had fled the country since Independence in 1975. The problem was that being a Marxist state, all vacated property automatically became the property of the government, available only to party members.

The office was in consultation with the Minister for Internal Affairs, a lady called Senhora Bombom Chocolate, a name surviving from slave times. Finally there was a suggestion. KJ was taken in an official car to inspect a site on which the European Commission might be permitted to build houses. As he emerged from the car he looked around in disbelief. Like Jesus looking down on Jerusalem, he was overlooking an immense rubbish dump, one of many informal refuse disposal areas that had appeared around the city when the 'Lixou Municipal' services gave up in despair. The mountain of rubbish stretched as far as the eye could see. Living in abject shacks, dump-dwellers were the recipients of the stench and debris that flowed from this non-functioning city. Turning to his escort, KJ asked: 'If we built on this site, what would become of all these people?'

'Oh,' was the reply. 'That's your problem. It would be up to you to get rid of the people and clear the site.'

Diplomatically, KJ made it clear that he had neither the heart nor the budget for such an enterprise. Such a task of slum clearance and resettlement would be a major aid project in itself. He mentioned that if some other suitable site could be found, HQ would be prepared to fly out an entire prefabricated compound of offices and houses, as had been done by other organisations, together with a team of builders and technicians to erect it.

At the fatal word 'prefabricated', the Senhora drew herself up to her full height which was not very tall.

'Pre-Fabricado?' she said. *'Pre-Fabricado? – Nunca! Aqui em Luanda, temos Normas Urbais!'* ('Prefabricated? Never! Here in Luanda we have Urban Norms!')

Gazing out on the pot-holed, dilapidated, rat-infested capital, with its rubbish dump in the foreground, KJ repressed a smile.

At Easter, Bernard, the small, dapper administrative officer, came to Harare for his Rest and Recreation leave. We went out to lunch. He told me proudly and enthusiastically that a house for the Delegate had been found. It was a three-storey house, built with the kitchen on the top floor for fear of fire. The staircase was an iron ladder on the side of the building. I thought of staff descending in rain or high wind with trays of canapés. And the dogs falling off. To cap it all, the house was situated next door to a panel-beater's yard! Bernard's hopeful eyes dimmed as he saw my expression.

'Well, perhaps it's not perfect,' he said, crestfallen, 'but . . . '

Stories filtered through from the team in Angola. As a representative of Western Europe, per se, the Delegation was an object of suspicion to those on the far left of the governing Marxist Party. The East Germans were in charge of state security. The team had been warned that all telephone calls would be monitored and that the hotel rooms and office would of course be bugged. Teams of white-overalled men came in to inspect perfectly functioning air-conditioning units, a task which seemed to involve minute examination of the rest of the room as well. Thereafter, KJ began each morning's office meeting – known as 'Morning Prayers' – with the jocular greeting: *'Bonjour les Russes! Bonjour les Cubans!'*

In the early weeks he paid his courtesy visits to the president, and to other embassies. These visits had their comical moments. The Bulgarian Ambassador, for instance, spoke no English, but employed a Portuguese translator. Shortly after the visit began, the ambassador made a remark, which was translated as: 'I wish you a good exit.'

'Exit?' thought KJ. 'Is he telling me to leave his office? To leave the country?' He decided to stay and see what happened. The conversation continued.

After some brain cudgelling he remembered that the Portuguese for 'success' is *Exito*. The ambassador was benevolent but the translator was weak.

It took some time to see the Russian Ambassador, who wished to ignore Western Europe. KJ did not wish to be ignored. After six months of being fobbed off with the *chargé d'affaires*, the visit was finally arranged. The ambassador himself met KJ at the car, escorted by a large burly man who did not look much like a diplomat but did look very much like a member of the KGB. A tray with glasses and vodka was brought in by a young woman wearing white gloves. A toast was drunk. At the end of the visit, the young lady, still wearing her gloves, came to collect the tray. She put KJ's glass very carefully to one side before carrying it out. Somewhere in the Kremlin his innocent Irish fingerprints may still be preserved.

One evening after office hours KJ was summoned from his room to the hotel reception. A young woman from the Department of Foreign Affairs was there to see him. He went down. The pretty young woman asked: 'Shall we go up for a drink?'

Up they went to the bar area. As they sat with their drinks, it seemed to KJ that the conversation was going nowhere very official. He also noticed that the buttons of the young lady's blouse had apparently undone themselves, revealing an expanse of alluring cleavage.

'Shall we go upstairs?' she said meaningfully, putting down her glass.

'Er – yes,' said KJ, thinking fast.

When they got into the lift, he pressed the button for ground floor reception and the lift went down, instead of up. By the time they arrived at street level, the lady was sizzling with fury. As he ushered her out she hissed: 'You're not wanted in Angola. We'll get you out!'

Shaken, KJ returned to his room, and spent some time poking behind pictures and into corners for hidden cameras, concealed to record the planned seduction scene.

The more I heard about Angola the more nervous I felt. But a visit to Luanda was mooted. The hotel room was there, and it would be useful, KJ thought, if I could see my future home. I was not enthusiastic – in fact I had gone into ostrich mode, hoping it might all go away. But new postings never do, and so the flight was booked.

Arriving at the Aeroporto 4 de Fevereiro, an appalling stench of urine and sewage invaded my nose. The terminal looked half-finished. Grey concrete walls and pillars towered to a ceiling layered with girders and pipes where bunches of naked protruding wires hung like Christmas decorations. In the chaos people formed straggly lines, handed in forms, retrieved luggage, and staggered from the fray bent double under the weight of suitcases, boxes, plastic bags and packages. Brooms, rakes, TV sets, bicycles and cages were disgorged onto the luggage platform, snatched up triumphantly and carried into the mob to be argued or bribed through customs and on into Luanda. As I stood irresolute in the seething crowd, near the sign '*Estrangeiros*' a uniformed driver appeared, waving the blue and yellow European logo. This was Antonio, and on his heels came KJ, carrying to my bemusement a small 'man bag' of the kind he had spent most of his life deriding as 'effeminate'.

'We were stuck in traffic,' he began, then caught my glance at the bag.

'Oh this? We have to carry so many documents. We don't dare go out without identification or we could find ourselves in jail.'

I saw the point, but I did wonder where that macho stance had gone.

Once we arrived at the hotel he went to check in. It might have been easier just to smuggle me upstairs. There was an altercation with the booking clerk. Apparently there were objections to KJ bringing a woman into his room. I could hear him repeating in ascending tones: *'Mas, e a minha esposa! E a minha esposa!'* (But it's my wife! it's my wife!)

Suddenly the Portuguese businessman next in line leant forward with a broad smile.

'Pode ser,' he said, *'Acontece – de vez em quando.'* ('It might be his wife! It does happen once in a while.')

Once in the plain, air-conditioned room, I looked out. Spread in an expansive half-moon was the Bay of Luanda, lined with tall buildings. The seafront was edged with dead palms, all beheaded for one Coeur de Palmier. The promenade was decorated with geometric mosaics in black and white, now strewn with rubbish. Leaking effluent pipes left oily traces on the once beautiful pavement. As we watched, a truck drove up. Two men jumped out with shovels and attacked the mosaic without ceremony, breaking it up and shovelling the stones hurriedly onto the back of their truck. When they had a good load they threw their shovels on top of the pile, jumped in and drove away. KJ looked at my stricken face.

'That's been happening every day,' he said. 'Someone is building a house and wants a few stones for the foundations. That's Luanda.'

Dinner at Le Meridien consisted of a small steak and frites. The downside was that it cost US$50 each night – a fortune for a meal in 1986. All food was flown in via Air France three times per week. Hence the expense. And hence the bright red tin trunk in KJ's room filled with tinned fish, dry biscuits, packet soups and a variety of tin-openers.

Breakfast the next day was Parisien: French patisserie, French ham, French cheeses, French coffee. KJ introduced me to his technique for staying alive. A ham or cheese sandwich made at the table and secreted in the briefcase for lunch at the beach.

The beach in Luanda might once have been beautiful. It was still frequented by shapely brown girls in Brazilian string bikinis playing ball games with handsome youths. But it was also used as a public toilet and dustbin by the hordes of homeless squatters forced into the city by the war. Black pigs grazed and unmentionable things lurked behind rocks. We sat on the sand and ate our ham rolls. KJ introduced me to *Amazeze* (Zulu for 'fleas') – the little stray dog who shared his meal every day.

Taking a deep breath and glancing nervously over my shoulder, I said: 'I have something to ask you.'

KJ looked nervous. 'What?'

Voice now down to a whisper, lest the rocks should be bugged, I said: 'The landlord in Harare says I can stay in the little house if we can pay him in foreign exchange. He needs to finance his wife in her studies overseas. Can we do it?'

I wondered why he was grinning. 'Is it going to harm anyone if we do?' he asked.

'Not really,' I said – then saw the joke.

In Zimbabwe people spoke in hushed voices about the punishments for infringing foreign currency regulations. I had somehow imagined that Robert Mugabe's government might have ears stretching as far as Angola. KJ lived with bugged air conditioners, and had entertained a KGB-inspired Mata Hari. Now I was whispering on a beach in Angola for fear of being heard in Harare. This was all becoming very James Bond.

We were invited to dinner at the French Embassy. The ambassador was a dapper little man. As the *Cuisses de grenouille* were served the lights went out. Candles were brought. We sat in silence, and listened as the deep thrumming vroom of generators started up, one after the other and all over the city, lights flashed up once more on the horizon.

We drove around Luanda. The streets were sandy, dusty, rutted and pot-holed. One hole was so deep that it had swallowed a yellow Volkswagen months ago. No one seemed to know whose it was, or whether there were any plans to extricate it. Filling the crevasse was not mentioned as a possibility. Litter had not been collected for several years. On an abandoned garage forecourt debris was piled five metres high to the delight of the hairy black pigs rooting around in it. At intervals along the streets, piles of stinking fish-heads were left, abuzz with black flies. Aimless stray dogs abounded, some hairless with mange. If an animal died, the body was left where it lay to swell and rot in the heat. It was a measure of the quality of life that no one seemed to notice any longer.

The city had once been beautiful. Exquisite colonial houses decorated Portuguese fashion, with blue and white ceramic *azuleijos*, decayed where they stood, shutters askew, roof tiles missing and walls daubed with Marxist slogans. Around the bay, the 'Marginal', dozens of once-pleasant waterfront restaurants were locked and abandoned, their rainbow-coloured chairs upended on the tables. On the city skyline multi-storey concrete buildings rose, skeletons surmounted by swaying cranes, exactly as they had been on Independence Day – the bones of abandoned hopes and dreams.

I returned to Zimbabwe sobered. I could see life in Harare as the paradise it was, but now had seen what could happen in a few short years. Nevertheless I, and others, felt secure in the thought that it would never happen in Zimbabwe. Zimbabwe was different. Zimbabwe was one country in southern Africa that would succeed. It was, after all, the food bowl of southern Africa. We human beings, perhaps fortunately, have very short sight.

Thinking about the visit, the challenges felt overwhelming. It also seemed to me that KJ was enjoying them immensely. He was energised, dynamic and full of authority. I noticed that he was wearing the new mantle of 'Head of Mission' with panache.

I have always been suspicious when people take a role too seriously. Roles are good tools and help us to operate efficiently in a material world. When we begin to believe that we *are* our role, there is a danger that the inner, essential person, the truth of us, is eroding. The job we do is not the person we are – and in the Diplomatic Corps, any honour we receive is to honour the country or organisation we represent, not ourselves. Foolish are those who take it personally. It will very soon pass on to the next incumbent.

We have all known teachers who became didactic bores, doctors who developed into arrogant bullies and actors who became confused, clowning chameleons in daily life. I didn't want to find myself living with a person who might be tempted to think he was 'Head of Mission' at home. Particularly not in my kitchen. So I went shopping.

I had seen something in downtown Harare that might be useful. It was in a souvenir shop in the new *Karigamombe* (cattle market) shopping mall. I bought one, parcelled it up and sent it off to Luanda in the diplomatic bag. A couple of weeks later KJ received the small parcel. It came with a card saying: 'Whenever you begin to feel that you are a VIP just put this on the nearest pile of Very Important Documents.'

He opened the parcel and found a half-circular Perspex paperweight. Inside was something that looked like a piece of bird's nest. Turning it over, he read: 'Contents: Best African Elephant Bull shit.'

He swears to this day it made him laugh so much that he forgot to be Important for fully half a day.

The housing situation in Luanda was slowly evolving. Roland found a house for himself and his family. Bernard likewise, though it was so tiny two people could not pass on the stairs. The Teddy Baar was left in the hotel with KJ. Then after a break-in and rape at another embassy an even smaller house became vacant. After more and heavier burglar bars were installed, the Teddy Baar moved in. As one who had worked in Central Africa, and had already survived smallpox and the plague, Teddy Baar felt he could cope.

KJ was last out of the hotel, like the good captain of a ship. Like divorce in Italy – 'There is no divorce in Italy and only Catholics can get it!' – there were 'no houses in Luanda' and only Marxists could get them. But there *were* a few Portuguese house owners who wanted to leave Angola and did not much want the government to commandeer their houses when they left – largely because they would not be paid for them. KJ was visited in secret by one such owner. He explained that he wanted to sell his house and leave. KJ could have it on payment of $50,000. If HQ would pay the Angolan Ministry of Housing $50,000, theoretically they would pay the money to Senhor. But there was the little matter of the 100 to 1 exchange rate. Government would make a small calculation and instead of $50,000, Senhor would be given $500 to start a new life elsewhere. This he could not afford. Phone calls were made to HQ.

Given the astronomical rents demanded from expatriates in many West African capitals, an 'advance rental' of $50,000 was acceptable for a house for the Head of Mission. A deal was struck that seemed fair to everyone. And KJ had a house.

He sent photographs. It was a small house in a small tiled garden. Every stone was meticulously picked out in white and outlined in cockroach-killer green. The main room was a masterpiece of nightclub décor, each wall a different colour – bright orange, turquoise, green, and red. Some walls had mosaic features, others were studded with embossed copper tiles. The ceiling was the masterwork. It was composed of rainbow glass panels, each illuminated separately at the flick of a switch for a moving light show. The red-painted staircase flaunted a swirling mural and the small windows were gaudy stained glass. But it was a house. A French firm, Stapem and Co, had been employed to strip it down and render it neutral and habitable. KJ would come back to Harare in a few weeks to help with the final packing and transfer of goods, dogs and Paddycat to the new home. It would then be fifteen months since I had first moved into the little house in Meath Road.

The final packing was almost as dramatic as the first. This time nothing could be left behind. The goods in the little house had, as usual, increased in geometric progression. The suspicious Janet assisted with suspicion until the end. KJ risked immediate divorce by presenting her with my new straw hat – *specially* trimmed with flowers to match a blue and yellow summer dress. As I scowled, she smiled.

One last night sleeping in the empty and denuded house. How many times have we done this? It is a ghostly sensation, living for the last few days or hours in a place which has been filled with life and happiness and is now filled with only the shreds of memory. Departing from a posting is a stomach-knotting time. So much life has been lived there, so many friends made, so much laughter exchanged, and now so many farewells said. The whole of life has been thrown up in the air and dispersed. Nothing remains but material debris packed in boxes.

The morning of the journey dawned. We arrived at the airport loaded with crates and boxes, two dog kennels, the cat-box, and the harp. The TAP clerk panicked. Surely these great and rich people could not be going to Luanda! No one of any importance goes to Luanda. They must be going to Lisbon! Ten items were checked in to Lisbon before we noticed. Telling KJ to see which country the pets had been sent to, I dived behind the desk into the luggage hall – it was the days before terrorism. Darting hither and thither I managed to identify six of the misdirected boxes. The rest had vanished Lisbon-wards.

6

Living in a Country at War with Itself

We arrived at the Aeroporto 4 de Fevereiro with dogs, cat, vegetables, typewriter, half our luggage and the harp. Some boxes had burst and some were missing. Paddycat had weed in his box from fright and was miserable. Stepping out of the plane we stepped into the hot room of a Turkish bath perfumed with a steaming miasma of blocked toilets.

We were ushered through customs, through the VIP lounge (*O Vipsh*) and into vehicles. As we rolled over the dusty, pot-holed roads we glimpsed the *Mousseques* – shanty-towns below road level, where refugees from conflicted country areas eked out an existence, and stunted papaya trees pushed up through the sunken level of human squalor and misery in an effort to reach the light.

Angola, 1986, was in the midst of war. The Land of the Blacksmith Kings, once one of Portugal's proudest possessions, was now a country depleted by 500 years of slavery and conflict. At Independence in 1975, Portuguese settlers, traders, artisans and professional people had fled the country. They took with them whatever they could – vehicles, machinery and plans for the public utilities of Luanda, including the public water system and the general hospital. A fleet of ships loaded with vast wooden crates waited in the harbour to transport the possessions of Luanda's Portuguese back to Portugal. Much that could not be taken was destroyed.

The MPLA,* which had led the Independence movement,

* MPLA – Movimento Popular de Libertação de Angola

controlled the government, first under Poet-President Agostinho Neto (the 'Immortal Guide of the Revolution') and later under President Jose Eduardo dos Santos.

But Independence brought no peace. Jonas Savimbi's anti-Communist UNITA* disputed the MPLA's ascendancy, and civil war broke out. With the Soviet Union and Cuba on one side, supporting the Marxist MPLA, and the United States and South Africa on the other, supporting UNITA, the country became a Cold War battleground. Fifty thousand Cuban troops were in the country, fighting beside Angolans and Russians against the West and bizarrely protecting American oil interests at the same time.

When we arrived, Luanda was awash with Soviet personnel and surrounded by a cordon of Cuban troops. There was a curfew and gunfire at night. Russian MIG fighters and helicopters roared overhead, and South African troops were operating in the south of the country.

In the midst of this military confusion the people of Angola were caught; fields were strewn with mines, towns and villages bombed, and food supplies cut off. With a coastline extending more than 1000 miles, Angola contained vast mineral resources, rich soils and micro-climates capable of growing ample food for the population. But Luanda, cut off by a cordon of troops, had no supply lines for provisions. In this climate of desperation, terrified refugees flocked in and the city built for 500,000 people, was crowded with 1,500,000 inhabitants.

Life was desperately hard. Industrial sites lay idle, the factories with plate glass windows broken, now inhabited only by squatters and a few hens. Public health had broken down, malaria was rife, cerebral malaria, cholera and typhoid were ever-present threats. Chemist shops were bare. Doctors could prescribe but to no avail. Water ran in the streets from broken pipes, and

* UNITA – União Nacional para a Independência Total

lacking elevators, professional people carried buckets up the stairways of their high-rise apartments.

People queued in long lines in the streets with gas cylinders on their heads, hoping for a refill before supplies ran out again. A few official shops doled out meagre rations.

The car pulled up in the Rua Damiao de Gois outside a small house behind a high hedge of spotted crotons. Upstairs a balcony was visible with thick prison bars. Eastern European embassies, friends of the leftist government, had been allocated large houses overlooking the sea but representatives of most Western nations lived in small houses such as this one. Once inside the gate we were in a tiny garden covered with ceramic tiles. Five ancient cycad palms sprouted from little squares of earth.

On the tiled porch three staff members waited. Wearing jeans and European Union T-shirts they made their obeisance. The plump Portuguese housekeeper Dona Adelaide, and Francisca her assistant, both curtsied, and Gaby, the young houseman, bobbed up and down like a cork on a choppy sea. Francisca and Gaby were thin and wiry. Gaby spoke some Portuguese. Francisca was from the country. She spoke only Kimbundu, and that rarely, as I would discover.

The house was now almost transformed. The last vestiges of bluebag blue and viridian green were being removed from the outside walls and the multicoloured main room was now painted cream. In the bedroom the bed had been made up with borrowed sheets, the corners neatly knotted, and Adelaide proudly pointed to a jam jar of spotted croton leaves on a chest.

'Fazem raizes estes!' she said. 'These will root!'

Immense work on the house had been done by an enterprising French company, Stapem, at correspondingly immense cost, since every nail and pot of paint had to be imported. There was no town water after noon, but the new underground water tank and pump were installed, and a generator was in place. This was fortunate, as not only was the town electricity erratic, but the three-phase wiring in the house had reduced itself to a smoking and variable two-phase system. At night it was candles and gas-lamps. We hoped for the best for the slightly squashed food supplies we had brought from Harare.

We hardly slept that first night. The bedroom had venetian blinds from floor to ceiling and the security lighting installed by HQ blazed in. Unsure whether to sleep with air-conditioning on or off, we alternately froze and roasted. The neighbours in their tiled courtyards waited until midnight to cook their *al fresco* evening meal with banging of saucepans, merry shouting and loud music. When we did manage to doze off, gunshots were fired in the street outside. Eventually we learned to sleep in eye-shades and ear-plugs. In the morning we peeped over the eye-shades and removed the ear-plugs, uncertain of what we might find.

On the first day, after a minimal breakfast, I was gazing in an exhausted stupor at suitcases strewn around the small hot bedroom when there was a loud banging on the door. It was Dona Adelaide, the housekeeper; energetic, bright-eyed and eagerly brandishing mop, bucket and dusters.

'I have to do the cleaning,' she said – with the sub-text, 'therefore please leave the room NOW!'

I scraped together enough Portuguese to say that I was not ready for her to do the room, and that she would do it, please, in my time rather than in hers. I hoped it was convincing. Dona Adelaide disappeared.

The phone rang. It was KJ. 'We are invited out tonight to *Futungo de Bellas.* Ceaucesceau, the President of Rumania, is in town.' Having established that *Futungo de Bellas* was the presidential palace, I fell on the boxes, desperately clawing out clothes and creating more chaos all over the floor, trying to find something to wear that was not creased to extinction, since the iron had not arrived.

The evening was a sit-down affair for several hundred people. Everybody who thought they were anybody was there. At the far end of the room, a hundred humble places away from the high table, we strained to hear long speeches above loud music. Most of them, as far as I could make out, attacked America and South Africa, though my Portuguese was shaky. But they were unlikely to have been in favour of either. Straight after the speeches the Rumanian Prime Minister stood up and left. Protocol dictated that we all had to stand up and follow him out. It meant that everyone missed out on pudding, which looked rather good, and we went casting sideways glances at the hundreds of little cakes. I hope they went to people who needed the food.

The next day Adelaide and I went shopping. I had seen the Loja Franca – the foreign currency duty-free supermarket – on the first visit. At that time it had been full of Toblerone chocolate, salami, outboard motors and slightly squashed Edam cheese. I was assured that this was temporary, that next week there might be nothing but washing powder and the week after, its Yugoslav entrepreneurs might get tired of not being paid by the Angolan government and close down. So it was a case of 'Gather ye outboard motors while ye may'.

For the moment, however, this 'Jumbo' supermarket still functioned. Shopping there was like gambling. Sometimes there were surprising things like yoghurt and peanut butter, or a few soggy apples. There was rarely any meat, bread only very occasionally, of an indestructible kind, no flour and no lots of other basics, but perhaps packs of ready-mixed doughnuts, French perfume or smart French shoes. On this first day there was tinned tuna, spaghetti and tinned tomatoes. Combined with some green peppers that Adelaide managed to acquire, we had a week of pasta. The Swiss Ambassador was there shopping with his red-haired wife. There was a shout and a commotion. His Excellency had put his foot through a rotten board and ruefully withdrew his dripping trousered leg from a drain that smelt of rotten meat and fish.

We visited a large local market, approached over a 6 inch deep carpet of rubbish and corn-husks. There was plenty of fruit, and vegetables and piles of gaping fish. All the produce was in small mounds priced at $15 or $20 – 15 or 20 cents at the unofficial rate. At that time the local kwanza – $US exchange rate had a discrepancy between the official and black market rate of 100 to 1. Eggs were 600 kwanzas each, which at the official rate of 30 to $1 made the price $20 per egg. For the honour of Europe, we were duty-bound to use only the official rate, and to fill all petrol tanks at prices fit for an Arab potentate, instead of just handing the attendant a couple of cans of beer. When the drivers went into the bank to change money at the official rate, as per instructions from HQ, bank clerks wept and tore their hair, and implored them to go out into the street and change it there instead.

Adelaide, in the market, spent her time making little noises of indrawn breath at the prices and shaking her hand from the wrist, as if she had been burned. I found the poverty, the squalor and the smells a shock. The meat was black with flies, there were poor hens and ducks tied by their feet, dying of thirst as they waited to be sold, and thin dogs with severely fly-bitten ears. I suppose I should have pitied the people but by a system of deals and exchanges they seemed to be keeping themselves clothed and fed in a fairly lively and spirited way, whereas no one seemed to care about the animals.

When expatriates employed domestic workers all meals had to be provided, and three quarters of their pay was put onto a Loja Franca card. That ensured food, and made employees in expatriate households extremely prosperous by local standards. Dona Adelaide cheerfully cooked for everybody at lunchtime, including the night-watchman, a stunning Cape Verdian called Francisco, with the longest eyelashes I had ever seen.

Some postings can barely be described. They can only be lived. In the first few weeks in Angola, the normal shock of a new posting was multiplied by the danger, violence and strangeness of the society. When not unpacking boxes or dealing with staff I gazed out through the inch-thick prison bars of my upstairs balcony at a desolate, dusty street, strewn with potholes. Sometimes in the morning, the fish-seller would come, a woman with a raucous voice who cried her wares in a medieval sing-song all the way down the street. She would take the plastic bath of fish from her head to make a sale, then wash the fish in the disease-ridden drain at the side of the road before handing it over to a customer. Here was a place where so many of the norms of life as I had known it were absent that the only expectation could be the unexpected. I may have written a thesis on Culture Shock but I was in desperation and near despair. The choice was either to laugh or cry. I didn't want to spend the whole time crying. It seemed better to see the funny side of whatever happened so I began to write long humorous bulletins to friends.

Extract from Bulletin 1, 31st March:

The house is large by Meath Road standards, but when the new dining-room table is extended to seat its 14 people it practically walks out the door. We have a large amount of beautiful cherry-wood furniture, some so far unidentifiable. Not all of it will fit, even if I decide just what exactly it is.

Kieran has found a housekeeper called Dona Maria Adelaide. Adelaide is energetic and cheerful and I am learning Portuguese at a great rate from her. She has chosen two domestic staff, a young couple, both with innocent, bright eyes – Gaby and Chica. Gaby seems bright and willing whereas Chica is struggling to learn to iron without putting all the creases back when she turns things over and I am struggling to put things into Portuguese like: 'When you put the iron down please don't burn the new ironing board.'

Bearing in mind our embryonic Portuguese, I think they are all doing very well not to laugh, particularly as Italian is throwing up some hilarious grammatical 'false friends'. As the cardboard boxes and cartons gradually reduce to about knee-height all over the house, one day, perhaps next week, there will be time to sit down and do some Portuguese grammar again. I have taken to wearing skirts with big pockets, so that I can carry a small dictionary with me since I am beginning to realise that Adelaide is a smart cookie with an answer for everything and I need to have my wits and dictionary about me.

I am getting used to housekeeping in Portuguese. Adelaide likes to clean with a product with the unlikely name of 'Soda Pop'. One day she asked me to get something else in the Loja Franca. It sounded like 'Oh vih!' I tried repeating it to her, but she just shouted 'Oh vih!' back at me several times. I was obviously being very stupid. Then I asked her to write it on the shopping list. There it was, clear as daylight – 'O Vim'. Vim!

'Oh, Vim!' I said. 'Si, O Vih!' Adelaide replied. It could have gone on all day.

Cooking terms are translated from other languages with a twist. Adelaide cooks *Esparguete* for lunch sometimes – spaghetti and chicken in a tomato sauce; *croasantjes* (croissants) puzzled me for a while, and *cha e scons* – 'tea and scones' delighted me – scones, in this amazing language being pronounced 'sconsh'.

The pets have settled in variably. The dogs are thrilled to be somewhere new, though Panda took a while to understand that the front garden was her territory. On her first day, she, a bull terrier, actually backed away from a small, gentle, half-starved Angolan dog that looked through the fence. Paddycat hibernates in the well of the spare room wardrobe where he thinks no one would look for a cat. He is frightened by all the noises – low-flying planes, trucks, gates, doors, shouting people, unidentified crashes, and, of course by Adelaide who moves very fast, slams things down and shouts loudly. She frightens me a bit too. It is all very Mediterranean, and I suppose the neighbouring cats all howl in Portuguese as well to make it worse.

On the day we arrived the city celebrated Mardi Gras – a bit late, but it was that sort of place, and in any case, in a Marxist society, Lent and Easter did not rate highly. No one took down the posters or viewing stands – perhaps they would do for next year. Lakes from burst water mains and inadequate drainage still lay in the streets, as did piles of rubbish. Council employees, thin women in rags, painstakingly swept litter into little mounds, but since the rubbish trucks never arrived, their dust mounds were dispersed every day by the wind, or flattened by passing cars so they started patiently all over again. There were not so many pigs in the streets as before, though Dona Adelaide kept one, she said, and some ducks, but there was a goat wandering in the street outside the house. On our second night Panda caught a large rat in the garden which thrilled her.

One effect of the unpacking process after fifteen months, was that we began to wonder why we ever acquired so much stuff in the first place. Luckily there was a good system by which second-hand clothes could be swapped for fish, so the pile for the *Kandonga* grew steadily.

Dona Adelaide's husband seemed to have useful connections. He was a small, nuggety Portuguese gentleman preceded by a large moustache, who drove a beaten-up old Renault deux chevaux through the battle lines to Bairra-do-Dando where he acquired wonderful fish. We had reposing in the freezer, thanks to him, a metre-long fish. That fish was one very good reason for keeping the generator going, as the supply line from Harare succeeded in producing only a lot of mouldy vegetables. We also acquired (somehow) a huge bag of powdered mashed potato from the SWAPO* stores – I hate to ask in exchange for what. And one night, Adelaide turned up at 8.30pm, hammering on the gate, bearing in her muscular arms five export boxes of fresh packed fish from, she said, a consignment bound for Russia. The possible ramifications were mind-boggling, but we quickly put it all into the freezer, pending a possible international incident. Hopefully, by the time Mr Gorbachev realised it was missing, it would be eaten.

In a society where poverty, swapping and making do were the norm, the whole economic and social situation seemed hopeless to Western eyes. It seemed obscene to expect to live by normal middle-class European standards. Already our priorities were beginning to change.

Not long after arriving in the house a 'Mission' from Head-quarters was announced. This would involve my first cocktail party for forty people. And I would have to do it somehow in a city without shops, using only what the Jumbo and the market could offer that week, starting from flour and $20 eggs. The menu would depend on what could be found.

I realised too, as I looked around, that the house was not finished. We had painters and workmen everywhere, the carpet squares for the main room were still in boxes and seemed to be of two different greens, and the furniture was yet to be identified and assembled. In addition the staircase was still painted its original bright red. There was work to be done. In fact there was always work to be done, just surviving each day, and trying to keep track of Adelaide, Gaby, Francisca, the men from the French company, Stapem, the painters, the drivers and messengers from the office. I would go into the kitchen and find various people being entertained by Adelaide, who seemed to think they had come to visit her, and held court, instead of letting me know they were there.

* SWAPO – South West African People's Organisation.

'*O Primeiro do Maio Mais Vermelho!*' (The Reddest First of May!) The Marxist slogan has appeared all over town – sort of like a white Christmas, only red.

I have a strange medley of staff in the house. Dona Adelaide is a dynamo. I haven't quite worked out how to control her enthusiasm yet. She has a way of taking the wind out of my sails, when I make a suggestion – with her famous 'Aie-eh!' which, as I interpret it, comes close to a Portuguese equivalent of 'Oh yeah!' I wear skirts with big pockets, and keep a dictionary handy but my Portuguese still being limited, it sometimes takes fifteen minutes with a grammar book to work out what I should have said after the event.

The two young Angolans shine with good will but are very new to domestic work. Apparently Angolans were never employed in houses in town before Independence, since poor Portuguese citizens, the '*degredados*', did domestic and menial work. Even Adelaide is a bit hazy about how things should be done, though she has a fertile fantasy of 'life in the great houses' which fills in the gaps. One of her fantasies concerned tea-towels. She took to getting rid of them after one use – I suspect transporting them home for herself. When we had gone through ten tea-towels in one week, I investigated and was told: 'We cannot use old tea towels in the house of *O Senhor Embaixador!*'

I assured her that O Senhor Embaixador had no problem with that, in fact he preferred them to be washed and used again.

Gaby and Francisca were just amazed at everything. Gaby initially showed promise, but his efforts to serve at the table entailed a lot of clenched teeth and a bottom that stuck out with concentration. Francisca spent whole mornings ironing one tablecloth, and the tablecloth emerged victorious. It seemed unkind to think of dismissing her since she was trying so hard, but meanwhile I was running out of dresses, and Kieran out of safari suits. I resorted to surreptitious ironing after hours. Francisca seemed to enjoy mealtimes. Her presence could at least be justified on the grounds that we were at least providing food for one more Angolan.

For some weeks we were infested solidly with painters and workmen. One day we broke the record with eleven people working in the house at once, fourteen including the staff. The situation felt desperate. I had just placed myself between the drills of the electrician and the hammering of the carpenter, for a few moments of peace and quiet in my study, when I looked up and saw a painter clinging to the balcony rails and peering in. These painters were quite a saga. They were employed to paint out all the bright colours with which the house had been decorated. It took them more than a month and many coats of paint. But they also spent a lot of time painting other things including themselves. The younger one was totally covered, from headscarf to feet, in white paint, the ladders were covered, the verandas were coated, the windows were spotted and the paths were splodged, and in between they did an excellent job on most of the pot plants, the lawn, Panda's back and the laundry basket.

One day I was between jobs, looking out into the street, when there was an almighty crash followed by series of clatters and a lot of thumping and shouting.

'Noisy lot!' I thought, and went back inside, feeling glad that whatever it was, was not happening here.

This was premature, because Dona Adelaide arrived breathless at the door to announce that there was a 'problema' with a painter who had fallen off a ladder and, I gathered, had 'broken his head'. He had indeed fallen off a ladder – about three steps – not with the usual pot of paint, but with a sheet of roofing material. He had a smallish cut on the head, which as head cuts do, bled profusely and gave rise to a splendid amount of shouting. When Panda very reasonably, being a dog, went to investigate, the shouting increased in volume, and I gathered that there was great fear that she might sniff the blood on the ground and instantly turn into a carnivorous monster. After much consultation, Dona Adelaide rather grandly sent Gaby to the office to fetch the official driver and the painter was taken off in great style to the local '*Instidudo de Saude*' for treatment, while everyone else stopped work for the rest of the day to talk about it. All very operatic. I'm sure the poor man had a bad headache that night, but I realised that the combination of the Mediterranean and the African sense of drama could enjoy a crisis to the full.

At our first formal lunch, for the Head of Division and Desk Officer from Brussels, I asked Adelaide to warm the plates.

'No, no, you don't want the plates hot, this is Africa!' came the jolly reply.

Instead of drawing myself up like the lady of the manor, I just gawped at her in surprise, thereby losing a round.

That lunch was memorable for a number of things. For a start, just as the guests were coming up the front steps, Francisca accidentally slammed the iron security grille on Panda's tail. Panda thought Polar must have bitten her and started a fight. I heard the snarling, and rushed into the kitchen to see three saucer-eyed staff members cowering behind the door as they watched the dogs demolish each other. I waded in, separated the fighters, flung one into the laundry and went to greet my first VIP guests with bloodstains on a new cream skirt. The lunch was also notable for Gaby's terror as he bit his tongue with the effort of serving the wine. He rushed around the table *accelerando*, collecting plates faster and faster, making everyone nervous and dizzy as he went.

KJ had installed a little electric bell which ran from the kitchen under the carpet, to a spot under the table near my toe so that I could press it when the next course was wanted. That was the theory but I was so nervous that my foot froze on the bell, and it rang endlessly. The kitchen door opened every two seconds, and three questioning faces peered in to see what was happening. And despite all the checking with books on table-setting and etiquette, we forgot to put out any forks for the salad. Adelaide, not to be defeated, dashed headlong into the pantry, and emerged triumphantly waving some tiny forks. So we solemnly ate our salad with cake-forks, po-faced, pretending it was just another rather odd English habit. To cap it all, I had proudly made an Australian Pavlova for dessert. Luanda boasts 90 per cent humidity. When it was ready to be served, it was brought to the table – no longer meringue but deliquesced into a sad mound of fruit salad and cream in the middle of a puddle of sugary liquid.

The cocktail party for fifty people was an even bigger challenge. We trawled the market and the Loja Franca for raw ingredients and worked for two weeks in the kitchen. We conquered puff pastry, fried prawns in batter, made the ubiquitous curried eggs, and experimented with tiny sandwiches using multi-coloured breads. Adelaide said she would do *Pasteis* which were tiny fish pasties, *ricois* – similar, filled with some sort of 'prime matter', and *forminhas*. The latter were a problem since she seemed to want little patty pans to make them in. When I produced muffin trays they would not do and she muttered about 'things being better in Portugal'.

However, she managed to produce fish balls and some crab pies which were wonderful except that in her enthusiasm she included pieces of shell as well. I tried not to watch the faces of the Exceléncias as they bit into them and just prayed that they would find handy ashtrays. When I tried one, I found four bits of crab shell, and a piece of glass as well. How on earth could I put all that into Portuguese! We had a slight problem with the serving. I had explained carefully that all three of the staff should take trays and go around offering the food to the guests. They did. Adelaide lead the procession, and Gaby and Francisca followed hard on her heels; too frightened to branch out on their own, so that everyone was offered the same things three times over in rapid succession.

After the cocktail KJ and the visitors disappeared for six days to rural areas. They returned with stories of whisky for breakfast, and whisky instead of drinking water, in places where the water supply was even more lethal than the Johnny Walker. They didn't have to wash in it, but they did have to remember not to open their mouths under the shower. When they arrived back in Luanda, KJ had to turn around in an hour and go to an official dinner, given by government for the visitors. None of the local officials had been invited in time. It ended so late that by the time it was over KJ's driver, Antonio had managed to get rolling drunk and almost ran down three women in the street. As people say here frequently: 'Ai ai ai!'

Paddycat slowly recovered from his culture shock. For a long time he spent his mornings hiding in the bowl of my wardrobe, to avoid the *confusão* that was Adelaide's idea of a good working day. However, when the staff had gone and things were calmer I took him for walks on his little elasticised lead and harness, so that if he tried to escape he promptly 'pinged' back. One evening we explored the front garden – ceramic tiles with five small cycad palms planted at intervals. He decided that each palm needed investigating, and insisted on circling them in detail. Unless I let go of the lead I had to follow. How do you explain to a quizzical Portuguese night-watchman why you are on your hands and knees, crawling around a dwarf palm at nightfall? And when PC took fright and bolted, KJ split his sides as I ran helter-skelter for the kitchen door, pulled by the cat.

The dogs became seasoned beach-goers. Polar wasn't about to go into the water a second time in his life (he tried that once in Zimbabwe) so he stayed on the beach, running away from the waves. Panda, however, got into swimming in a big way. She liked to go right in and say hello to swimmers, who, being Angolan youngsters, shrieked and squeaked when she came near, which only made her all the more keen to join in the game. Panda and KJ breasted the waves, both heads held high, and all paws flailing.

In order to get to the beach we had to drive through the cordon of Cuban troops that surrounded Luanda. Panda sat virtuously in the back but Polar Bear, all 27 kilos of him, liked to climb laboriously through to sit on my lap, grinning and panting with excitement. We had to pull up at a military checkpoint. The Cuban guard would come to check the car and stuck his head in at the window eyeball to eyeball with Polar Bear, who was showing all his teeth in his best smile. Drawing back hurriedly, Cuban guard tripped over rifle and asked nervously: '*Sao Maos?*' ('Are the dogs fierce?')

'Muito Maos!' KJ would reply with conviction. ('Yes, they're really bad!')

And we would be gestured on our way with a rapid: '*Vai! Vai!*' It worked every time. Thank you Polar.

The food situation went from the ridiculous to the sublime. Having lived for two weeks on fish, tinned ham and spaghetti, KJ went with Lena, his PA, to one of the oil company supermarkets and at huge expense, came home with – Oh Joy! – not only meat but eggs and yoghurt as well. It cost four times the normal European price, but how wonderful to see an egg again! Then we discovered a large wholesale ship's chandlers, which sold food in industrial quantities. This had all the fascination of gambling. One might go there on Tuesday for 50 kilos of potatoes, but come away with no potatoes, just 25 kilos of courgettes or 10 kilos of bacon instead. It was not ideal – the food was then shared out among the office staff – but it was primitively comforting to have food in the freezer.

Freezers were a lifeline. The Danish Embassy had nine of

them. We eventually had four. We collected food and stored it away for the future. We ate fish and rice ourselves and kept our frozen treasures for guests. Adelaide was very impressed with the freezers, though her way of making things fit in was to hammer them down with a hefty fist. I made a note to myself to look up Portuguese for 'Don't hammer.' Perhaps 'Gently' would do, but would the lady know that concept?

Our first visit to the 'Angoship' ship's chandlers introduced us to the concept of '*Confusão*', meaning predictably, 'confusion'. Watching the *confusão* in Angoship, it occurred to KJ that it was not all bad. The overseer of the *confusão* sat on a high dais, and orchestrated the show. As people ran hither and thither, dragging boxes and crates, shouting and disappearing through doors, *confusão* became an art form. The other Portuguese word much used was '*esquema*' – a scheme, but not only a scheme. It meant to find a way, to know someone, to get by, and cleverly to extricate oneself from an impossible situation. Everyone had *esquemas*. Angoship epitomised the way Angolans coped with their impossible lives in an impossible economy. There was already *confusão*, voluntary and involuntary. They then created more of it, so that they could, under its cover, organise *esquemas* and manage to survive. Boxes departed from Angoship, fell off the backs of lorries or off Russian ships, plastic buckets were exchanged for chocolate or fish or babies' nappies and somehow, in this happy *confusão*, people managed to get by.

Prior to Angoship, we had fish – wonderful fresh fish – even lobsters, all obtained by Dona Adelaide's husband who really knew how to exchange a case of beer. It was a beer economy – in fact I never met anyone who drank the stuff. It seemed to be used purely as a form of currency. One night at a cocktail party I overheard a mock argument among diplomats as to the relative merits of 'convertible' and 'non-convertible' beer, and which brands might come under which heading. When a load of beer was unpacked in the Loja Franca, there was a near riot, as people stampeded to buy a case for $US11, which they would then sell in the Kandonga for 1100 kwanzas or swap for other things. One morning we drove past a large, filthy market near the old bull-ring where a queue of 200 people were waiting patiently, each with a case of beer on his or her head to exchange for black market kwanzas.

To go to the markets we went through *Mousseques*: slums built of cardboard, boxes and corrugated iron. The roads between the houses were more lakes than paths. We heard that people slept on their tables when it rained as the houses quickly filled up with water. Malaria, in particular, worsened in the wet season. We took malaria preparations constantly, although it didn't do to read the list of side-effects. Apparently our eyesight, our digestion and our memory could all suffer damage. But would malaria be preferable?

Hospital conditions were bad. In the public hospital, operating theatre equipment, electricity and water supplies had all been destroyed or sabotaged at Independence. KJ was in the midst of discussions to restore it to something resembling a medical facility. Stories abounded of conditions on the wards – in the maternity hospital, women were said to be four to a bed, with no sheets, since they had already been stolen. They were forced to go to their deliveries naked and were likely to find their clothes gone on their return.

Another unsolved problem in Luanda was the mentally disturbed population. Before Independence there were three psychiatric hospitals. Since the new government provided no food for inmates, and no wages for warders, the occupants had been released. Now there were wild-haired '*malocos*' wandering the streets, dressed in rags and living off the plentiful rubbish dumps with the dogs and pigs. One day we were driving near the Cinema Karl Marx past a raised dais where a white-uniformed policeman usually directed traffic. But on this morning, the energetic policeman was stark naked! One of the unfortunate '*malocos*' was living out his power fantasy, causing drivers to swerve as they did double-takes at what they saw.

Sitting at home in the Rua Damiao de Gois, in my barred and air-conditioned prison, or going to various embassies to pay courtesy calls on ambassadors' wives, the world seemed crazy. Here we were, for the purpose of helping the people of Angola, and here was I driving around in an air-conditioned Mercedes, with flag, while the people of Angola slogged along in the mud, carrying buckets of water and gas canisters on their heads. Worse, there seemed little chance of meaningful contact between the two worlds.

On Sundays we went to a little church on the Ilha. It was on the waterfront, at the end of a long narrow isthmus. It was staffed by Italian nursing nuns who had created real community there. They seemed to know and love everyone who came. The priest preached lively sermons, calling on various members of the congregation by name, so that they squirmed as they gave the wrong answers. The singing was raucous but heartfelt, naked children played with the emblem on the front of the car, and old women came draped in Arabic robes which always snagged on the pews as they went to communion. The harmonium squeaked and must have been the original one installed 500 years ago.

But even there at the church, normal contact was difficult. We were regarded as 'celebrities', ushered to front seats and called up by the padre to shake hands for the kiss of peace. It was wearing to be regarded with such reverence.

One Sunday on the way to church, a truck had gone off the side of the isthmus leading to the Ilha. It was perched drunkenly on the steep stone sea-groin, front wheels in the water. 'They need a tractor,' we thought.

At the church, a bishop from the north of the country presided, a saintly old man who read the Gospel as if he'd been there. We were asked to give him a lift back home.

On the way back, with the bishop on board, we came to a

halt. The truck was still there but people had been busy. Another truck, even larger, had been summoned to pull truck No. 1 up from the sea with a thick wire hawser attached to both bumpers. This being Angola, truck No. 2 had somehow managed to fall off the *opposite* side of the isthmus, and was now in the same drunken predicament as truck No. 1. The wire hawser was stretched taut across the road between the two at waist height, effectively halting traffic from both directions. People had left their vehicles and were enjoying heated arguments about the best way to solve the problem. One party wanted to cut the hawser and let the traffic through, in which case, presumably, both trucks would have slowly toppled into the sea. In the end cars inched around some buildings, gingerly grinding over boulders on the steep stony bank, and we eventually deposited the bishop at his rather decrepit Bishop's Palace.

Next door to the Bishop's Palace stood the mausoleum where the body of the national hero and poet, President Agostinho Neto, was kept deep-frozen for viewing on official occasions. The Diplomatic Corps was summoned to attend these events. Pens and sharp objects were removed from their pockets before they filed past the body, in case they were tempted to puncture the refrigerated glass case. The 'Immortal Guide of the Revolution' had died seven years before, but each year, dressed in black, the family of the defunct Presidential Hero sat around the corpse and looked on.

This business of being one of the 'great ones' also meant I had to think carefully about what I wore in the house. I noted the look of grave shock on Dona Adelaide's face one morning when she caught me on the stairs, barefoot and in shorts.

She gazed at me with eyes wide and said in a shocked voice: *'Descalçada, Senhora?'* ('What! No shoes, Senhora?')

In a country where shoes were a measure of dignity, the 'Senhora da casa' could not go barefoot.

Meanwhile, the Senhora da casa was pondering little things

like how long our clothes might last if they were continually scrubbed on a washing board and dunked in bleach, and trying to solve the mystery of how fourteen litres of oil had been used in a month.

I was beginning to understand culture shock better since I was becoming a walking example of my own studies. I knew that things would probably get worse before they got better. Six months, the books said! At times I found myself feeling extreme irritation and negativity towards local ways of doing things – like dropping saucepans in the yard next door at 1am. However, since regaining a sense of humour was supposed to be a good sign, perhaps writing funny bulletins to friends was a sign of hope.

Another sign of hope was the small art class on the balcony of the British High Commission. Perhaps it was a frivolous activity for idle expatriate women, but the effect of spending a few hours each week in creative pursuits was miraculous. The company was an antidote to our solitary lives. Trixie, our art teacher, brought ideas out of her bottomless suitcase – paints and paper, silk and textiles to dye and embroider, crayons and airbrush techniques. It was a tonic to share stories of the constant crises and mishaps that made up life in Angola, and to find that we were not alone. In the gaps between creative bouts, we feasted on cherry cake provided by Rosemary, the British Ambassador's wife. Rosemary was my model. She was kind, cool, poised and calm and carried out her duties to perfection. But when we heard her stories of knife-fights in the kitchen between her Angolan cook and Cape Verdian butler, our lot didn't seem so bad after all.

Among the trials of Angola were the number of things that went missing – our new stair-carpet from Paris, for one, which got lost en route. We bore with the bright scarlet stair treads for three weeks, but then, just before the big cocktail, painted it white. Neither the stair-carpet nor the missing suitcases from the airport turned up. Not, that is, until KJ went out to the luggage depot one lunchtime to enquire. Having been told that the cases were not there, he spotted two of them on a shelf.

'There they are!' he said, noting as they were brought that they were extremely thin and empty. He pointed out to the official in charge of lost luggage that the zips and locks had been broken, and that most of the contents were missing.

'Prove it!' was the reply.

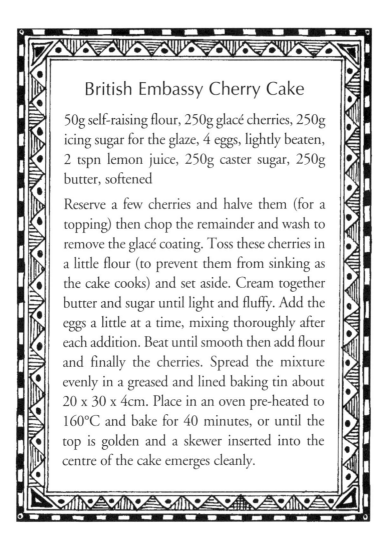

British Embassy Cherry Cake

50g self-raising flour, 250g glacé cherries, 250g icing sugar for the glaze, 4 eggs, lightly beaten, 2 tspn lemon juice, 250g caster sugar, 250g butter, softened

Reserve a few cherries and halve them (for a topping) then chop the remainder and wash to remove the glacé coating. Toss these cherries in a little flour (to prevent them from sinking as the cake cooks) and set aside. Cream together butter and sugar until light and fluffy. Add the eggs a little at a time, mixing thoroughly after each addition. Beat until smooth then add flour and finally the cherries. Spread the mixture evenly in a greased and lined baking tin about 20 x 30 x 4cm. Place in an oven pre-heated to 160°C and bake for 40 minutes, or until the top is golden and a skewer inserted into the centre of the cake emerges cleanly.

7

Adelaide and the Ambassadors' Bones

We went on leave early in the year to attend the wedding of our friend Mary – apparently none the worse for being lost in the Chimanimani Mountains. Jostling, dirty, noisy old London felt safe in comparison with jostling, dirty, noisy Luanda. I spent the first week or so rushing into supermarkets, gazing at the food, marvelling at the many brands of everything, and the piles of fresh fruit – not to buy, but just to be reassured that there was still plenty of food in the world, despite the extraordinary situation in Luanda.

How did people survive there? The secret was the thriving black market in currency, beer, cars, stolen TVs – an entire alternative economy. If a car was taken to the garage, in all likelihood the following day the office driver would need to go and retrieve missing bits of it from one of the black markets. This probably suited the driver, since he may well have had a little payoff from the garage in the first place. The black markets were immense, covering many hectares, and some of them were dangerous. They did, however, have the most wonderful names. There was '*Cala boca!*' ('Keep your mouth shut'), and '*Desculpe Senhor dos Santos!*' ('Sorry Mr dos Santos!') and best of all '*Tira Bikini!*' (translated as 'It costs so much you have to sell your knickers!') Everyone knew about the black markets, and they were teeming with customers and inventive salesmen. Adelaide's favourite vegetable market was on the edge of one of them. We saw vendors selling single plastic bags to shoppers, a young man who had opened a 'coffee stall' with a jar of Nescafé, a spoon, hot water and three wooden boxes to sit on, and best of all, a little boy who had managed to get his hands on a roll-on deodorant which he was selling for a mere ten kwanzas per underarm swipe.

When we arrived back from Europe it was the depths of what passes for winter in Luanda. The *Cacimbo* was blowing the mist in from the sea, the skies were greyish, and it was cool. This meant that we could wear clothes with sleeves, instead of wanting to wear nothing at all, and despite all the noise outside in the street, we occasionally sat with open windows in the evenings.

This 'cool' season brought with it a circus of animal antics in the neighbourhood. First, there was disturbance among the local cat population. A little tabby cat, whom we nicknamed 'Miss Pretty', came into season, and spent her nights leaping daintily across rooftops and walls, calling in an astonishingly loud voice like a piercing counter-tenor, and sending all the local tom-cats raving mad with desire. The feral choir sang oratorios all night. A parrot in the house behind ours talked incessantly and spent his days gnawing holes in the fence; a neglected Alsatian pup played noisily with a broom, and a monkey in the same yard chattered and clattered. Then the small female dog next door came into heat. Seven male dogs lived in the street. For five nights they fought and yelped – just as we got to sleep they would start all over again. Panda was beside herself trying to see it all through the front fence. The real fun began when Miss Dog was ready and the local dogs all queued up to take their turn. A mighty cheer went up in the street. I looked out. Fifty-eight little boys were lined up on garden walls to watch the show.

On the first night back from Europe, however, food shortages had hit our own kitchen. Adelaide had left the house spick and span but apparently hadn't thought that we might want to eat on our return. Although the fridge was polished to a high shine, it was completely bare. After a meagre supper, KJ ambled out to talk to Senhor José, the large and avuncular senior night-watchman. Drawing up a chair, Senhor related, in dramatic Angolan detail, the alarms and excursions that had gone on in our absence.

It went something like this: One night, Senhor José was watching faithfully on the front porch when he smelled something.

'Was it smoke?' he asked himself, and going around to the kitchen door, he decided that indeed it was.

What should he do? The house was locked, he had no key and if he did not do something the Senhor Embaixador's house would certainly burn down.

'Perhaps it is electricity?' said Senhor José to himself, so he found the electric mains and turned off the electricity.

'But perhaps it is gas?' he then asked himself, so he found the gas cylinder, and disconnected that too. But still the smell continued, so he found a broom handle and pushed open the kitchen door, inside the barred grille. There inside the kitchen, was billowing smoke.

'The Senhor Embaixador's house *is* burning down,' said Senhor José, and immediately betook himself out the front gate to the family over the road who were the proud owners of an old, well-worked, and much-washed 10-ton truck.

'The Senhor Embaixador's house is burning down,' said Senhor José. 'You must take me to the house of Senhor Roland immediately.'

So climbing into the 10-ton truck, they thundered off through the unlit streets, over the potholes and drains, to the house of Senhor Roland, Economic Advisor. It is not on record whether he was surprised at this visitation – probably not, this is Angola – and he had, after all, been visited recently by a uniformed gang who held a loaded Kalashnikov to his chest. But Monsieur Roland did not after all have any keys, so he joined the crew in the 10-ton truck, and all three thundered through the night to the house of Monsieur Michel, the head of Stapem, the construction company who worked in the house, a gentle bearded French giant, who had a fine command of the very best French adjectives on occasions such as this. Monsieur from Stapem, rooted out of bed, took the keys of the house, and joined the team, which turned and thundered back in the opposite direction, watching anxiously for columns of smoke in the distance.

They arrived at the house, and the smoke was still there. Senhor from Stapem opened the kitchen door with his key and what did they find? Bones! Soup bones on the stove, in a saucepan, smouldering and sending up clouds of foul-smelling fumes. Senhor José did not remember exactly what Monsieur from Stapem said at that moment, but it was probably something pejorative about housekeepers from southern Europe.

Meanwhile, at the very same moment that the Gang of Four in the 10-ton truck was thundering through the unlit streets, the redoubtable Dona Adelaide was lying in bed beside her husband, looking at one of Dona Pamela's recipe books, when she suddenly sat up and screamed: 'The Senhor Embaixador's bones! I've forgotten the bones!'

Hoisting her small husband out of bed in his pyjamas, she insisted that he should drive her back to the house in their little old banger.

When they arrived, what did they find?

Not only the Senhor Embaixador's smouldering bones, but Senhor José, the night-watchman, and the man with the 10-ton truck from across the road, and Senhor Roland, the Economic Advisor, and Senhor Michel the head of Stapem, and Uncle Tom Cobleigh and all standing in the kitchen.

Senhor José's story ended there and he waited respectfully while KJ gave him a beer and a pat on the back for his resourcefulness and the extreme keenness of his nose. But I rather like to imagine that, in the best Latin tradition, the scene in the kitchen might then have taken off, with the entry of the night-dressed and curler'd Dona Adelaide, into a fully orchestrated Final Act Quintet, with everybody recounting in ascending counterpoint the story of the heroic deeds of the night, nobody listening to anyone else, Dona Adelaide's stentorian Dramatic Soprano soaring over all – and perhaps a part for Bones Obligato from the saucepan.

The first social event on the calendar after our return was a dinner to celebrate the arrival of the new French Ambassador. After the requisite forty-five minutes at the Egyptian National Day cocktail, we went to the home of the First Secretary of the French Embassy to meet his new boss. The First Secretary was a large, bluff bachelor who lived in a tall narrow house, with an outside stone stairway at the side. As we went past the downstairs kitchen, we smelt a cheesy and buttery aroma. Soufflé? Mmmm! We glimpsed a small Angolan houseman working hard, then climbed to the roof terrace and sat over a drink as cooking smells wafted three stories up from below. We sat . . . and the smells wafted . . . and we sat . . . and no one mentioned the time, and we talked . . . and ate nuts . . . until finally, after the host had gone up and down the stairs several times we were called to the table. At 10pm.

At the dining table, there was a soup plate at each place. On each plate was a phallic object, long, skinny, pink and naked. In fact, a lukewarm tinned frankfurter, covered with an awful cold sauce the colour of a frightened tomato. We chewed through the concoction with dead-pan faces, conversing politely about the price of lobsters in Luanda and world politics. No one commented. No one laughed. No one left a scrap. The rest of the meal was an impeccable steak and salad, followed by pineapple dessert. We still wonder what happened to that delicious cheese soufflé. And what was said to the cook after we all went home?

Another memorable dinner took place at the Chinese Ambassador's residence. He lived in an apartment in one of the better tower blocks. The décor included an emperor-sized Chinese screen and two ten-foot-high fringed and carved lamps like mini street lights. The Chinese Ambassador spoke only Chinese (it was said). In attendance were his two interpreters, one for Portuguese and one for English. It was a formal twelve-course Chinese banquet. Each guest had a member of the Chinese Embassy sitting at his or her elbow, to ensure that food was served and eaten, that glasses were filled regularly with potent rice wine, and tossed back with the exhortation '*Kampai!*' As a non-drinker, I found these multiple toasts a serious challenge and eventually compromised by just touching my lips to the glass. It was a choice between the Chinese tradition of hospitality, or a ferocious migraine the next day. And mindful of Mrs Bakewell's Chinese experience I examined each course nervously for evidence of unfamiliar meat that might have been dog.

The conversation struggled as each remark was translated from Chinese to English, and from English to Portuguese, and back again. When a joke was told, we all had to laugh three times. Phrases were translated into Chinese, and emerged twice as long. Did I really say all that? By this laboured method the Chinese Ambassador grilled his diplomatic guests mercilessly. At the end of the evening, there was a distinct coolness in Sino-European relations. One of the senior western ambassadors emerged from the evening saying: 'Bloody hell! The bastard milked us all night and gave nothing away himself!'

I was always diverted when high-ranking diplomats let their diplomacy slip. There was the occasion when the Egyptian Ambassador dropped his guard at a cocktail party. KJ referred to the city of Luanda, and the large jovial gentleman emitted a spontaneous guffaw saying: 'Haw, haw, call it a city!' and we had all laughed before we realised it was probably sedition.

Once on the way back to Luanda at Harare airport, we met an urbane ambassador just back from leave in Asia. KJ remarked that he was just in time for the National Day Parade, an awful event that involved endless hours standing in unbearable heat as ragged columns of troops filed past.

'Oh God,' said the ambassador, 'I thought I'd managed to miss it. Isn't there a later plane this week?' Luanda was a bit like that.

And there was the wonderful moment when I asked one of the ambassador's wives how things were going with a high-ranking visitor from her home country, who was staying in the Residence. She looked at me for a moment, then burst out: 'I hate 'im, I hate 'im, I hate 'im!' Incessant demands she could deal with, but the last straw was being asked to clean his shoes!

On the other hand, I have to confess to a diplomatic gaffe of my own. Reinhild, in her coffee morning lessons, had made clear that there was only one meat that could safely be served to all cults, creeds and nationalities, and that was chicken. It was something I should have remembered. In Angola, chicken was plentiful. It was available from Angoship in large cardboard boxes of twelve closely packed carcases neatly wrapped in plastic. We ate it constantly. After we had been eating it for some time I looked at the label and noticed that it came from Eastern Europe. Wondering why the boxes were so cheap, the word 'Chernobyl' floated across my mind.

Be that as it may, we were fortunate to have a house that more or less functioned, and food in the freezers. Not so fortunate was the Indian Ambassador who, like KJ, had been living in the Hotel Presidente for more than a year and was becoming ever more depressed and pessimistic. We decided to cheer him up a bit and invited him for a meal. I delved into the freezer to find something really special – not chicken – to give him a treat. It was only when I was about to serve up, that I realised what I had done. I was about to serve fillet steak to the Indian Ambassador. He looked at it, and at my dismay. Smiling, he said, with beautiful diplomacy: 'Well, I'm sure it's a foreign cow!' And ate it.

At this time, the household staff still consisted of Dona Adelaide, Francisca of the tablecloths, and Gaby, serving at table with clenched teeth and protruding behind. Francisca continued for her probationary period, without ever producing anything that was actually ironed, despite demonstrations, pep talks and entreaties. Out of her depth, she lived in a daze, deaf to everything, including Adelaide's shouts, and doorbells. Apart from the celebrated occasion when she slammed the door on Panda's tail and caused a fight, she gave no visible sign of animation whatsoever, with the possible exception of staff mealtimes which she enjoyed. So at the end of the month, Cisca was given notice. She accepted the news with the same stolid expression with which she greeted everything else. But during her final week, her unconscious spoke loud and clear.

On Reinhild's advice I had bought from the Indian bazaar in Johannesburg, many yards of white damask cloth to make a frightening number of large-scale tablecloths and napkins. These had been hemmed by a friend of Dona Adelaide's in return for a generous amount of flour and sugar. On their return these brand new and spotless damask tablecloths were given by Dona Adelaide to Francisca, together with four bottles of bleach, and the instruction: 'Wash them!'

So she did. In neat bleach. The results were predictable. Lots and *lots* of shredded white damask dusters and no tablecloths. I suppose we were lucky that Francisca didn't stay longer than a month.

About this time, the Danish Embassy closed down in Angola, for reasons of security. The ambassador's wife was very anxious to find a place for her young housekeeper, Maria da Conceição a small, smiling convent-educated young woman who, it seemed, could run a household, and was charming into the bargain. Cão came to join the team, and went quietly about her tasks, keeping her eyes well down, and not responding too much to Adelaide's more dramatic excesses.

After Francisca went, Gabriel did his very best. Dona Adelaide, large and bossy, set her staff ten jobs, and shouted them from one to the other. As time went on Gabriel looked increasingly distrait and desperate and made more mistakes. When Dona Adelaide was on leave for ten days, he improved, since I explained things quietly and clearly one at a time. But a few weeks after she returned, we were in the kitchen one night, wistfully discussing how nice it would be to have someone efficient and bright working in the house, like, for instance Francisco, Senhor José's nephew – he of the long eyelashes, when lo and behold, Gaby rang the bell at the gate. There he was on his motor-scooter, asking if we would mind if he switched jobs with Francisco. His church had asked him to become a catechist during the day, and he wanted to be a night-watchman at night. We were dubious about the quality of his catechesis, but jumped at the chance, before he changed his mind. Dona Adelaide was highly put out that she had not been consulted. We rather suspected that Gaby was looking forward to peaceful days as well as quiet nights.

So Gabriel the houseman became Gabriel the night-watch-men. The first night he was asleep by 7.30, the second by 8.30, and on the third he managed to stay awake until we brought his hot supper out at nine. He was gently told that night-watchmen are not supposed to sleep, conducted round the tiny garden with instructions on how to use the gas siren and what to do if 'Ladrões' arrived in the night to rob the house. A few days later Gaby was late for work. He explained light-heartedly that they had had visitors at home and disappeared. At about 10pm, Paddycat had not reported in for duty so I went to find him, in case he should be locked in somewhere. The door to the outside room where the dogs had their kennels was closed. Thinking that Panda had slammed it with her interminable ratting activities, I went in nightgown and bare feet to open it. What was behind the door but Gabriel sound asleep on a lovely soft mattress of padded bags, ears covered with a woollen balaclava – dead to the world. It was that old game of 'hunt the watchman' again.

I crept upstairs, and told KJ of my discovery. Taking with him the gas-powered alarm siren, 'O Senhor Embaixador' crept downstairs and across the yard, and sounded the hooter close to Gaby's ear. Watching from upstairs I saw the balaclava'ed Gabriel emerge from the outhouse door like a Harrier jump-jet closely pursued by an enraged *Delegado*, mock-belabouring the miscreant over the head with little strips of paper bag. Our night-watchman fled, covered with bits of fluffy paper, shouting as he went: *'Não me bate Senhor, não me bate!'* ('Don't beat me, Senhor, don't beat me!')

Panda and Polar Bear arrived on the scene, dancing and apologising and wagging in all directions, wondering what they had done wrong and who they ought to help. Poor Gaby was last seen on his motor scooter in the distance, high-tailing into the night.

As I wrote to a friend at the time: 'It may sound harsh and colonial, but bearing in mind the two armed attacks on other EU houses in recent weeks, the job of night guard does have a serious purpose – not to fight burglars, but to raise the alarm. No doubt all guards sleep, but they really do need to be a bit more intelligent than to take to their beds before the house lights are out. We are now interviewing friends of Francisco for the job.'

In September the diplomatic wives thought they should do something for the community. A dinner-dance was planned, to buy sewing machines for a women's co-operative. A disused sports centre was found with vestigial kitchen facilities, and a large courtyard that could be decorated for the occasion. Everyone cooked their best, we sold 200 tickets, and turned up in dinner-dance clothes and sparkly shoes. A local dance band had been found and coloured lights were installed. Even the town electricity supply was holding out. In this 'cool' season the heat and humidity were high, but not unbearable. Twirling on the dance floor to a Salsa beat, I happened to glance down. There among the stiletto heels and dancing shoes was a black moving mass – thousands of cockroaches, driven from their darkness by the lights, the smells and the noise, scurrying in circles as we danced. Unlikely as it sounds, at precisely that moment, the band began playing 'La Cucuracha!' As we whirled and stomped our feet in the small spaces between the black hordes, the precise rhythms of that dance became crystal clear.

After the Cockroach Dinner-Dance, a group of us went to visit the women's co-operative to present them with their new sewing machines. In an old house, with bare boards, twenty women were seated on wooden benches, taking part in a 'literacy class'. The 'class' involved one better-dressed woman, reading to the rest from *The Works of Karl Marx*. We couldn't help hoping that life with sewing machines would be a lot more fun.

At home the garden suddenly took off in a growth spurt. We planted a papaya tree and marked its growth on the wall every evening – an inch a day. KJ built large wooden plant boxes in the back courtyard, to relieve the heat and monotony of the pale blue ceramic tiles. We planted tiny cuttings and seedlings obtained from the once-glorious Botanical Gardens – now overgrown and covered with a white fungus which dripped from the trees. The old gardeners there were more than willing to donate a bundle of cuttings and a load of compost in return for a supply of whisky. Now, after five weeks, the rockery was covered by burgeoning plants – petunias and portulacca and African marigolds already flowering. There was even a small tree in the middle like an umbrella. And I had a new plant in the garden. It was the national flower of Angola. A member of the ginger family, it was called 'Rosa de Porcellana' – the Porcelain Rose. The flowers were ten centimetres across, waxy petals in rose formation, in exquisite pinks and reds. With so little beauty to look at, I went out and crouched in the searing heat to caress it several times a day.

With the garden came snails. Suddenly there were hundreds of them, on every surface, chewing the new plants. I was beside myself. What was to be done? Snail poison – even if it were obtainable – was out of the question, because of the pets. I was advised to try saucers of beer and oatmeal. The theory was that the snails would have such a feast that they would then become drunk and easy to catch. This was astonishingly successful. Except that I now found myself burdened with hundreds of comatose snails. It was a moral dilemma. I could not bring myself to murder them in cold blood. On hot nights I collected them in bucket loads. What to do with the slumbering innocents? After a long, long time in deliberation, in desperation I threw them over the fence into the neighbour's concrete 'garden' to take their chances.

In October we had our first tropical storm. The rainy season *should* have been from January to April, but there had been no rain for months. But one day about 5pm the sky turned a ghastly yellow and dazzling heavenly floodlights lit the city like a stage set. The clouds opened and the street was full of screaming as local children and dogs all ran for cover. Roads were awash, and debris raced downhill in a river towards the lower end of Luanda. There would be lakes in the city for days, and driving would be fraught with peril since only experienced drivers could know where the gigantic potholes were. No doubt there would be a few more cars lodged in craters when the flood-water cleared. And sadly, the stagnant water would herald more outbreaks of malaria and other diseases.

In November the gods descended from HQ again, with consequent red carpet, rushing about and genuflecting in every direction. Fortunately there was no Adelaide-assisted cocktail this time, just a large lunch to do and some smaller ones All the visitors and the advisors were scheduled for a three-day trip around the country to visit projects. I looked forward to three days of peace.

One of the main thrusts of the projects was to get agricultural production going again in war-torn areas. Word was that there was an excellent corn harvest in the south of the country near Lubango. It seemed a splendid opportunity to take the great ones along to see the harvest and subsequent celebrations. A 727 plane was commandeered by government to take the VIPs to Lubango and from there a military helicopter was provided. There were no seat-belts – passengers just sat firmly, held on to the edge of the rough benches with their fingernails and prayed. The young pilot was Russian trained – perhaps recently – and was a bit sudden in some of his manoeuvres. The flight reached the site of the corn harvest, where proud local dignitaries and farmers were visible standing in a cleared space next to the field. The pilot should have landed easily near the official party. In his youthful enthusiasm he miscalculated, and landed in the middle of the harvest field instead. The helicopter blades prematurely harvested the mealies all in one go, and with a deafening din like a hailstorm, corn cobs went flying like bombs, scoring direct hits on more than one dignitary.

After such a dramatic beginning, egos were dusted down and the programme proceeded. Village pumps were inspected, irrigation projects, projects for growing bananas and corn, each separated from the last by miles of dusty and desolate road. At each project a team of local officials, dressed in their best, anxiously shepherded the '*Exceléncias*' to give the very best impression. At night the travellers were put up in government guest houses, of varying degrees of decrepitude. The exception to this was the night in the Palacio Comunal of Lubango, redolent of vanished colonial grandeur with its marble floors and columns, but even there the visitors had to choose between using the dubious local water supply or cleaning their teeth in whisky. On the last day they travelled to Namibe, and from there miles into the hinterland to see a field. Obviously it must be a very special field. The journey took three hours on a hot and dusty road filled with such enormous potholes that the cars either jarred over them or shot off the road altogether to avoid them. Arrived at the destination, KJ looked frostily at the 'special' field and asked crossly: 'What is the difference between this empty field and the empty fields we saw three hours ago near the town?'

The visiting Deputy Director General from HQ was an old experienced Africa hand, nearing retirement. He was tired. And he did not want to miss his plane back to Europe that night. Local officials wanted to serve a meal. Back and forth went the discussion – if they were to go to the next village for the meal, lovingly prepared by the local community, would he catch his plane? Eventually they sat down to lunch, hoping for the best.

The guest of honour was still agitated. Everyone was tired and hungry. The first course of succulent local lobster had just been placed in front of them, when a car screeched to a halt. Out jumped a uniformed army officer with a torrent of rapid Portuguese. Without explanation or lunch, the entire company was bundled into cars and a headlong race across the countryside began, rumbling back over the potholes towards the airfield. Deaf to all questions, the colonel in charge of security bundled the VIPs on board their small planes, almost leaving behind a few minor officials in older, slower cars. Breathlessly, the planes took off almost before the doors had closed. The connecting flight was waiting in Lubango. Once more it was a military plane with benches and no seat belts and, taking special precautions such as flying out to sea and spiralling in to land, they were taken back to Luanda.

It was only after the event that they heard the reason for their hurried exit. South African forces were converging on the area, and had reached the port of Namibe. All civilian planes had been banned from the area. Hot on the heels of the VIP plane, the armies were about to enact the ferocious Battle of Cuito Cuanevale.

The period leading up to Christmas was hot. While KJ and his minions were away, inspecting projects and dodging war-zones, the electricity supply faltered. Night after night, one air-conditioner after another stopped working. I became adept at picking up my pillow and moving from room to room – sleeping around, you might say. One night when all of them had packed up, Paddycat and I crept downstairs. I was standing at the main electricity control board in my nightdress, flipping fuses up and down, hoping to improve matters, when I heard clicking sounds on the other side of the wall. I had to giggle. Senor José, the senior night-watchman, had opened the fuse box on the outside, and was doing the same thing, each of us cancelling out the other, and both congratulating ourselves when the power came on again.

Christmas in Marxist Angola was officially called 'Family Day' although many people still went to church anyway, and the same kinds of present-giving and festivities seem to go on as anywhere else. It was just more difficult to organise. Socialist wealth-sharing had an effect, however, in that the pre-Christmas weeks in the office were studded with visits from various government officials carrying the message: 'You have wealth, how much of it are you going to share with me for Christmas?'

This was euphemistically called '*Incentivos*'. *Incentivos* could be defined as the oil that made the social wheels go round. It translated, it seemed, not as 'Incentives' but as 'Helping each other'. We capitalists might translate it differently. However, it could cause considerable problems if one's favourite bank official refused to transfer any money due to insufficient Christmas *Incentivos*.

Dozens of pigs grazing on the city's myriad rubbish dumps mysteriously disappeared during the weeks before Christmas. The piles of litter became, in effect, 'Installations for Urban

Farming' ('*Instalacões por agricultura urbana*'), the pigs reclassified as 'Useful Civil Servants'. There was also private enterprise pig-farming – one urban legend told of a pig kept in a bath-tub on the tenth floor of an apartment block. From time to time we shrank from the agonised sound of an animal being slaughtered. We put our fingers in our ears and prayed that it would be mercifully brief, then reached for ear-plugs for the night, knowing that a very noisy party lasting until 4 am was on the way. Angolans, like their colonisers the Portuguese, loved a 'festa' and didn't want the fun to stop, and since there was a curfew no one could go home between midnight and dawn anyway. They also loved very loud music, and a lot of noise in general – a safety valve in difficult times.

We decided to repay a lot of invitations at once, by having a Christmas party, with turkey brought from Harare (one of the Jolly Butcher's 'luxury stuffs'), peas (frozen) from France, plum pudding and fruit mince from Australia, and table decorations ferried from London. We even managed to get a Norwegian pine tree in a pot in exchange for a bottle of whisky. I delighted in doing a full English Christmas with all the trimmings, although it entailed cooking from 4am on several mornings to get it all done. It was worth it for the expressions on the faces of guests as they gingerly tried plum pudding and brandy sauce, or took their first bite of a fruit mince-pie, not knowing what to expect.

The jovial Cardinal of Luanda came in full cardinal's regalia, to the not altogether pleasant surprise of Marxist ministers and members of government. As the evening wore on, one high-ranking diplomat after the other crept into our little TV room, where a lively discussion was sparkling between the Cardinal and the Marxist ministers – intelligent human beings at opposite ends of the ideological spectrum. In a non-threatening environ-ment both sides were willing to discuss the hitherto taboo subjects of the war and the economy. Both were able to admit that mistakes had been made and changes were needed. It was probably the most useful and exciting function we had ever held. As I refilled plates of mince-pies and Christmas delicacies to fuel the discussions, it occurred to me, for the first time, that perhaps – just perhaps – I was not wasting my life after all.

8

Adelaide, the Galloping Gouvernante

Dona Maria Adelaide Lousada, (' 'dlaide' for short) – house-keeper, supervisor, cook, and general factotum – warrants a chapter all to herself.

Dona Adelaide was a large blonde lady in the very pink of condition, probably in her late forties, much given to pony-tails and curls and the wearing of artificial flowers in her hair. She clothed her ample form in tight jeans and T-shirts and bright dirndl skirts, with a few gay earrings to complete the picture of the 'Swinging *Gouvernante*' (housekeeper) of modern Luanda. She was sometimes seen precariously perched on the pillion of Gaby's motor-scooter. She wore an overall in the house, a demure garment from Harare in blue or green, but nothing daunted, and despite the heat, Adelaide insisted on wearing the overall and apron on *top* of her other clothes with another apron on top of that for good measure.

The first warning of Adelaide's presence in the mornings was a resounding slam of the front gate, followed by an ominous pause until she reached the iron-barred gate at the side of the house. This stuck, and was unstuck daily by a karate chop from an espadrilled foot and solid forearm to such effect that for several minutes the whole house resounded with a sort of kerchung-kerchung-kerchung – fading diminuendo into the distance. This was followed by cheery '*Bom dias*' to the dogs, '*Muito Bom Dia*' if the morning was very good indeed and a chirrup or two to the cat. There might be an 'Ola Polar!' to Polar Bear, or an 'Anda Panda!' to Panda – both original Adelaide witticisms. If there were no '*Bom Dias*' we knew it was a Bad Morning. Perhaps Dona Adelaide had been splashed with something unmentionable (and there was plenty of that around) on the way to work, and it was likely to be a Bad Day for the household in general.

In the early days of Adelaide's regime, the next frightening stage of her arrival was a wide-flung dining-room door as she burst into breakfast. With lots of *'Muito Bom Dia*'s she would energetically stride across the room, scrape open the curtains and clatter up the iron security shutters while we cowered behind the teapot. We were too subtle at first. KJ's early acid comment of: 'You're very early, Dona Adelaide,' received the jolly booming reply: *'Sempre, Senhor, sempre!'* ('Always, Senhor, always!')

An unspoken battle raged over the first few weeks. The earlier Adelaide stormed in, the earlier I got up to wash, dress, meditate and do some yoga, and the earlier breakfast became. The alarm was going off before 4am. Breakfast was on the table by 6.30. We were beginning to think we'd have to get up at midnight to have some peace. Finally with extreme bluntness, we conveyed the message that we really didn't need the lady to come an hour early to work in order to de-curtain us at coffee.

Once that was clarified, I would scamper upstairs at the first sound of the advancing troops, with Paddycat hot on my heels, taking with me anything I didn't want swept away. Occasionally I heard the sound of horse's hooves in the house and knew it was Adelaide going downstairs in wooden-soled mules.

I tried not to hear the forceful clearing of plates, the slamming of cupboard doors and the resounding clatters and jangles as the crockery and cutlery were all dumped into the sink together

When Adelaide's radio was turned on in the kitchen it became her territory for the morning, a jolly, noisy domain surrounded with invisible proprietary notices so that I tiptoed out the front door and went the long way round to water my plants, then hesitated nervously outside the kitchen door for a few moments, thinking carefully about which Portuguese remark I would make when I entered.

The kitchen was particularly sacrosanct at staff mealtimes which were very important, and took great preparation and table-setting with napkins, and a flower or two. Breakfast for the '*pessoal*' took up the first hour of the morning, and lunch the last, and no matter what other domestic urgencies might press, that was that. If I suggested that they should speed up a bit or that there was something important to be done I received a 'look' and the lunch continued. To do her justice, Adelaide seemed to achieve these wonderful '*almoços*' with astonishing economy at the local market, returning from the '*Praça*' with my big cane basket, which she loved, sprouting *gindongo* (chilli) which they swore gave protection from malaria, *kiabos* (a green vegetable) and the dreaded *fuba bombom* – the manioc root which was ferociously cowed into submission with a pestle and mortar. It looked and tasted exactly like a great, grey bath sponge of the most rubbery variety. It bounced

Adelaide had other talents too, of an acquisitive nature, evolutionary traits developed during long years in Luanda. We acquired, I never dared to ask how, not only our huge bag of dehydrated potato from SWAPO stocks, and the 20 kilos of fish that fell off the back of a Russian trawler, but such unlikely objects as plastic buckets, mops, hose-pipes and birthday cakes, all unobtainable in the shops, but spirited in by Adelaide from her network of contacts.

In Angola it was all about contacts, friends, *esquemas* (schemes) and favours owed and repaid.

'There is nothing available in Luanda,' it was said, 'but you can find everything if you have friends!' And somehow it worked.

Conditions for living were almost impossible, and for many situations the only answer was a philosophical shrug of the shoulders accompanied by a rolling up of the eyes and the words '*E Assim!*' ('That's the way it is'). There was a wartime spirit in operation. Anyone who managed to acquire something – a dozen eggs, for instance – would immediately share with friends. If people needed something, they asked around and it would be found. If there was a birthday, everyone brought what flour, sugar and butter they had and a communal cake was made.

But to return to Adelaide, she also seemed to have powers verging on the paranormal. In her presence strange things happened. Handles snapped off, screws flew out, tin trays twisted, shelves leaped out of refrigerators and forks bent – just like Uri Geller, except that Adelaide insisted it was all perfectly explicable because these products were not made in Portugal and were therefore extremely inferior in the first place. I often got the impression that it was somehow my fault as she held up yet another bent bread-knife or dented saucepan, saying, with a curl of the lip: '*E fracu!*' ('It's weak!'), sometimes adding, 'They make them much better in Portugal!'

Dona Adelaide very much enjoyed her cooking – doing it, eating it and experimenting. I tried, innocent that I was, to teach her how to make a basic salad and French dressing, and French fries. She more or less got the hang of it, but after one repetition got bored, I think, and the chips began to emerge from the kitchen in ever more varied shapes, sizes and degrees of sogginess. The salad acquired daily more exotic additives of any vegetables or nuts that the cupboards or the *Praça* could yield. This spirit of invention and playfulness gave Adelaide a lot of pleasure. She never gave serious credence to the actual text of the menus I worked out each week. They were obviously meant to be only the basic theme on which she would perform bravura improvisations.

I frequently went into the kitchen to find Adelaide down on her knees in front of the glass oven door, admiring her productions and exclaiming: '*Linda! Linda!*' ('Pretty! Pretty!') to herself, or to the oven contents, or to the dogs or anyone else within earshot. She often brought a dish to the table exclaiming: 'This is delicious!' as she placed it before us.

One day she brought in two large sugar-bowls of something unidentifiable for dessert. Seeing our mystified expressions she said in the jolliest manner possible: 'You just eat that now and I'll tell you what it is later!'

We did our best with help from Panda and Polar Bear under the table. It turned out to be sweet potatoes in solid little balls, in a luscious creamy caramel sauce. Worth repeating for the sauce, but not in sugar bowls and not in industrial quantities.

The part Adelaide liked best of all, though, was garnishing. Everything had to be garnished, and came to the table strewn with lots of parsley, pieces of carrot or mint or sliced lemon, or whatever else I had hidden in the cupboard for some special occasion. The only thing I ever made which earned her unstinted approval (*'Lindissima!'*) was a salmon soufflé in the shape of a curved fish. It had a whole spiralled cucumber coiled around it and mint leaves between each slice. This was the way things should be in Adelaide's opinion. But as guest after guest tried to pick up a little bit of cucumber, they ended up with three metres of spiralled vegetable hanging from their forks!

Dona Adelaide's ideas and mine often clashed at times when it mattered, for instance when we had visits from The Great Ones from HQ or dinners for the Diplomatic Corps. She felt that my planned menus were distinctly lacking in imagination and fire, and did her best to improve them. Having consulted *The Good Housekeeping Cookbook*, and *Larousse*, and *The Joy of Cooking*, I would write out a menu most of which could be cooked in advance, on the principle of damage limitation, leaving only some simple vegetables for Adelaide to produce at the last moment while I greeted the guests. But what appeared on the serving dish would be not simple boiled potatoes with parsley and butter as I expected, but some splendid Portuguese mixture of every vegetable available at the market that day, bubbling in garlic, tomato and oil, and doing vigorous battle with the delicately poached chicken in cream sauce. Adelaide never saw any problem – her invariable reply was: 'I've done this instead, it's much nicer!'

Roast chicken metamorphosed into a hundred desiccated chunks, avocado starter mysteriously became avocado dessert, and ice-cream transmuted by alchemy into the ubiquitous 'Pudim flan' or 'crême caramel' – and lots of it, so the *pessoal* could have some too. When these creations were brought to the table, and I saw them out of the corner of my eye, I had to maintain charming conversation with the guests, not betraying by so much as a flicker the inward gnashing of teeth as yet another *cordon bleu* attempt bit the dust.

Dona Adelaide was a great inventor. Unexpected objects could be used for unexpected purposes. I suppose, when you don't have many uses for cake forks, they do look handy for eating salad with. A fine sharp Sabatier knife probably does look like a good saw for cutting through chicken bones and lobster shells, or for doing up the odd screw inside a radio, or poking inside a live toaster. Iron window grilles are obviously tailor-made for defrosting chickens in the sun. But the one I liked best was the day I went through the kitchen just before lunch to find Adelaide humming a merry little tune and just popping an egg into the Senhor Embaixador's soup to boil it for her lunch.

Water was another source of contention. The water in Luanda was undrinkable – sewage seeped into it and teeth were cleaned at one's peril. So in the beginning, everyone drank gallons of expensive French bottled water each day. Eventually the water purifier arrived. Then we had a cholera scare. In the poorer areas of Luanda people were struck down in their hundreds. KJ called on Emergency Aid and flew in hundreds of cholera beds and thousands of bottles of rehydration fluid for the devoted Italian nuns who were nursing the victims. Sadly, desperate and ignorant relatives stole the rehydration fluid from bedside tables to sell on the black market. Such a level of ignorance and desperation is almost beyond comprehension.

In the midst of all this, KJ telephoned London and urged me to bring back plenty of permanganate of potash without fail. Initially we had a few purple salads, but after a while people learned how much to use and the great importance of dis-infecting all fruit and vegetables was much applauded all round. Then we had the *big visit* from HQ. We were all at sixes and sevens with that nightmare – a lunch and a dinner on the same day. Adelaide's excitement, panic and palpitations knew no bounds. I went into the kitchen just in time to find her holding the precious and expensive imported lettuce under the lethal tap water, ready for the consumption of the Highest of High Directors.

'What are you doing?' I enquired in my best Portuguese.

'Oh,' said Adelaide, 'we can't possibly use the chemical for *these* visitors, it might stain the lettuce!'

On the same night we had a slight misunderstanding about coffee. As the coffee tray sometimes came in looking a bit mismatched, to say the least, I always prepared it beforehand, foreseeing, I hoped, all creative possibilities. But on this night – everyone wanted tea. This was not foreseen. The order was relayed. A long, long wait. Panic time in the kitchen. Then the tea came, obviously the fruit of long discussion – served in the coffee pot. I sent it back with a request for a teapot, and fresh, non-coffee-flavoured tea. Another long wait. This time it came back in the hot water jug. Things were obviously getting desperate in the kitchen. So finally I went out and made the tea myself to an audience of Adelaide's stolidly turned back and a strong sense of dark brooding discontent. But the real mystery of the story is that, when we calculated it, we found that Dona Adelaide had, by that time, made tea for us at least 150 times – and always in the teapot.

Things were always frenetic and panic-stricken when there was entertaining to be done. Not having done this kind of catering before, I was quite nervous enough. But my nerves were as nothing to the red alert emanating from Adelaide. I would get up at 4am to cook in advance for dinners and functions. If not, the smallish kitchen would be full of every pot we possessed, as Adelaide created her lobster mayonnaise and the staff lunch, and descaled fish, all at the same time. Every available surface would be covered with wet tea-towels – I limited her to ten at a time and she used them all – and I would find myself putting the finishing touches to a dish, keeping my elbows very close to my sides, while Adelaide whizzed from side to side at the speed of an ice-hockey player, looking steadily more apoplectic as her gestures got wilder. She used a special Rugby tackle to fell me if I tried to demean myself by getting the roast potatoes out of the oven. It might sound as it we ran a very disorganised kitchen. It's not true. We had lists, and time-tables, diagrams of the way to set the table and clear, clear instructions, but Dona Adelaide was equal to them all, and imposed her joyous sense of *confusão* over everything she did.

Adelaide loved to give unsolicited advice about everything. It was delivered in a manner halfway between severe criticism and a loud command. She told KJ that he must destroy the compost he had carefully prepared for the garden, because it would bring flies. To make the point she shouted 'Moscas! Moscas!' for two days as she huffed and puffed around the kitchen with the fly-spray. Eventually we had good compost and no flies to speak of. When, again, poor KJ transplanted a struggling passion vine into one of his huge flower boxes, we were told peremptorily: 'Those things never grow in boxes, it will die, they need earth.' After a few weeks it was covering a wall.

I was ordered one day to dig up my precious papaya trees which were the only shade in the blistering hot back courtyard: 'That kind is male, it never has fruit, it's useless!'

When, after a few days, it remained where it was, the lady brought a sharp stake from home with instructions to plunge it through the unfortunate tree's heart, to turn it into a female. The biology left us thoughtful.

She gave advice about the swimming pool too. The would-be pool was about the size of four baths put together, and it was empty when we arrived. Adelaide eyed it speculatively, and said we should keep chickens in it. We listened but felt life was complicated enough, and in any case, the poor birds would have fried in the heat of their concrete prison. Then, as nothing had happened, one day I saw the dread light of invention in her eye, and she told me we must fill it up with earth, '*E Feio!*' ('It's ugly!'), and make a big garden there with hanging baskets. Not a bad idea. We thanked her, but we did intend that some day it should be a pool when we could work out how to get some pool paint and a small pump. For a while longer it remained, and then we had a shower of rain. Adelaide rushed through the house spraying furiously and shouting: '*Mosquitos! Cheio do mosquitos!*' ('Full of mosquitoes!')

'It's that pool,' she said. 'Why don't you get a plug put in the bottom so you can let out all the water?'

But gardening was Adelaide's real passion. Plants grow visibly in the steamy heat of Luanda, and it was touching to see how people in the poorest houses added poetry to their hard lives with a row of flowering plants around their house in old tins or jam jars.

'Plants only grow well if you steal them!' Adelaide told me, and she loved to purloin cuttings on her way to work. She either presented them to me for the garden, or planted them herself where she thought they ought to go. Sometimes she chose one of my vases to decorate her kitchen with them while they rooted. We always did our cooking surrounded by her little posies standing on the bright coloured pot-holders she admired. She didn't think my flower arrangement were much fun, and often popped in a few brighter flowers to improve them or scattered a few other pots and jam jars around the reception room to help along my boring sense of décor.

When we went away early in the year I left her in charge of all the pot-plants including a treasured collection of tiny flowering cacti brought from Zimbabwe. Arrived back in Luanda, I found all the cacti drowned, and rotting in their pots. I showed her several sodden pots and explained, yet again, that these were *Plantas do deserto* and only needed water once a month. What was the lady's reaction? Adelaide looked very fierce indeed and said: 'Who put water on those plants?' Never at a loss for words, our Adelaide.

The next time we went away everything was in good shape. The dogs were flea-free, plants growing, roses shooting again. I left Adelaide with all the pot-plants that could not be over-watered. As I had shown her the effects on the cacti, this time she decided not to be caught out again, and nothing was watered for the entire month. I suppose 'Who' was the culprit again.

However, the really big Adelaide event of 1987 was her wedding. She told me about it almost by accident, a week or so ahead, when I was telling her that we would be having two big functions before Christmas.

'Oh,' she said, 'You can't have it on 18th. My wedding is on that day!'

As she had been talking about 'my husband this' and 'my husband that' for the past nine months, I was slow to react. I assumed that she already had a husband, and that this was a wedding she was attending, as in 'my doctor' or 'my dentist', without involving the full possessive case. However, it transpired that this was indeed to be Dona Adelaide's wedding. After nineteen years of happy cohabitation and three children, they would tie the knot in their middle years. Adelaide was rapturous about the event, and played the blushing bride to perfection.

As the day drew near, Adelaide wafted round the house and

the tune of 'I'm getting married in the morning!' kept playing in my head. With two days to go I asked if she had a pretty dress to wear. She hadn't done much about that, she said, but some-one had loaned her a blouse that might do if she let it out a bit and she might find a skirt somewhere. Feeling a great pressure of noblesse oblige I invited her to come and see if I had a skirt she could borrow, to go with the blouse. Adelaide's eyes lit up, not at a skirt but at a silky white flowing dress last used for a harp recital at Reinhild's Christmas party in Harare. 'Just right for a bride!' I could see her thinking. She was full of confidence, pronouncing that we were really the same size, only in different places. (Now that's one to remember!) Luckily it was the time of elasticised waists so the lady wriggled into it, with the expression of a little girl who had just seen a fairy. She whirled off, rejuvenated and with shining eyes, after giving me a big kiss.

We were invited to the wedding lunch. The invitation depicted a little cartoon dog, saying 'I'm having a party'. We expected it to be interesting. Adelaide had told us about her friends, how they dropped in to eat together in the evenings, and once she told us she was going to a *festa* to eat 'goat's stomach poached in blood' for lunch. We were right. It was interesting.

The wedding *festa* was held at one of Luanda's few restaurants, on a road out of town. It was near the prison but very difficult to find. There were no names on the streets, and it was a new district, with higgledy-piggledy dirt tracks and thousands of 'new' houses, all looking like the oldest slums in the world, full of mismatched stones, and lean-to corrugated iron fill-in walls surrounded by pot-holes and litter. We finally found the 'Ristorante Mae Joanna' – a triumph of the human spirit in such an environment. With some difficulty we located the small front door, and inched past several workmen up to their knees in fresh concrete and wheelbarrows. Was it a late face-lift for the wedding, or merely Mae Joanna's on-going developmental process?

We went through a small whitewashed courtyard bright with

sunflowers and entered the main hall, a large barn with a cement floor and long tables covered with colourful cloths. It was set up with hundreds of little bread and butter plates, each containing a few fish balls, little cold pork chops and a variety of little cakes – the whole besieged by battalions of enthusiastic flies. They must have been pork chops because Adelaide told us she had killed her poor pig for the occasion. But it had been a very small pig. Had she mastered miracle of the multiplication of the pork chops? My mind flitted briefly to the pigs on the rubbish dumps.

The walls were freshly whitewashed, and the ceiling too, but there that Angolan disease of inconclusiveness had set in since, to install the many hanging electric bulbs, ceiling tiles had been removed. These remained stacked in a corner, and whole metres of ceiling lay bare to the naked wires, rafters and spiders above. But the centre of the room boasted one true glory – a glittering chandelier, proving to anyone who dared doubt it that Mae Joanna's was a Real Restaurant.

Around the walls on hard wooden and metal chairs sat other early-comers, lulled like us into believing the hour written on the invitation, though they should, being Angolan, have known better. The guests displayed, as does Angola, a marvellous spectrum of colours, shapes, sizes and forms of dress, all one community of celebration and all, like us, drinking local draught beer or warm coca-cola with no fizz.

Finally after an hour and a half, the happy couple arrived, fresh from the civil ceremony at the Portuguese Embassy, looking newly married and radiant. Gentle little Senhor Pinto wore shirtsleeves and his best trousers. Dona Adelaide was positively blooming and ten years younger in her billowing white silky dress, golden hair decked with a white ribbon bow and streaming down her back in ringlets. With a smile of great sweetness, the bridegroom made a speech.

'Senhores and Senhoras,' he said 'Now we are here, so you can all begin to eat!'

Flies notwithstanding, everyone fell on the little plates. I remembered Adelaide and the *moscas*. The company nibbled port chops and fish balls and cakes until the main courses were served from aluminium baby-baths – more fried fish balls, followed by steaming goat and vegetables and a spicy feijoada or bean stew. We sat back and watched everyone enjoying themselves; children in frilly clothes, others in jeans and plastic sandals, men in best white shirt-sleeves and the very occasional suit. The women wore cotton dresses of varying formality, and one or two ancient grannies wore long, draped Arabic robes. Groups formed and reformed. A young disabled man with a long, puckish face became a Pied Piper, and limped around the room starting serious conversations with groups of small children who dogged his heels in a junior conga.

Adelaide announced that she was going to 'Open the *Salao*!' We all flocked to the neighbouring room – the Salon in question – startlingly decorated with primitive life-size murals in gaudy colours, apparently depicting the exciting adventures of a gigantic tree-rat. There to the accompaniment of an ancient disco, the '*Salao*' was opened as the happy couple performed an expert foxtrot while we all applauded. And then we went back to eat more goat stew, and to await the cutting of the monstrous four-tier cake, seemingly made from rough-cast concrete, and decorated with many coy little bridal figures.

We didn't stay until the end since, like all good Angolan parties, it went on until breakfast-time next morning. Adelaide didn't stay either. She went to the beach after a while, she said.

It was the first close encounter we had had with the microcosm of Angolan society, with its mixture of colours, friendships and interrelationships. Everyone was in a state of happy comradeship: government officials, the gardener from the Botanical Gardens, the old man who painted the house, the Minister of Fisheries, a few doctors, vets and lawyers, and the boss of the factory where Adelaide's husband worked. There was no Anglo-

Saxon awkwardness or awareness of class or racial differences. Joyous embraces were exchanged by friends who, in most European societies, would never have had the chance to know if they liked each other or not, since our social mores would decree that those so different in race, occupation and lifestyle should never meet, and should live in a state of difference and separation. Just to see such egalitarianism made all the tribulations of Adelaide's regime worthwhile. Well, almost.

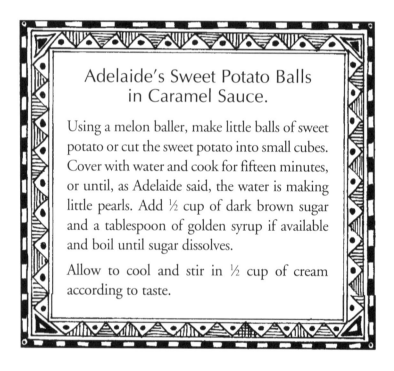

Adelaide's Sweet Potato Balls in Caramel Sauce.

Using a melon baller, make little balls of sweet potato or cut the sweet potato into small cubes. Cover with water and cook for fifteen minutes, or until, as Adelaide said, the water is making little pearls. Add ½ cup of dark brown sugar and a tablespoon of golden syrup if available and boil until sugar dissolves.

Allow to cool and stir in ½ cup of cream according to taste.

9

Senhor Cruz and Co.

After Cisca's departure, Conceição had joined the household. Charming, polite, and tranquil, she went about her work, ironed and folded to perfection, and acted as blotting paper to Adelaide's turmoil. When Adelaide was not there she took over her duties with quiet efficiency and cooked fragrant fried linguado for lunch – a flat, sweet fish, and succulent *Moamba de Frango* (chicken in tomato and peanut sauce).

Handsome Francisco, erstwhile junior night-watchman, became gardener and houseman. He, like Conceição had an innate courtesy and dignity. Now at last the house might have a chance of operating smoothly. My Portuguese was improving, and while Adelaide still scored points and always had the last word, I didn't mind so much. I sometimes caught a mischievous glance from Ção, implying that she found Adelaide pretty funny too, and was on my side. And Francisco was the possessor not only of film-star eyelashes but of excellent arm muscles. There was no local bread to be had and he became house kneader-in-chief. Together we produced ever more elaborate bread recipes and rolls – knotted, plaited, cottage loaves – we could do them all.

Shortly after her arrival Ção became pregnant with her third child. She carried on working since her husband's salary as a government telephonic engineer could barely support the family. In due course her daughter was born. There had been much discussion about names. I thought an African name might counteract the Portuguese influence a bit, but the household was having none of it. Ção didn't see herself as African. Despite her appearance, she thought, spoke and cooked in Portuguese. Adelaide was all for a saint's name. So it was no surprise when the new baby was called 'Maria de Fatima'.

Maria de Fatima made her debut in the house at two weeks old. She was a doll-like baby with a face like a flower, as tranquil as her calm and smiling mother. The next problem was, where would she be while Ção did her work? Conceição was clear: 'She will sleep on the couch in the TV room.'

Fearful that she might roll off, I bought a large basket from the market to serve as a cradle and upholstered it with pink frills. Maria de Fatima slept away her mornings, only waking for food. But we were not expecting Panda to take a hand. Wisely Ção had insisted that the animals be formally introduced to the baby and that the dogs should sniff her well. Panda decided that this was a puppy and she was on duty. She sat in the TV room while Ção worked, guarding the baby carefully. As soon as Maria de Fatima awoke, Panda would run and tug at Conceição's dress until she came to attend to her progeny. We were all entranced.

Then suddenly, the household changed again. There must, after all, be miracles. I had prayed fervently every day that Adelaide might find a wonderful job somewhere else – preferably back in Portugal. It didn't happen quite that way – perhaps I didn't word it quite right – but one day KJ's Portuguese secretary announced that an excellent Portuguese cook who could do *everything* was looking for work. The chance seemed too good to miss.

For a whole month we stewed over how to exchange Adelaide for someone who could cook well and would not make our lives an ongoing circus. We felt that a long period of notice might not be a good idea, in case the powerful Adelaidean unconscious rampaged around the house washing tablecloths in bleach and scrubbing yet more of the silver with Brillo pads. In the event, we decided that, like washing up, the only way to get it done was to do it. For days before, I nervously dosed her with calming flower remedies, ostensibly for her heart palpitations.

KJ told her one afternoon after lunch that we could dispense with her services. She heard the news and said brightly: 'That's OK. I was offered a better job last week.'

So she cooked one last chicken, and skipped off to Portugal for a month's holiday with a waggle, convinced to the last that she had been quite the best housekeeper that any embassy had ever had the good fortune to employ.

For some time we continued to find broken, cracked and splintered objects in kitchen drawers, and we never fully solved the mystery of the missing screws on the downstairs toilet seat. This was tricky for honoured guests, since if they were so foolish as to actually sit on it, the whole apparatus immediately disintegrated into six pieces and pinched them where it hurt.

For the first weeks, living in the house without The Presence was surreal. I expected the gate to emit its kerchung at any moment and frequently looked over my shoulder.

Our new cook and Major Domo, Senhor Cruz, bore no resemblance to Adelaide in any respect. He was a small, slight little man, with smooth, thinning black hair and a pleasantly ugly face composed chiefly of rather protuberant eyes. One of our guests likened him to an elf. This puckish appearance was heightened one rainy morning when I went into the kitchen to find him solemnly cooking the breakfast for the *pessoal*, wearing a pair of white long-johns which clung to legs of frighteningly stalk-like fragility. I wondered if he habitually travelled with spare long-johns in case of sudden emergencies. And if so, what kind of emergencies did he expect?

When he came for his initial interview he was overwhelmingly reverential, bowing from the waist and continually washing his hands Uriah Heep fashion. He punctuated his conversations with dramatic rolling of the eyes, clasping of the hands and the raising of operatic arms and eyeballs for heaven to witness.

Senhor Cruz used his histrionic talents with such exaggerated sincerity and conviction that KJ and I were struck dumb with a sort of hilarious exultation. Surely this time we had found a paragon among cooks – in particular since, when KJ gave his spiel about the evils of cooks who drank on duty, our Man in the Kitchen struck the appropriate horrified pose and intoned (with his hand on his heart): '*Nunca Sehnor, nunca!*' ('Never, Senhor, never in my life have I been seen to drink!')

All this and sobriety too! Senhor Cruz began his regime brilliantly by orchestrating a reception for thirty people with such tranquillity and efficiency that when I went into the kitchen at 4pm to check on the pitch of the hysteria, I found the entire meal prepared, and the staff sitting demurely to afternoon coffee. I merely had a jam tart popped into my mouth and was told to go and rest.

In contrast to Adelaide, who never moved at anything less than a spanking trot, Senhor Cruz moved with the utmost silence and care, bending slightly from the waist, and if transporting a particularly precious dish, carried it prayerfully with two hands, and placed it reverently at a precise angle. He would then step back three paces, fold his arms and wait respectfully for the reaction. The first time I saw him in action, he was wearing an old blue and white T-shirt as if it were a dinner-jacket, as he hovered and washed his hands in the fashion of a nineteenth-century butler. He subsequently instructed me on what he considered 'comme il faut' for him to wear, but graciously made do with the standard white Harare drill suits that were all we had to offer, and which I had previously considered rather fine.

Like Adelaide, Senhor Cruz was full of ideas, but seemed at least to understand that it was my house rather than his. Like Adelaide too, he loved arranging flowers but instead of bunches dumped in jam-jars he preferred vast and trailing arrangements which languished across the tablecloth and writhed around the salt and pepper. We still had vases of flowers dotting the kitchen, and my morning tea tray came each day decorated with a tiny exquisite water-lily-like arrangement of flowers and leaves. Tea was delivered with an unctuous tap on the door and a respectful 'Sona Pamela' – the Cruz elision of 'Senhora Dona'. We were amazed and amused in equal parts.

The poor man was longing to cater for more lunches and dinner-parties. Unfortunately KJ was away for the first month of his stay. He regarded it as a great challenge to impress the Senhora with all that he could do and I struggled with an unending succession of lobster mornays, fish done a hundred ways, the Portuguese versions of stew and the amazing progression of nursery puddings which are the delight, it seems, of all Portuguese cooks. At times Panda and Polar came to the rescue. Thankfully I had persuaded him that I detested being hovered over while eating.

While struggling with his lunches I often listened to the BBC World Service. At just this time there were constant news items about Lech Walesa and the strikes in the Gdansk shipyard. They were events that changed history, but I didn't expect Polar Bear to be quite so interested in International Affairs. He listened to the radio attentively with his head on one side. As he was not the brightest of dogs, I was intrigued by this. Then he began to bark once every time 'Poland' was mentioned. The BBC was saying his name!

All the pets seemed delighted with the change in staff. Polar was no longer shouted at all day for being lazy, and as soon as he heard Senhor Cruz arrive, he rushed down the stairs, sturdy little hind-quarters working energetically to see about tit-bits in the kitchen. We would soon have to see about a little reducing diet as well. Panda was less easily impressed and was therefore wooed even more assiduously. Paddycat took time to get the new staff trained to his liking. He was given about four breakfasts and freshly cooked fish at lunch-time. To obtain this he stalked into the kitchen making a noise delightedly interpreted by the staff as '*Çāo ,Çāo*' (Portuguese abbreviation for *Conceição*).

One morning I was at the telephone when Senhor Cruz arrived to speak to me. I realised that he was not speaking, but apparently chirping from the region of his chest. It was so surprising that I was struck dumb with the telephone in my hand (mind you, this happened to me quite often in Portuguese conversations). I gazed at him, wondering if heart pacemakers make chirping noises like hearing aids, and whether it would be polite to ask about the sound. The little man suddenly plunged his hand into his cook's apron and produced a tiny golden chick which he was keeping warm and happy. He had found it wandering in the road on his way to work. Its name, he said, was 'Isadora'. It lived on muesli in the staff room for a few days, and I lived on tenterhooks lest Paddycat or Panda or Polar should discover the possibility of fresh poultry on the hoof.

We had several weeks of seeing what Senhor Cruz can do. He had some good recipes like lobster soufflé, strewn with bread-crumbed prawns. The rest depended on a heavy coating of oil and garlic, and a lot of béchamel sauce, but he displayed enormous ingenuity in the serving.

The first buffet he did had as its centrepiece a huge seafood mayonnaise, a *Mayonnesa de Lagosta* consisting of lobster and vegetables in a liberal coating of real mayonnaise. It was delicious if hugely calorific. It was decorated with three lobster shells standing on their hind legs, waving their antennae. At least there were three until Polar Bear saw it from afar. Polar had never seen anything so enticing in his life, but his object was not mere aesthetic pleasure. I arrived to the sound of tremendous crunching under the table, and dived just in time to rescue two lobster shells with drastically reduced radar equipment.

Then our new Major Domo approached me with an in-spirational idea for the next dinner party.

'If,' he said, 'we get a big live chicken, I will kill it here in the yard and then I can do a wonderful dish. I will cook it so that it is served at the table head and all, as if it is alive and looking at the guests!'

My face must have betrayed my feelings, since he suddenly stopped and said: 'Wouldn't you like that?'

He subsequently served another new recipe for lunch – large fat squid swimming in a sauce made of their own ink. Struggling, KJ hinted diplomatically that perhaps this was not his very favourite dish of all time. A conversation was then heard from the kitchen about how, of course, not everybody liked everything, did they, and there was no accounting for tastes . . .

We also had adventures in the quest for 'lemon delicious' pudding. I thought it would be a good idea, with its light sponge and lemony sauce underneath and gave Adelaide the recipe translated into Portuguese. I don't quite know what Adelaide did, but it turned up on the table in a tin pie dish, the consistency of rubber and about half an inch thick. Then Senhor Cruz tried. On that morning I was drawn downstairs and into the kitchen by a strange rattling. I found, in the biggest saucepan, full of boiling water, the lemon delicious pudding bounding around perilously in the best china soufflé dish. This method did, in the end produce a sort of blonde soufflé pudding, but not lemon delicious. There was no end to the surprises.

About this time we acquired a new driver as well as a new cook. This is how it happened. On one of the many trips into the hinterland poor KJ managed to pick up some virulent tropical parasites. On the very night that he was to go to London to the Tropical Diseases hospital, his driver, Antonio, nicknamed 'Little Napoleon', turned up almost too late to catch the plane and merrily drunk. While no one could blame the residents of Luanda for taking a drink to ease their woes, it was unwise for an official driver on duty. As it was the third offence, and warnings had been given, KJ was Not Amused, and fired him on the spot, leaving the office to find a replacement.

A week or so later there was a knock at the kitchen door. When I opened it, there on the step was a skinny little man in black trousers and a white shirt. To my astonishment he began to bob up and down doing rapid knee-bends and reciting: *'Faz-tudo! Faz-tudo!'* ('Do it all! Do it all!') over and over again.

'Silly little man,' I thought uncharitably, 'Is he trying to impress me?'

But it transpired that his misguided parents really did christen him 'Do it all!' in the spirit of Figaro, the 'Factotum' from the Barber of Seville. But like so many names of that ilk, it backfired, and they might more wisely have opted for *Faz-nada* (Do nothing) since his gifts were quite the opposite of his name. Faz-tudo was superbly inept, not only as a driver, but at opening doors and gates, and even at carrying boxes. He invariably dropped everything while he was ringing the front bell which always stuck and short circuited as soon as he touched it. He even forgot to put on the brakes of the official car one day while opening the gates, leaving KJ in the back seat of a runaway official car.

Faz-tudo put the most enormous efforts into everything. He turned up hours before he was needed, driving me mad, and did everything with his whole heart, soul and body, using maximum energy and the largest, wildest gestures, and tripping over his feet to get it right. I never knew whether to find him endearing or irritating. He never dared to drive at more than 40 kilometres per hour, slowing to 10 whenever a large pothole hove into view, which in Luanda, was about every ten metres. When he came to an intersection we would spend a long, long time in the centre of the road, and other cars wove imaginative patterns around us while Faz-tudo frowned with concentration, clenched his jaw and bit his tongue. Finally he judged that there was sufficient empty space ahead and with one last delay, surged forward desperately, just too late as the next cohort of cars bore down. I took to driving with him with my eyes shut. We seemed to have a rare talent for choosing staff who were polar opposites. No one could be further from the character of 'Little Napoleon' who was so full of bombast, panache and alcohol.

I was aware as I wrote bulletins from wartime Luanda to friends, that they contained little but domestic comedy. It was like Stendahl's novel *The Red and the Black* where the hero finds himself walking through a confused landscape, and realises he had just walked through the battlefield of Waterloo. Or Auden's poem 'Musée de Beaux Arts' in which as Icarus falls, the dogs get on with their doggy life and the ploughman ploughs.

We forget that history and world events happen in the midst of life. In Luanda, although there were hundreds of armed soldiers in the city, and gunfire at night, and battles of crucial importance to the southern African scene being fought, I was chiefly aware of the rattling of perfume bottles in the stifling little bathroom as I took my bath in the mornings. The vibration of Chanel and Estée Lauder was caused by Russian MIGs and Antinov planes as they roared overhead, on their way to the appalling bloody battle being fought at Cuito Cuarnevale. At night we saw the battle on TV. One scene was repeated over and over – a clip of the body of an Angolan soldier being crushed into the mud by a tank.

During the day I looked through thick bars, and saw, across the street, funeral processions wending their way to the cemetery, many of them with heart-breakingly tiny white coffins. Stories were told every week of bandidos, of violent break-ins in the city and shootings in the black market. We lived among death, sorrow and disaster, as people in Angola had done for hundreds of years, since slave-traders began their depredations along the Angolan coast. Forty per cent of the slaves taken from their homes to the New World came from Angolan ports. There is to this day a stone chair near the port where the bishop performed mass baptisms, before captives were branded with a cross and sent on their way. In all ages, disaster and death take place as vibrant life carries on all around. We are all, in different ways, ambling unaware through the fields of Waterloo.

It occurred to me that when we did finally leave Luanda, the thing I might miss most of all could be the silence and solitude which that life behind bars gave as a curious back-handed gift.

With Senhor Cruz fully in charge, however, I felt confident in going away on our next leave, since all was going so well in the house. Senhor Cruz, his eyes brimming with sincerity, kissed my hand and urged me not to preoccupy myself with nothing. (*'Não preocupar-se de nada Sona Pamela!'*) I gathered that on return the house would be shining and the garden redesigned and ablaze with flowers. He had been scurrying back and forth to the hard currency supermarket since, due to a change in management, all credit had to be used and cards recalled. At his suggestion we bought great quantities of beer and coke to 'future-proof' the house against inflation. The store-room shelves were piled up to the ceiling with these stocks, so there would be no chance of the staff running out of items to barter for vegetables during our absence.

The staff were reliable, the weather was cool, Lena, KJ's PA, promised to come in every single day to check on the animals, so for once, even though this was Angola, it seemed that I could catch the plane with a tranquil mind.

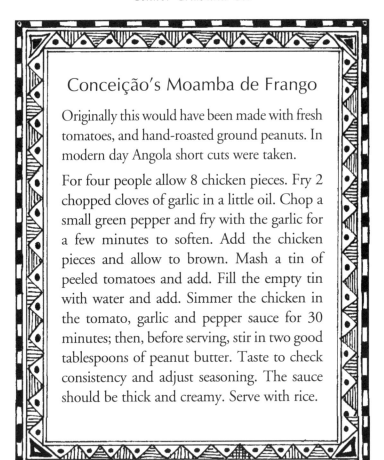

Conceição's Moamba de Frango

Originally this would have been made with fresh tomatoes, and hand-roasted ground peanuts. In modern day Angola short cuts were taken.

For four people allow 8 chicken pieces. Fry 2 chopped cloves of garlic in a little oil. Chop a small green pepper and fry with the garlic for a few minutes to soften. Add the chicken pieces and allow to brown. Mash a tin of peeled tomatoes and add. Fill the empty tin with water and add. Simmer the chicken in the tomato, garlic and pepper sauce for 30 minutes; then, before serving, stir in two good tablespoons of peanut butter. Taste to check consistency and adjust seasoning. The sauce should be thick and creamy. Serve with rice.

10

Senhor Cruz – Saint or Sinner?

We arrived back in Luanda on 15th August – dia Quinze – and the weather was relatively cool and pleasant. We were serenely confident that all would be well with our new paragon Senhor Cruz in charge. Lena had telephoned and told us that in his surpassing virtue Senhor Cruz was even sleeping in the house at nights, so worried was he by our long absence. She assured us that everything was just perfect, and that the only possible problem might be that the dogs were slightly fat. In gratitude for all this fidelity we had looked for special 'thank you' gifts for the staff, and found watches for all three of them, including a rather stunning 'gold' one for Senhor Cruz. We were sure he deserved it for his efforts, and looked forward to seeing his large eyes grow even bigger with astonishment when he saw it.

In fact little Senhor Cruz looked quite ill when we arrived at the house. He was unshaven and yellow, and unlike his usual smart white-clad self. The kitchen seemed uncharacteristically at sixes and sevens, with everyone barely arrived from the market, baskets and packages strewn everywhere, and a surprising feeling of scramble in the air.

As I walked through the house there were 'artistic arrangements' everywhere. The kitchen fridge was festooned with long strands of creeper, and at strategic points there were 'shrines' in front of photographs of us. I resolved to get rid of the Hindu temple effect as soon as I decently could, i.e. just as soon as Senhor Cruz left the house. On the upstairs veranda – my beloved refuge – the plants seemed rather peculiar. All of them were dripping wet, and yet they looked as if that was the first water they'd seen in weeks. Others had miraculously meta-morphosed into altogether different plants.

In the cantina, the store-room where the Senhor had so kindly volunteered to sleep at night, all seemed normal – until I pulled aside the floor-length curtains designed to shield the household stores from curious eyes.

We had left the shelves piled to the ceiling with cases of beer and soft drinks – several hundred dollar's worth. Now the shelves were empty. Doing a quick calculation, at the normal rate for staff food, that amount of beer for exchange should have lasted six months, as an insurance against inflation. How had they managed to eat so much food in only the same number of weeks? Even to my jet-lagged brain, this seemed very peculiar indeed. Had the stores been moved? What was going on?

We called the staff into the main room, to receive their gifts. The reaction was as astonished as we could have wished from all of them, but Senhor Cruz's eyes almost popped out of his head as he opened the parcels containing his new watch and his smart black trousers, waistcoat and bow tie, fresh from the uniform shop in Regent Street, and just as he had wanted.

We had an early night. The next morning there was no jam or honey or marmalade for breakfast, in fact a lot of things were missing that I thought should have been left, but remembering Adelaide, I just concluded that throwing things out of other people's fridges must be a Portuguese pastime and thought no more of it. The day passed with an odd atmosphere in the house, but unpacking took up most of the time.

Then on the second night back, Senhor Domingo, the senior night-watchman, and Francisco's uncle, once more drew up a chair in his domain on the front veranda, beckoned to KJ to join him, and began his story, just as he had done for the tale of the Ambassador's Bones.

'Things are not right!' he said, 'Not right here at all.'

KJ was then made to swear that Senhor Domingo had not

divulged anything, for should anyone suspect that he had, he was afraid of vengeance involving a bit of local sorcery or poison. So having sworn to keep the source a secret, O Embaixador was then told the complete and unabridged history of the last six weeks, and the perfidy of Senhor Cruz.

It seemed that little Senhor Cruz, who 'Never never!' took a drink, had fallen from those starry heights during our absence. Having organised himself to be the custodian of several hundred dollars worth of beer, and then to sleep in the cantina, temptation had proved too strong, and the little man had set about drinking solidly through the lot. After achieving this monumental task, it seemed a pity to stop there, so he searched for the key to the cocktail cabinet, and demolished the contents of that as well, embezzled the grocery money and even borrowed from Francisco in order to continue. Now Senhor Cruz, drunk, could probably cook better than most people could when sober, but in those heady weeks that was too much to expect of such a dedicated toper, and the poor staff, including hungry and thirsty night-watchmen, were neglected, while the little Senhor disported himself in the store-room with the liquor, and apparently with sundry boy-friends as well.

We were disappointed and shattered by these revelations. We didn't want to believe it but it seemed to add up. Though Francisco and Conceição maintained a buttoned-up silence, they emanated such icy disapproval of Senhor Cruz that it was obvious they could say a great deal if they chose. KJ from his long experience of Africa knew well that nothing would be said by the rest of the staff unless we made it obvious that we already knew some of what had gone on. Then we would learn the rest. So the following day I began by tackling Senhor Cruz about the accounts – not done of course – and with much urging he produced an untidy and fudged version which accounted for six cases of beer and doubled or trebled all the market prices.

'Oh Sona Pamela!' he said (probably praying hard), 'You must never, never come to the market with me; you would die of shock – it is now so expensive.'

Feeling more and more like store detectives, we established, from independent witnesses, as they say, that in fact market prices had halved, being the growing season. So waiting until after lunch, with an eye to getting lunch cooked and not being poisoned, Senhor Cruz was invited into the main room, and tackled by KJ in amazingly fluent and trenchant Portuguese.

Increasingly incandescent, KJ taxed him with one misdemeanour after the other. The little man quickly realised that he no longer had a leg to stand on, as one after the other was kicked from under him and the carpet pulled out as well. The Senhor's little head sank lower and lower on his chest and his shoulders hunched. He experimented with crossing his hands over his heart as in a deathbed scene, and then tried clutching his head in his hands and passing a hand over his brow. So absorbed in his rehearsal of operatic gestures he was, that he jumped visibly when KJ asked: 'Do you want to continue working here?'

'Oh yes yes, yes!' he replied, quite overwhelmed with his own sincerity.

He was given very clear conditions – repayment of $100 of the consumed alcohol from his future pay, and total and immediate drying-out. We were always optimists.

There followed two weeks of apparent reform and relative peace, except that Senhor Cruz did seem rather more noisy and self-confident than he used to be. In any case, I was busy dosing Polar Bear with drugs imported from the four corners of the earth against his skin condition which had flared up in our absence and – not surprisingly – had gone unnoticed. In the evenings I discovered that a great many objects from the kitchen cupboards were missing and broken about which, of course, nobody knew anything (the ghost of Adelaide walked again) and I spent many hours scrubbing smoke and dirt from kitchen stoves and walls. It was also fascinating to open cupboards and bookcases and discover empty bottles stashed away. There were even, to my great puzzlement, red wine rings on the tops of the highest wardrobes. Did Senhor Cruz and his friends do their drinking on the top rungs of ladders?

It was also necessary to resuscitate poor Paddycat from near death of diarrhoea and dehydration. What had he been given to eat? The poor little chap was extremely ill. We asked around in alarm and discovered that the only vet in town belonged to the team on the other side of the ideological fence – the East Germans. The situation was desperate. It looked as if we could lose our beloved Paddycat. The East German Ambassador's Residence was a few doors away, surrounded by guards, alarms, lights and security fencing. There was nothing else for it. We walked down to the fortress and rang the bell at the gate. Just then the ambassador drove up in his car, recognised KJ and courteously invited us in. We came straight to the point: 'Our cat is very ill. We are afraid he is dying. We believe you have a vet in your team. Can you help us?'

The ambassador, a bluff pleasant man of country stock, took in the situation immediately. Looking kindly and concerned, he too forgot about the Cold War. He got onto his radio telephone and called the vet: 'You must come immediately,' he said, 'and save the cat of Europe.'

And that was how we found ourselves in the East German veterinary clinic with a sympathetic lady vet, who looked grave and poured gallons of rehydration fluid into poor Paddycat, by now limp and almost comatose.

'Give him nothing for twenty-four hours,' she said, 'and if he survives, bring him back to see me.'

Fortunately, Paddycat was a big, strong African cat. He turned the corner that afternoon, with non-stop Rehydration, Reiki and Rescue Remedy, and after several days of eating only puréed carrots and drinking water, made a full recovery. It was a victory of humanity over ideology. But since he was the light of my life – perhaps even more than the dogs – it did nothing to bias me in favour of Senhor Cruz.

The final crunch came one Saturday morning three weeks later when we were enjoying a peaceful breakfast on the upstairs veranda. There was rattling and banging at the front gate, and, looking out through the bars, we saw Conceição and Senhor Cruz apparently playing hide and seek. Each time Ção opened the gate, the Senhor banged it shut, laughing merrily and shouting playful teasing remarks at her. He was in high good humour, and spent an enjoyable morning hugging and kissing the cat, and ambushing me all over the house. As I retreated from him he followed and tried to initiate long and obsequious conversations, all of which involved much hand-kissing and bowing – and in general, managed to spend the entire morning doing absolutely nothing.

At 11 o'clock we went into the kitchen to look for coffee. No coffee, but Senhor Cruz was humming a little song as he polished a perfectly clean electric plug. Half an hour later, he was still polishing the same plug. KJ disappeared precipitately into the staff room to nose around for stored bottles. And there they all were, lined up in a drawer. Doom descended. Senhor Cruz conceded defeat, wringing his hands and walking backwards as, with an approximation of tears in his eyes, he assured us that he forgave us and bore no ill-will towards us: 'Of whatever manner, Senhor, of whatever manner,' he repeated.

Surely there was some mistake. Shouldn't that line about forgiveness have been ours rather than his?

Obsequious to the last, Senhor Cruz backed out of our lives. He disappeared entirely from view for a few days; we presumed on an almighty bender to celebrate the end of yet another promising job. But he surfaced a week later at the office asking for his holiday pay and his big lobster trays. He was neither repentant nor crestfallen, merely hoping to the last to persuade KJ not to split on him to other international organisations.

So here ended the second lesson. From then on we did not employ a cook. My kitchen was peaceful and I did not play games of hide and seek with the kitchen utensils and culinary tools. I just had to work harder, and if necessary, get up even earlier if there was entertaining to be done. Conceição could barely conceal her pleasure at being number one helper in the house and did brilliantly at cooking ironing and advice-giving. When I was not there she was more than capable of holding the fort so that I wondered why we ever needed anyone else.

We had still not experienced all the surprises that Luanda had in store for us but we just hoped that the remaining ones might be funny rather than disastrous. I suspected that we were not the only establishment in Luanda lurching from one comic-opera episode to another. This particular comic chapter could end happily with a good rousing chorus, Cão preparing *Moamba de Frango*, Paddycat fleeing from Francisco's vacuum-cleaner, and the Senhora sailing downstairs to make, at last, a real 'lemon delicious' for pudding.

Lemon Delicious Pudding

The dessert that proved so difficult. It should be a light sponge cake with a magical tart lemon sauce beneath. Usually served with ice-cream or cream.

1 cup white sugar, ½ cup flour, ½ teaspoon salt, ½ cup lemon juice, 2 tblspn grated lemon rind, 1 tblspn melted butter, 1 cup milk, 2 eggs, separated.

In a medium mixing bowl combine sugar, flour and salt. Stir in lemon juice and rind, butter and milk. Beat egg yolks until thick and pale, and add to the lemon mixture. Beat egg whites until stiff but not dry, and fold into the lemon mixture. Pour into a buttered casserole. Place in a larger pan. Pour hot water to about 1 inch deep in the larger pan. Bake at 350°F for about 40 minutes, until the topping is set and golden. It should be cake on top with a lemon sauce beneath. Serve warm with cream or ice-cream.

11

Hunting for Food, Rats and Bandidos

Poor Faz-tudo did not survive his probationary period. Despite his good will, he was just too great a danger to himself and everyone else as a driver. He was paid off and encouraged to seek less challenging employment, and the indefatigable Lena at the office produced yet another candidate from her network of contacts. Agostinho had been one of the fleet of drivers at the presidential palace. He was young, bright, efficient, and helpful. And as KJ would find, driving for the President had given him confidence and panache.

The first inkling of how useful these qualities could be came when KJ needed to visit Cabinda, north of Luanda. The reason for the visit was very Angolan. *Someone* had made a big mistake and 300 tons of food aid had accidentally gone to Cabinda Port. Government was responsible for the distribution but the only facilities at Cabinda for off-loading were said to be three small floating barges, and there were no goods sheds. There were numerous UNITA soldiers in the area but no one seemed to know how many local people would benefit by the food. And too, Cabinda was dangerously near to the border with Zaire, where many things went, never to return. To cap it all, there was no ship to bring the cargo on to Luanda where it might stand a chance of being unloaded and distributed before it was stolen.

KJ persuaded some government officials to go with him to see what was happening. He went to the airport on the appointed day and found the usual chaos. A plane to Zaire was taking off and the airport was heaving with passengers. The VIP lounge was closed and someone had gone home with the key. The normal entrance doors were completely blocked by several large Zairoise ladies. They were wearing brightly coloured robes and head-dresses, they were laden with suitcases and large packages, and they had all arrived in the doorway at once, so that their expansive derrières were stuck fast. Knowing that the plane to Cabinda was due to depart, KJ panicked and strode back to the car, where the faithful Agostinho was waiting.

'Is there another entrance to the airport?' he asked.

'Get into the car!' said Agostinho. 'Sit in the back and look important!'

Doing his best to oblige, KJ sat up very straight. Agostinho rapidly reversed out of the passenger parking ground, revved the car and roared around to the military airport next door. Armed soldiers manned the entrance barrier. Agostinho made an imperious upwards gesture, which fortunately was taken to mean: 'Raise the barrier!'

Propelled by self-confidence they shot through and onto the tarmac, careering past rows of Russian MIGs and Antinovs. Thankful that no one had yet fired a Kalashnikov, KJ couldn't help remembering that the military airport was often the scene of shootings and stray bullets since frightened Angolan recruits received short shrift if they tried to escape from troop planes and scooted across the tarmac, rather than face battle.

Spotting the plane for Cabinda at a distance they screeched to a halt. The plane was just being loaded. KJ breathed a sigh of relief, but could see no sign of any of the government officials who were supposed to be making the trip.

He went to the pilot, an efficient older man in shirtsleeves, who was supervising the loading.

'Is this the plane to Cabinda?' he asked.

'Yes,' was the reply.

'Where is the party from government who are travelling today? They don't seem to be here.'

Light dawned in the pilot's eyes. This was obviously a novice in Angolan ways.

'This is the plane for Cabinda, yes of course, but this is *yesterday's* plane. *Today's* plane leaves *tomorrow!*'

When they did arrive at Cabinda, by tomorrow's plane, which was by now today's, what did they find? In Angola, expect the unexpected. Cabinda was and is an oil-rich enclave, buzzing with European and American oil companies. Equipment had been borrowed, the food was unloaded and stacked neatly in the port. Evidence was produced that it was being distributed to needy districts. The local Commissario invited the visitors to lunch and took them shopping in the market, before they returned to Luanda on yesterday's plane. KJ arrived home carrying a small table carved with elephants from the market.

Back in Luanda, another potential scandal was brewing. Five million dollars' worth of food aid was alleged to have gone missing. There were rumours that armed soldiers came to the port at night, to commandeer food and load it onto army trucks. Once more, though this was really the government's responsibility, KJ thought he should make enquiries. He needed to know if any of the food aid was actually being delivered. He requested a visit to the warehouse facilities together with the minister and government officials responsible. There were many delays. 'The minister is unavailable'. 'He is out of town!' 'Not this week!' 'Maybe next Tuesday or the Thursday after!'

Finally with the minister, his minions and a military escort, KJ set out for the outskirts of Luanda, to one of the huge industrial sites, now derelict. The convoy drove on rutted roads among the deserted factories and warehouses, with much discussion as to whether it was this building or that one over there. A warehouse was pointed out. The convoy stopped and the group got out of their cars. A large, heavy door was pushed open, and KJ caught a glimpse inside. It was piled high, from floor to ceiling, with crates of Moet et Chandon champagne –

for the use of Russian, Cuban and East German army officers. The door was hastily closed and the visitors were hurried back to their cars. There was more consultation and more searching among the jungle of old buildings. A second warehouse was pinpointed. It looked exactly like the first. The cars pulled up. The group alighted and walked to the door. This warehouse was piled high with Johnny Walker Black Label whisky crates. Once more the curious fact-finding delegation had found more than it bargained for. They were again hushed up and hurried out.

After another twenty minutes of weaving on rutted roads, a third warehouse was found. It was at the very edge of the industrial site, near one of the huge black markets. On the other side of the wall was a seething mass of humanity buying, selling, trading, bartering, fighting, shouting, like a scene from Dante's Inferno. For a third time a large door was pushed open. There was the food aid, clearly labelled, stacked in immense piles, as far as the eye could see. KJ was just beginning to feel relieved when his hair stood on end. At the far end of the building, adjacent to the black market the wall of the warehouse was not quite complete. In fact it stopped at shoulder height. The food aid was being stored next to the black market in an open building.

When he pointed this out to the minister and the government officials, there were some inventive explanations. Perhaps the best one was: 'You can trust Angolan people. No one would ever steal food from the government!'

Hearing the story at an evening function, the jovial Egyptian Ambassador commented, with a twinkle in his eye: 'Your food is to feed hungry Angolans. You may be sure it will be stolen by Angolans and that they will eat it.' Philosophical though it was, KJ was not sure that this line of reasoning would appeal much to HQ.

It may not have been related to these investigations but shortly afterwards the office was burgled. It was in an old building in

Rua Rainha Jinga, up a dark set of stairs. The door was barred by the heaviest of security grilles, with a mechanism that locked into three iron stays in the wall. On a second gate was a steel padlock, guaranteed to foil the most expert thief.

Not so. One morning the grille was open. The foolproof tripartite locking mechanism had been surgically removed and placed on the floor inside the office The padlock was beside it. In the Holy of Holies – KJ's office – the lock had been expertly picked. Nothing was stolen but confidential documents were neatly arranged in rows on the floor. It was clearly a message to Western Europe – 'Watch what you are doing!'

Meantime back at the house in the Rua Damiao de Gois, we had our own issues to deal with.

For our entire stay in Luanda both electricity and water went on and off with maddening irregularity. After some of the Cuban troops withdrew, UNITA blew up two pylons near the city. As a result, half the town was without water and electricity for days on end, a tragedy for those who had hoarded food supplies in their freezers for months.

Luckily we were in a part of Luanda where the electrical cuts were frequent, but short, probably because the Cuban Ambassador lived at the end of the street, and 15,000 Cuban troops were fighting on the side of the government. So our freezers stayed frozen. This was fortunate because one of them was full of lobsters. I placed them there myself.

Shortly after we arrived a tall, weather-beaten fisherman had arrived at the gate carrying two large canvas bags of fresh prawns and lobsters which were plentiful in local waters. He announced himself as the European Commission Fisherman. The fish were good, the price was good, and we took him on.

Seafood was the province of Adelaide, Senhor Cruz, and now, Conceição. The fish delivered, the kitchen would be covered in silver scales for half an hour and then all would be stowed neatly in plastic bags in the freezer. One Saturday afternoon when KJ was away, there was a ring at the front gate. It was the fisherman. Remembering that we were short of fish, I opened the gate and in he came with his canvas bags. He tipped out his haul. Twenty lively lobsters tumbled out and began walking around the blue-tiled courtyard on their claws. Shouting at the man to catch them, I went for the housekeeping money to pay him. A dreadful thought occurred to me. What was I going to do with them? Conceição was not there. I was certainly not going to drop them into boiling water. The fisherman would take away his canvas bags, and the weekend would be a nightmare, with twenty lobsters at large being chased around by two lively bull terriers. The kindest way to euthanase a sick tropical fish is to put it in a little water and place it in the freezer so that its vital functions gradually slow down to zero. Would this work with lobsters? It seemed the only option. With the fisherman in tow I opened up the freezer room and together we put them one by one into the largest freezer. As the lid was closing on them, they began squeaking, as if to say: 'It's getting cold in here, boys, what's happening?' I felt like a murderer!

We had other livestock too. Luanda was a rat's paradise. They loved it because there had been no rubbish collected for years. The drivers took ours away. I hated to think what they did with it. When it went, our yard was clean and tidy but not necessarily those of our neighbours. All Luanda houses had Arabic-style tiled courtyards, with round drain-holes to carry away water. These drains made a Rat's Underground throughout the city, and they poked their heads up anywhere they chose, to see what the pickings might be. Being a sports girl, Panda loved an exciting rat hunt, and spent much of her time with her nose down the holes, hoping one might come along as she sniffed delicious 'parfum de rat'.

Rats turned up everywhere – in the garden, in the kitchen, in the store-room, and even in the laundry basket. A family of them nested in the clothes dryer and one set up shop in the generator and chewed through the cables. We really needed the Pied Piper of Hamelin, but rather than use poison or traps we let the dogs deal with them instantly and instinctively. When a rat was spotted, my strategy was to call Panda and shut her in the room for the thirty seconds it took her to despatch it. If my exit was cut off, I sat on a table, eyes tightly shut, and feet tucked under, well above the level of battle. We had a scoreboard on the back of the kitchen door. By the end of our stay, it read 'Panda 31, Paddycat 1.5 (that one was *very* small), Francisco 3, Agostinho 1, Polar Bear 0'.

One day, as KJ was about to go to work, the driver started up the car, and something large flashed out from under the bonnet.

'Was that a rat?' asked KJ.

'No Senhor, it was not a rat, it was the cat,' was the calm reply, and Antonio prepared to drive off, as though this was an everyday occurrence.

Panic ensued, departure was delayed and we searched for Paddycat who had taken refuge under the compost box. He was looking distinctly offended and licking himself rapidly. The only trace of his disagreement with the fan-belt was a piece of fur missing from his tail. No more little siestas inside the car engine, then.

We also had mosquitoes in abundance. Once (*Nos dias dos Portugueses*) the city had been spray-misted regularly. Now things were different. At evening functions, as a matter of course, the hostess issued guests with mosquito repellent before they went outside for drinks and the room would be full of elegantly dressed guests energetically spraying and rubbing their arms and ankles. There was a choice between taking daily anti-malarial preparations with side-effects, or risking malaria, We could opt to take a preparation with the bizarrely frivolous name of Fansidar, which would wipe out the illness in a day or two.

The local population walked around heavy-eyed, in the grip

of constant low-grade fevers. While we were there, Agostinho suffered cerebral malaria, returning to work a shadow of his already slim self. Francisco contracted cholera and was hospitalised, relying on cooked chicken from the house for his food. KJ was supervising a project to renovate the 800-bed university hospital. Everything from the operating theatres to the lift shafts had been sabotaged at the time of Independence. Everywhere else in the city there was a desperate need for repair, rebuilding and reconstruction. The housekeeper of a friend said one day in despair: 'Madam, when will this Independence end!'

Another aspect of the misery of life in the city was the level of crime and violence. Naturally, when people have nothing there will be those who help each other and those who steal from their neighbours. There were constant hold-ups, armed break-ins and shootings. M. Roland, KJ's economic advisor, answered the door one night to face a group of men armed with Kalashnikovs, and his Italian engineering advisor, 'the Teddy Baar', also had a midnight visitation. A member of the French Embassy's aid team was shot and his body thrown into the bushes on the Miramar hill. No action was taken until with a sudden flurry all the bandidos in town were inexplicably found and rounded up.

Night after night the police raids were headline news on Angolan TV, and the desperados were paraded in front of the camera. They were a thin, tough and ragged band, glowering at the camera through their hair and trying to look fierce. When they were sentenced to be shot by firing squad as a public example, KJ and the other diplomats became increasingly nervous that they might be summoned to take front row seats at the executions. People began planning reasons why they might have to be out of the country. Then suddenly it was all over. Some bandidos had been shot, mercifully away from the cameras, some had been imprisoned, a few pardoned. Life felt marginally safer again, and the city went on with its life – until the next time.

Now that things were a little more secure in the city, and some parts of the country were back in government control, we had a short respite from the daily tension. Ambassadors from Europe, with their wives, were invited on a trip out of Luanda to see European development projects in the southern town of Namibe, near the Namibian border. Most had not been further than the beach at quilometro 14, and those of us who had, had seen very little. Ruined and smelly government guest houses, game parks where the game had been poached from helicopters and eaten by the army, and long, long lunches in derelict beach shelters were the sum of the tourist attractions. Angolans cheerfully made the best of it, but the possibilities were less than enticing.

We would leave very early, before the military planes began flying, and we eagerly presented ourselves at the airport at 6am, in comfortable clothes and shoes. The airport was cool and eerily deserted. We waited on the tarmac. Minutes ticked by. We looked around for something to sit on, and perched on a pile of concrete girders. There was no sign of the government ministers who were accompanying this grand tour. Obviously they regarded the 6am starting time as a joke since they turned up, fresh and breakfasted at 7.30. We saw why today's planes tended to take off tomorrow. Finally we took off, in high spirits, laughing, shrugging our shoulders and saying, 'This is Angola!'

At the town of Namibe we were met by KJ's friend Fernando Faustino Muteke, the Governor of Namibe Province. He was a huge bearded man, fierce and piratical in appearance, with a laugh like a lion's roar. A small crowd of local people had lined up to greet us at the Palacio Communale with its columns and marble staircase. As we were ushered in to the inner reception room we noticed a sybaritic feast laid out on a long table. Breakfastless, we licked our lips. Inside the faded gilt reception room, observed by portraits of dignitaries, we were welcomed at great length by the governor and his cohorts. We stood on the right foot and then on the left for what seemed like a long time.

But when we emerged into the entrance hall, looking forward to some of that food, not a scrap remained. The citizens of Namibe had demolished the lot.

Hungry and thirsty, we moved on to the next visits – all by now, two hours behind schedule. We were taken to a banana-growing project and dutifully walked up and down between the rows, inspecting irrigation ditches and new pumps. There were long speeches about new seeds and the hopes for multiple yielding crops. Back into the buses again, and off to see an olive grove being harvested. The trees were ancient, gnarled and beautiful. But curiously, there were many branches lying on the ground. While the bumper harvest was being extolled, KJ strolled over to one of the workers and asked about the branches.

'Oh,' he was told. '*Não temos escados.*' ('We don't have any ladders.')

And so, the workers of the New Angola simply tore down the branches of their ancient trees to make the harvest easier.

Back in Namibe a fleet of cars was waiting. The Governador must have mustered every car in Namibe for the transport of the Excelencias. We were bundled into them, in twos and threes. The vehicles had seen better days, but the drivers were, to a man, dressed in suits and ties for the occasion. KJ and I were in an old vehicle, which banged and rattled along. We had no idea where we were going. The two Angolan men in the front seats ignored us and talked non-stop at the tops of their voices – discussing local events and scandal as we bumped along. Along the desert road the scenery was desolate and eerily beautiful. Suddenly we saw, by the side of the road, the famous Welwitschia Mirabilis plants, six feet across, sprawling out over the white desert sand like leathery, multi-limbed monsters.

'Stop,' we shouted, and when that didn't work, 'Pare!'

We unstuck the door and clambered out to gaze at the extra-ordinary sight, reminding each other that these plants might be 500 years old.

We drove on, further into the Namibe desert, the loud chatter in the front seats unabated. Dramatic angular sand-hills appeared on the horizon. We wondered whether we were travelling parallel to the coast near the *Baia dos Tigres* where, the story goes, a hundred years ago, some dogs swam ashore from a shipwreck. They survived by catching fish, and by running along the edge of the surf with their mouths open to catch the spray. A pack of dogs still lives there, evolved over time to live in this astonishing way. We looked westward and wondered.

Finally, after an hour of bumpy driving, we approached a settlement. White and glaring in the midday heat was a moon-scape of salt works – small huts, little hillocks and sacks of salt stretching out across the desert. In the blazing sun, the mine workers of Salinas stood in a line, dressed in their best clothes, waiting to greet the 'great ones' who were coming to see them. Endemic Angolan lateness and delay had kept these simple good people in the searing heat for hours. We walked the length of the line, shaking outstretched hands and greeting people warmly. It was all we could do as they stood in simple dignity. Then our Angolan hosts turned their backs, leapt into the convoy of cars again and roared back the way they had come. There was no explanation, to us, or to the salt mine workers. In the unbelievable heat and grinding hardness of their lives, they had been put on display, so these 'important' folk from the city could visit the salt works. What possible sense could it have made to them? I felt ashamed to be part of such arrogance.

For another hour the car bumped and rattled back over the desert. There were yet more visits to be made. Transferred into hot buses we were taken to see a fish factory. There was a distinct fishy smell, but no visible workers and no sign of production. We were presented with a flat piece of metal which might one day be a tin into which fish would be put. We have it to this day.

The buses continued on to another site. As we followed a line of people past dilapidated buildings, we met the first visitors coming back. I called to the French Ambassador's wife, an intelligent and humorous person: 'What is there to see?'

'Oh!' she said, 'We have been to see a bridge that isn't there!' And so it was.

At last, by 4pm, we were driven back through the town of Namibe, into what had once been a botanical garden. Among the sparse vegetation were concrete tables and ancient wooden benches where we collapsed with relief. Mercifully, there was water to drink. Plates of food materialised, carried by local women. Seated opposite to me was Paloma, the dark-eyed wife of the Spanish Ambassador. A cooked lobster surrounded with salad was placed in front of her. She took a piece of it onto her plate and prepared to enjoy it with a smile of anticipation. There was a sudden stir and a message began to ripple up the table. Angolan officials began to run about in a sort of panic. It seemed that we were not to eat here after all. For KJ it was a moment of déjà vu. We were bundled back into buses. Paloma, in hungry rebellion, departed with a tomato in her hand. It was back to the airport, back on the small plane. Everyone was hungry, exhausted, dismayed, astonished and amused in equal measure. No explanation was ever given.

We had all been in Angola long enough to have mastered the Angolan shoulder shrug. *'E Assim!'*, 'That's the way it is!' We arrived back in Luanda – for once, thankful to be there, even hungry, thirsty, tired, eye-sore and dirty. Whether it was rats, bandidos, mosquitoes or mad journeys into the hinterland we were learning at last to shrug and say: 'Ah well, this is Angola!'

12

Panic, Potholes and Packing Cases

In January 1989 we had an extra few thousand people in Luanda for the SADCC* conference. This is a union of Southern African States aiming to encourage self-sufficiency, and to reduce reliance on South Africa. The EC sponsored the conference and the Angola office became a temporary Conference Factory.

Two dozen visitors were arriving from HQ, all on different flights. It would be a struggle to accommodate them, since apart from the Hotel Meridien, the only other hotel in town had been stripped of its basins and sanitary ware by departing Cuban troops, and guests were reduced to buckets in the bathrooms. There were interpreters coming, journalists, agriculturalists, legal and engineering specialists, political scientists and economists, and government representatives from all of the SADCC countries and members of the European Commission. Chris Patton, then a junior minister, was coming from Britain with his henchmen, and the Portuguese Deputy Foreign Minister was coming with his team. It would be the first visit to Africa of the new Spanish Commissioner for Development. And at the same time Luanda chose to hold a Trade Fair – not that Angola had much to exhibit, but it was hoped that other countries might.

The whole exercise was made more interesting by the issue of new radio-telephones in the office. We practised charging them, chose call-signs, and tried calling each other – Alpha 1, Alpha 2, and everything through to Theta. People learned not to leave them switched on when one evening the Teddy Baar was broadcast reading a bedtime story to M. Roland's children,

---

* Southern African Development Coordination Conference.

and snippets of private conversation floated through the sets. We all remembered with a chill, remarks we would not have wanted broadcast.

Food was stockpiled to cater for all the breakfasts, snacks, lunches, dinners, and cocktails that might be required. Menus were planned, timetables were set. We were ready.

The city of Luanda too, was preparing for the great week of events. The potholes in the road were overdue for repair. Unfortunately there was no asphalt available for the purpose. But there was a lot of beach sand. All the potholes were carefully filled up with sand, tamped down and the surface was painted over with a thin layer of tar. It looked convincing, and with luck might possibly survive one motorcade.

When the arrivals began, we realised that this would be a new and superior level of *confusão*. The radio telephones crackled and squeaked day and night, drivers scurried to and from the airport, lost visitors, picked them up and were directed to four different addresses by different members of the office staff. From time to time KJ was summoned to the airport to meet a particularly V-VIP. One of these was the Portuguese Deputy Foreign Minister.

Though now a prominent figure on the international stage, he was at the time a young minister, recently promoted, and very proud of it. He was also rather small. As the ex-colonial power in Angola, Portugal aroused powerful emotions and the Diplomatic Corps was expected to greet this visitor at the airport. The TAP plane landed and taxied in. The Dip Corps was lined up along the red carpet. The Deputy Foreign Minister in his dark suit appeared at the door of the plane, waiting to make his entrance into Angola, his short figure outlined in the light as the gangway trundled across the tarmac.

There was a problem. The gangway designed for a smaller plane was two metres short of the doorway. The Deputy Foreign Minister stood, looking down at the gangway, and the welcoming committee stood looking up at him. Then someone on the plane had a bright idea. This was a modern plane. It had its own gangway. A button was pressed and the internal gangway concertina-ed itself down, stopping two metres short of the ground. Trying to retain his dignity the Deputy Foreign Minister remained standing at attention in the doorway. Finally a third bright idea was broached. The DFM should come down the plane's gangway as far as he could, and then hop over onto the Angolan ladder. He crawled over gingerly like a crab and arrived at last with his dignity in shreds, to shake the hands of a Diplomatic Corps which, if not quite spluttering with laughter, was having considerable difficulty keeping a straight face.

Sometimes on these occasions, a Monsieur, Herr, Mijnheer or Senor would arrive with fanfare and imperial delusions. This time 'Signor Obnoxioso' tested our diplomacy. He began badly, turning up late and decidedly the worse for wear to his own formal reception. Guests invited to meet him were left, hands outstretched, with no paw to shake. He cancelled the planned programme and made other appointments around Luanda at impossible fifteen-minute intervals. He bellowed commands, slighted government officials and propositioned the pretty ones.

His wife, Signora Obnoxiosa, arrived unannounced on her husband's coat-tails. A sharp-featured person with sunflower yellow hair, she entered the room with attitude, and dominated every social situation. She was one of those women who despise their own sex. In conversation with a mere female, her eyes constantly flickered across the room, seeking the next male she could use to serve her purposes.

Meantime we, the 'catering staff', had been working overtime. By now we were wise, and cooked interesting local foods for guests from Europe, since expensive imported delicacies invariably led to sotto voce remarks about people 'living in luxury in the tropics!' Conceição would do her Moamba de Frango, and Francisco had graduated from breadmaker par excellence, to chef of the Cape Verdian *feijoada* and *cachupa*, a tasty mixture of plumped-up corn kernels, beans, garlic and spicy meats. There would be a lunch at the house for forty people. Buffet lunches are easy to serve but the food has to be plentiful, and I had been rising at dawn and staying up until all hours, cooking ahead.

To warn us to be on stand-by for guests, KJ would use his radio telephone and call: 'Alpha 2, this is Alpha 1, the cars are just rounding the corner.'

The call always came as I was on my knees struggling with the plug on the hot-tray, or juggling the last hot dish out of the oven.

Since it was a working lunch, only women who were 'honorary men' (so to speak) were invited – women who had a relevant role in the conference, and were part of the discussions. Signora Obnoxiosa was neither, but came anyway, and monopolised the Angolan Minister of Planning, to everyone else's chagrin.

On these occasions, after greeting the guests, I was happy to revert to the role of cook, to do it well and with full concentration, without the complication of being 'front of house' at the same time. But it did mean mad conversations through the kitchen wall, like: 'Alpha 1, this is Alpha 2, are you ready for desserts yet?'

We had cleared the main courses, the gazpacho, the salads, the lobster mayonnaise, and the local hot dishes, and set out the desserts. The kitchen door opened, and friends from Swaziland and Zimbabwe crept in for a hug, a laugh and a bit of a chat. Then the door opened again, in the midst of the steam of washing up, and I looked up to see the tall, handsome, black-bearded figure of the Commissioner for Development, looking down at me, every inch the stunning Spanish Grandee. He had come in to say a courtly thank you for the lunch. Any woman might have gone weak-kneed, wishing that she were not wearing an apron, that her face was not shiny and her hair not standing on end!

Finally, by the middle of the afternoon, the retinue swept off to some urgent meeting in their fleet of cars. We had cleared the tables. I was about to take off my shoes and collapse when unceremoniously the front door burst open. It was 'Signora

Obnoxiosa' back again with a group of people including a grossly obese gentleman bizarrely concerned with famine relief. She flounced in, with a toss of her yellow head, and to my appalled astonishment began to hold a meeting then and there in the centre my living room.

The ten days were long. Very long. Signor Obnoxioso bellowed for service, insulted hosts and cancelled dinners at a whim. Mercifully the last day came. Signor had decided to leave early – perhaps some of his schemes were in danger of backfiring. He was invited to the house, for drinks and a substantial snack before catching the plane.

The sound of high-voltage braggadocio arose from the reception area as I prepared snacks in the kitchen. Fetching something from a cupboard, my eye lit upon a box of Senokot, a dramatically strong medication for constipation. I was filling vol-au-vents with mushroom pâté at the time. It was exactly the same colour as Senokot. Just supposing, I thought. Just supposing il Signor Obnoxioso were to get a *really* bad dose of the runs on the flight back to HQ. Just supposing . . .

That was our last mission from HQ in Angola. After two years I was beginning to feel, if not comfortable, then at least able to cope. No longer a frightening threat, Luanda had become an interesting challenge. Now it was almost time to move. West African countries like Mali were mentioned. KJ had suffered more than his share of tropical diseases – Dengue fever, tropical parasites, undiagnosed low fevers – and it was time for a healthier post. He pleaded for a second term in Swaziland and after some demurring, got it. Life there would be cool and manageable again, and he spoke the language fluently.

But first we had to leave Luanda. We began to make enquiries. They told us, at one of Luanda's two forwarding agencies, that there were no packing cases in Luanda.

'There is a war,' they said. 'There is no wood. All the wood in

Angola is beyond the cordon of troops and through the zones of fighting. But we can made you packing cases from imported wood. Each case will cost you US$ 250.'

We reeled with shock. Understandably HQ was not in favour of this option. From the standpoint of a European country where everything was available, our requests must have seemed truly bizarre.

The second forwarding agency which also did not provide crates, asked: 'Can the goods be flown from Angola to Lisbon, and then on to Swaziland via Johannesburg? That would be the safest route.'

HQ was back on the phone in a flash – or as near as Angola ever did to a flash when it came to telephone calls.

'Lisbon,' they said, 'is in Portugal. Portugal is in Europe. We see no reason for your goods to make a detour of several thousand miles via Europe.'

Despite the fact that from the Angolan point of view *everything* went *everywhere* via Portugal, we had to admit that they had a point.

We consulted the forwarding agent again. They came up with Plan B. Goods could be sent via Zaire, where they would be stored in a warehouse for three days prior to being flown out to either Johannesburg or Harare. We queried the wisdom of trusting our lifetime's treasures to a warehouse in Zaire.

'No sir,' they said at the forwarding agency. 'We can ensure that there will be no problem. All you have to do is to pay an extra US$500, and the people in the warehouse in Zaire will be happy and will not steal your goods.'

We felt they should be too, and contacted HQ once more . . .

'Request permission to pay $US500 bribe to warehouse in Zaire not to steal our goods!' Predictably, the correspondence went on for quite a while.

We were running out of time. There were two working days left before Easter and we were due to leave the following week.

International phone calls, as always, entailed hours of waiting. Emergency mode set in so KJ decided to try the 'Incentivos' route. After speaking to a contact at the telephone exchange, a bottle of whisky from our cupboard changed hands and the call to HQ miraculously shot to the head of the queue. The official at HQ came on the line. He had studied the dossier. He pointed out that Johannesburg was in South Africa. South Africa was not recognised by the commission for political reasons. Goods could not be sent via a country which officially did not exist. 'You may take your goods from Luanda to Harare,' he said.

Now this was hardly satisfactory. We had arrived from Harare, but we were not going back there. KJ had just said: *'Quand je suis á Harare je suis nul part!'* ('When I'm in Harare I'm not anywhere!') when the line went dead. And that was that. Despite hours of trying, it was impossible to restore the connection. The Easter weekend loomed. We were posted to Swaziland and only authorised to fly as far as Harare.

Left to our own devices we needed crates. We telephoned everyone we knew. People were helpful. Embassies gave access to their junk rooms and KJ went trawling through their rubbish piles. The British Embassy had received a delivery of new furniture and had boxes. The Spanish had a strong crate. The Belgians donated wood and packing paper. Stapem provided nails, screws and reinforcing materials. An assortment of boxes began to assemble in the back courtyard, and His Excellency KJ spent the next few evenings straightening metal strips, repairing, strengthening and putting in extra screws.

We also had the dogs and Paddycat to consider. PC had his wooden box, but this time he would be travelling in the cabin in a special tartan cat-travelling-bag. It came from Paris, a gift from M. Roland, and it had a furry lining, air-vents and little Perspex windows. Cat-like, he was not impressed, but I was. I was longing to waltz onto the plane carrying my cat in a purple tartan bag with fur lining and Perspex windows.

The dogs would be in travelling boxes. But first they had to be weighed. We had weighed them at home but that was not enough. It had to be done at the airport. They scrambled out of the car, always ready for another adventure and set off along the path. A group of Angolans instantly levitated to the other side of the road, one old man saying audibly, of Polar Bear: *'Cuidado, e um ourso!'* ('Be careful, it's a bear!')

In the TAP office, bored staff members barely looked up. Perhaps they saw bears every day. We explained that Panda and Polar were there to be weighed. Polar Bear was sitting on my feet. Panda was straining at the leash, desperate to get around the back of the ancient settee in the office. It had lost one leg, and was keeling over, the upholstery was filthy and torn, and she was absolutely convinced that there were rats down the back of it. She was probably right. I held on tight, knowing that if I let go she would be up on the couch, scrabbling for all she was worth, stuffing and rats flying everywhere.

We were taken into a back room where they were weighed on ancient scales. We each stepped on ourselves, holding a dog in our arms. When the calculations were made, their weight was exactly what we had put on the forms. A waste of time. Panda left reluctantly, still eyeing the settee. I wished I had let her go just to see the fun.

Having spurned the offer of the forwarding agents to make $250 packing boxes, we could hardly ask them to do the packing into our home-repaired containers. And, besides, we had had packers in before, and had ended up with less than expected.

So during the long Easter weekend we packed. Boxes were filled and every item listed and numbered. Just as the goods reached the top of the box, we found the box for the toaster, now at the bottom. We had arguments about whether the dogs' blankets should be taken, and whether another special sunhat should be given away. We spent three hours on Good Friday, trying to fit the sound system back into its polystyrene box. When it was all done we telephoned the forwarding agents again.

'Very good,' they said. 'We will send out men to collect the boxes. The boxes must be left open. We will take them away and seal them at our warehouse later.'

'No, Senhor,' we replied, '*we* will seal the boxes in our house and only *then* will they be transported to your warehouse.'

After some muttering it was agreed and we watched the boxes sealed and removed, with dramatic straining and heaving and a certain amount of devastation to plaster and paintwork. At the truck in the street outside, everyone in the neighbourhood gathered round and marvelled that the truck's magnificent lifting mechanism was working that day.

Truck and crates gone, we looked around the house. Under the brown paper and plastic bags that were strewn around, objects were crawling out. Half of the breadboard, barbecue forks, books, a mirror that had been in full view, a box of socks. There was nothing for it. These things would have to go as accompanied luggage.

We were travelling in several stages which meant packing three ways. I would go to Harare with the dogs and Paddycat, and then on to London while they stayed in Philippa's Kennels. KJ was going direct to HQ for a briefing, and we would meet up in Britain for a brief break between postings.

The cases stood in rows. KJ had one small overnight bag for his few days at HQ. He liked to travel light. My load included two large cases for London, three suitcases for the first month in Swaziland, several boxes containing everything left behind after the packing, two bull terriers, a large tabby cat smouldering with discontent, and one crated Celtic harp.

Meantime farewell invitations were coming in. There were goodbyes to attend, all bitter-sweet. Everyone cooked their best treats and I struggled to take small helpings of dessert. There were presents and hugs and promises to stay in touch.

Departures from Luanda were special. We had spent our time there enduring the endlessness of it all, hardly daring to hope that one day we would escape. When friends came to the end of their term, the Diplomatic Corps went en masse to the airport to say affectionate goodbyes – something that happened in no other posting. We would all sit there rejoicing for the friends who were leaving and wistfully thinking ahead to the time when it would at last be our turn.

There was a war-time mentality in Luanda. We needed each other, Angolans and expatriates alike. We shared what we had, and helped each other whenever we could. There was an un-spoken agreement to keep up our own and each other's spirits. No one complained, everyone was cheerful and there was enormous affection between relative strangers. We had all seen what happened to friends who gave way to negativity. Once someone began to complain, the situation would overwhelm them. They would rapidly go downhill, succumbing to de-pression, over-use of alcohol or illness. None of us wanted to go any of those routes. So we took R&R leave when we could and supported each other to the end.

Our airport farewell was almost unbearably moving. Everyone was there and I loved them all. I thought of all that we had been through, of Conceição and her children, of Francisco and Agostinho, of Senhor Cruz and even of good old Adelaide. I thought of the house and how harmonious it had become, of the art class on the balcony at the British Embassy and the haven of creativity that it was. I didn't want to leave. The struggle had been so hard, and it had created equivalently strong bonds.

Someone in an airport uniform came into say that Paddycat could not come on board the plane. I resisted, firmly clutching the cat-carrier, and he gave up. The flight was called. There were multiple hugs and goodbyes, and carrying Paddycat in the tartan bag I climbed up the gangway. Anxious about the dogs being frozen or suffocated in the hold, the harp being crushed, and Paddycat disgracing himself in the passenger cabin I settled in for the flight, trying not to hear the muffled meows from somewhere around my feet. Every time I put my fingers through the air holes to stroke him, he bit.

Arrangements had been made with a friend called Joe, in Harare. Joe owned a Big Game fishing business on Lake Kariba, and would be at the airport with one of his vehicles. I had no worries on that score. Clutching cat and carry-on bag I watched as piece after piece of luggage appeared on the Harare carousel. With two hefty luggage trolleys trundling behind in charge of porters I emerged to find . . . no Joe and no transport!

The dogs were across the tarmac in a cargo terminal, no doubt bewildered and desperate for water and piece of grass. I vastly over-tipped two porters to watch the baggage and with one five kilo cat and hand baggage, trudged over the concrete to fish out the bull terriers. It was now 5.30pm.

'It is late,' the cargo attendant said. "We are closing. You must come back tomorrow.'

'But my dogs are in there, they need water and food, they might be dead by then!'

As I was dancing up and down, the most blessed sight in the world hove into view – the van of 'Pet's Express' Travel Agency, all efficiency. The dogs appeared, looking owlish. The whole circus was loaded onto a *bakkie* and we roared off through the night to Philippa's Kennels where the animals, at least, would have a safe haven for the night. Rather than bed down with them I phoned a friend.

Postscript. When KJ arrived at HQ the next day, his first appointment was with the official in charge of travel arrangements. The gentleman rose to meet him, saying: 'If any mistake was made in your arrangements it was to think that Harare was the capital of Swaziland!'

Was this an omen? Had Angolan *confusão* now reached as far as HQ? And would it follow us to the new posting in Swaziland?

Angolan Avocado Dessert

In Europe we normally think of Avocado as a savoury or a salad ingredient. In Angola it was most often used for this green dessert.

Take two or three perfect avocados. They must be very ripe and creamy, with no brown spots inside or strings. Remove from the shells and mash with a fork. Add the juice of half a lemon to taste, and a dessertspoon of sugar. Adjust the sweet/sour taste. Pile into glass dessert dishes, and swirl some cream on top. Place in the fridge for half an hour before serving.

Angolan Banana & Papaya Mousse

Another very easy dessert. The two tastes combined form something which is neither one nor the other.

Take a medium papaya. It should be very ripe and orange inside. Remove the flesh and mash in a bowl with two or three bananas and the juice of half a lemon. Pile into glass dessert dishes. If a firmer texture is required, dissolve one envelope of gelatine – make sure it is blended carefully throughout the mousse – and chill for two hours before serving.

13

Gazing at Sheba's Breasts –
life and death in the magic kingdom

Why did we always travel on April Fool's Day? We landed at
Matsapha airport clustered in its bowl of mountains, and were
welcomed as old friends by the two smiling drivers Sam and
Mr Dlamini. Panda and Polar Bear emerged wagging from
their boxes. They sat in the back seat, and Mr Dlamini's neck
disappeared into his collar as of old. On the way up the
Malagwane Hill into Mbabane, Paddycat's neck, on the other
hand, extended to giraffe proportions as he sniffed familiar
scents. We drove past the Animal Welfare Kennels where he
had first chosen us, and down the road where our new house
looked over the Ezulwini Valley. Once at the house, he got out
of his box, stretched and said: 'This is home!'

From a morose cat who had seemed to be declining into
grumpy old age he metamorphosed overnight into a young,
cheeky, scampering pet. I knew how he felt! Here there would
be no sticky heat and humidity, no gunfire at night, no rats,
no malaria, no cholera, only peace and birdsong and a sunlit
mountain view that stretched into forever.

The house was at the bottom of a steep road, on a sloping
five-acre block of land. On the steps my three new companions
were waiting – the staff. There was Gloria Khoza, a stout
middle-aged lady on solid legs like upturned bottles, a felt hat
rammed on her head to signify that she was a married woman.
Bona Matsebula, in her twenties, had a broad smile and greeted
us with a little bob, and Mr Mabuza, the gardener in grizzled

middle age, stood holding his hat in his hands. He was dignified, and about seven feet tall.

Once in the house, the entire Ezulwini Valley – the valley of heaven – spread in front of us. In the distance were the twin peaks of Sheba's Breasts. I could hardly bear to stop looking long enough to explore the rest of the house. Perhaps this was just as well.

The house was thirty years old and coming apart at the seams. There was mould on the walls and moss in the gutters, the kitchen ceiling leaked – we cooked under an umbrella on rainy days – and there was only one functioning ring on the stove. Our predecessors must have had angelic patience. The bathrooms were pure 1960s. One was bright pink, and the other was a cold dank dungeon with a green bath and black tiles. Everywhere were bare floor boards, and in the middle of the main room squatted a square brick pantry, like a heavy toad.

The furniture was made of rough pine boards. Everywhere there were hollow pine boxes of all shapes and sizes. Sometime in the 1970s these modular objects had proliferated like the brooms of the Sorcerer's Apprentice. In theory we were supposed to pile them up and use them as cupboards, bookcases, and coffee-tables and who knew what else. The windows were hung, not with curtains, but with metre-wide strips of gathered material, in varying patterns of red, blue and white. But however they were hung, they just looked like strips of cloth.

In the garden a lawned area dropped down to a lower level of trees and forest. Old hydrangea bushes were flowering in every colour from green and pink-tinged white through to the deepest electric blue, and beneath them were hundreds of day-lilies. There would be a year of magical discoveries as plants showed their faces to the sun. A tiny oval swimming pool in bad repair lay on the edge of the view, creating a mini-Hollywood vista, and crying out to be framed by bougainvilleas in Ali Baba pots.

On the first morning, mist modestly shrouded Sheba's Breasts, like a diaphanous shawl. Birds were singing in the garden. Near the gate, a smartly uniformed young day-guard indulged in an endearing spot of fantasy as, knobkerrie over one shoulder, he practised smart military about-turns.

We felt like Odysseus coming home after seven years. Things were the same but not the same. Our old house on the Golf Course Road had been at the opposite end of town. I would set off from home with confidence, turning left and right, but always landing somewhere unexpected. The mental map had re-activated, but details were filed in reverse.

We had also come home to a new ruler in Swaziland. In September 1981, King Sobhuza had celebrated his Diamond Jubilee at the age of eighty-two. Thousands including Princess Margaret had attended the celebration. That was the last time he appeared in public. He died at eighty-three, the longest-reigning monarch in the world.

The old king had seventy wives and many more concubines. In a polygamous society how do you choose an heir? In Swaziland, it is not necessarily the son of the first, or 'great', wife. In 1968 a boy had been born to the king by a young wife, Ntombi La Tfwala, of the Ndwandwe tribe. His birth name was Makhosetive (King of Nations) because he was born in the year of Swaziland's Independence. He would become King Mswati III.

To guard against their assassination (and the possible assassination of the king himself), heirs apparent were usually sent to another country to await their inheritance. A number of King Sobhuza's presumed heirs had already spent many years overseas in exile. Most of them, in the end, pleaded to come back home, succession or not. This child of the king's old age was his own choice, and the choice of the Committee of Elders, and after primary education he was sent to preparatory school in England.

After the old king's death a power struggle broke out between traditionalists and modernists. The prime minister was dismissed but declined to go, and in the interim the queen regent ruled. Because of the upheaval the young heir was recalled to Swaziland two years earlier than planned. He dissolved Parliament and called for new elections and at the age of eighteen was crowned king, assuming full executive power on his twenty-first birthday. He would rule for the rest of his life as 'Ngwenyama', the Lion of the Nation, in tandem with his mother, known as the Great She-Elephant, the 'Ndlovukathi'. It was a large burden for such a young and relatively unprepared man to carry.

We arrived back in Swaziland just after the young king's twenty-first birthday. He had already been king for three years. There were conflicting rumours: 'The young king is completely under his mother's thumb, and under the influence of traditionalists in government', 'The young king will be a modern monarch who listens to the young people of the nation', 'The young king is as wise as his father, Sobhuza', 'The young king is a teenager who stays up all night playing games.' All we knew so far was that he was a handsome, fresh-faced young man with clear eyes and a ready smile. He was amazed to find that KJ could speak to him in fluent Siswati. Time would tell.

It should have been heaven. There was no stress, the climate and the view were idyllic, there were old friends to rediscover, a shopping mall and supermarkets which stocked all that we could want. The country was full of craft markets, boutiques, studios and workshops; there were excursions to Johannesburg to look forward to and restaurants to try. And yet, looking out over the mountains, I felt depressed and useless.

In Angola life had been a challenge from dawn until bedtime, and gunfire crackled in the night. I had struggled to control the staff, and to make the house into a harmonious place, filled with colour and plants and music, protected from the accumulation of dark history that hung like a miasma in the very air. Now that role was gone. I had lost my purpose. It was as if a wall of negativity vanished into nothing. Leaning on paper and falling through, what was there to struggle against? What was I *for*? It was another side of culture shock and one I had not expected.

Once more, time would tell. I would discover that Swaziland was its own microcosm, with layers of cultural complexity, endless possibilities and many needs. In KJ I had a cultural coach, who could answer the dimmest questions about why and how things were done. He came as a European diplomat, but spoke the local language with a fluency Swazis did not expect. From his years in the area he had deep knowledge and a sensitivity to the culture that would enable him to bypass barriers. Before he was known and accepted, he had some fun in lifts and in meetings, overhearing remarks in Siswati that he was not supposed to understand.

Back in the house we unpacked. As we stowed away our goods, we found rolls of architects' plans in a cupboard. They were the entries for a 'Competition of Ideas' to rebuild the leaky old house. The hills and valley of Swaziland were an architect's dream and inspired designs that incorporated the landscape. The winning design was striking but had been turned down by HQ as too expensive.

One sleepless night I crept downstairs at 3am and curiously unrolled the plans. The winner had heavy jutting pillars and massive frowning lines which were out of sympathy with the flowing curves of the landscape. Even worse, the entrance was on one level, the dining room on another, and the entertainment area on a roof terrace. I could imagine trays of food being transported up staircases and across balconies in howling gales. The second design was Swedish. It had futuristic conical black chimneys on a white building. It lacked appeal. The third design had a clear barrel-vaulted roof running from front to back, open to 'the Valley of Heaven', bringing in light and warmth on dull, misty days. It embraced the landscape. It was a house in a garden and a garden in a house. I was excited. If changes had to be made, this was the architect to do it.

The architect was contacted. He was Richard Stone, a strong, stocky young man with sandy hair who came in as if he had been called to his execution. When told that there might be a chance of refurbishing the house with a modified version of his plan he looked stunned. Perhaps contracts didn't usually come so easily. The South African rand (to which the Swazi lilangeni was pegged) had recently been devalued and money committed for rebuilding would now go much further. A new proposal was sent to HQ and we settled down to wait for the reply.

Meantime we got on with living in the old house. It was winter. People who have never lived in Africa cannot imagine how frosty high veldt winters can be. The house was draughty and the wooden floors were cold. At a craft centre we bought hand-woven rugs and their cream and apricot colours glowed on the pine floors. The bathrooms were hideous but at least the water was hot. Every morning in the bath, we listened to the BBC World Service news. In mid-April the bulletins were full of happenings in China, in Tiananmen Square. With the rest of the world we cheered for the students through the rest of April and May, marvelling at their bravery and the break-through of freedom in Beijing. And then on 3 June, the promise of new life was interrupted by death, as armoured personnel carriers lumbered into the square, and hopes and students were crushed.

Polar Bear had not been himself. He had arrived in Swaziland with a cauliflower ear from shaking his head too hard to rid himself of ear mites. After the ear was fixed surgically he did not recover well. His chronic skin condition had been exacerbated by the Angolan heat and constant antibiotics had taken their toll on his system. We tried tonics, and homeopathic remedies but nothing seemed to help. In July we were due to go on leave and, despite my deepest misgivings, we had to go, leaving staff and friends in charge. The vet said he was improving but eleven days later, he died.

He was playing in those eleven days, but on the last day was really ill. I had done some courses in Reiki healing. Unaware of his state, that night from London, I sent him special thoughts and prayers. I felt that we were close and fell asleep with a mental picture of him bathed in light. At exactly that time, 1am in Mbabane, Polar Bear got up and went up the long flight of concrete garden steps to where his friend Mr Khumalo, the night-watchman, was sitting. He stood in front of him, looking up very seriously as only Polar could do. Then he went round to Bona's door and barked, and finally to the front gate, where he gave two more very loud and strong barks. He was saying his goodbyes. At 5am the next morning he was found dead in his kennel. I so profoundly hope that we did contact at some level and that he knew how desperately I wanted to be with him. Not to be there when needed is one of the sorrows of the travelling life.

We ex-pat women spend days, weeks, months and even years coping in large houses, alone with the staff and the loving devotion of our animals. By far the most devoted was Polar. He early decided that he was my dog, and rarely left my side, sitting so that we touched, clambering up laboriously whenever he could to balance his 27 kilos on my lap. In Angola he sat at my feet in the well of my desk as I typed, heaving great sighs that unplugged the electric typewriter and unset the margins. Every afternoon at precisely 5.10 his great white head with the black ears and the shiny boot-button eyes came out from under the desk. He would take my wrist gently in his strong white jaws, to let me know that KJ would be back in five minutes and it was time for the 'great game of squeak'. How did he know? He loved the game so much that he would welcome KJ with an excited bark on each step of the staircase as he came down. Round and round the house the dogs would run, as we squeaked a plastic toy first at the front door and then at the back, until we were all hot and exhausted. Not the brightest of dogs, Polar Bear was all the more loveable, as one loves a specially needy child. He knew how to love and did so unconditionally.

It was a heavy-hearted homecoming. We were grief stricken to be met by only one dog. We found a torch and went out into the dark to the west-facing hillside where we had asked for him to be buried. The earth was covered in flowers by understanding friends and there in the dark we cried.

Mr Mabuza had dug the grave, hollowing it out under a shelf of rock, as for a chief. Polar Bear was buried with honour, wrapped in his blankets, wearing his collar, with a squeaky toy and a ball by his side. The staff came solemnly to his burial, friends came, and read a Walt Whitman passage about animals as they threw earth on the grave.

I think I could turn and live with animals, they're so
               placid and self-contain'd,
I stand and look at them long and long.
They do not sweat and whine about their condition,
They do not lie awake in the dark and weep for their sins,
They do not make me sick discussing their duty to God,
Not one is dissatisfied, not one is demented with the
               mania of owning things,
Not one kneels to another, nor to his kind that lived
               thousands of years ago,
Not one is respectable or unhappy over the earth.

Every morning we awoke with hope, then heavy remembrance. Little rituals pointed up the empty space. Each night we found ourselves staring at two little piles of good-night titbits on a plate, while only Panda's dark-eyed face looked up at us. Polar's kennel and food dish had been removed by the staff, in accordance with the Swazi tradition of razing the hut of someone who has died. Wrapping him in his blankets, it was as if they buried him with his sleeping mat.

We made the little hillside grave into a garden. These things we do for ourselves, to assuage our grief. I imagined Polar's spirit frisking around my feet as I worked there to create a small mirror of his unconditional love. People who have loved animals will understand. Others, without that love, will not. Our pets become closer as they age, twining themselves around our hearts, and when they go, the tearing of those bonds leaves jagged edges. A small stone plaque was made, incised with a bull terrier's head, on a piece of green-veined verdite.

POLAR BEAR

Richmar Meneer

Indoda

1980–1989

Unconditional Love

We survived just one month as a one-dog family. KJ was keen to get another dog and set about building a puppy run. Only half-thrilled, I remembered too well the awfulness of bull terrier pups, like miniature tanks with teeth. We hoped to find the right puppy and that Panda would accept him. He would not be Polar but he would have his own endearing qualities and would win our hearts in his own way. I began phoning kennels in South Africa, tracking down breeders who might have a puppy, revising Afrikaans expressions in the process.

Finally we travelled into South Africa to find the new member of the family. I was sure Polar would approve. He was Star – kennel name Galactica Skiapasko – twelve weeks old. He alternated between preternatural goodness and fearsome bouts of nipping. We first saw him looking out of a wire kennel with questioning eyes. When he was handed over he had been washed and his fur was white and soft. He sat quietly on my lap all the way from Pretoria, except for some fierce barking when he woke up and saw a strange white puppy reflected in the wing mirror. When he tumbled out of the car, Bona saw him and called spontaneously: 'Oh what a nice little dog!'

Panda greeted him and played for a while until the thought struck her: 'This thing is going to live here!'

At which she growled, turned her back and sulked.

It took a few days to bring her round. One Saturday morning, out in the garden, she seemed to think: 'Perhaps it can play?' And she put Star through a session of rigorous gym. She chased him, jumped on him, knocked him over and sent him rolling down the garden slopes. Star bravely entered into the game, running back to me with an 'Am I doing OK?' expression on his face. When it was all over, he was accepted as a playmate and that was that. Panda sauntered off, secure in her position as Senior Dog.

Paddycat established himself in his own way. One day he squeezed through the pantry window, and lay down non-chalantly in the puppy yard. Star barked and play-pounced. PC ran a few yards, then stopped and put out a paw, claws extended. The puppy, already running, shot past, claws raking his side as he went as in a scene from a Garfield comic strip. The cartoon ended with a self-satisfied licking cat and a be-wildered dog. Hierarchy was established.

In his first week Star fell into the swimming pool, upset a cup of tea over himself and brought KJ crashing down in the garden by jumping at the back of his knees as I struggled to contain my mirth. He was a brave little chap. When he heard his first thunderstorm he dashed out into the middle of the lawn, to bark at the thunder. And he barked ferociously at a large sack of oranges that Bona was dragging around the kitchen floor, so of course she dragged it even further and faster to tease him.

He was long, silvery and lissom when he came – hence the name 'Star' – but he grew apace. Different pieces grew at different rates. At first his ears were too big, and we thought we had a bat-eared dog. Then the face caught up and the tail was too long. When that evened out the front end and chest barrelled out like superman, leaving his back legs looking as if they belonged to someone else. Eventually he harmonised, and I hoped he would one day be like his father, who was Supreme Champion of South Africa. His name had scope for creativity. People said 'Morning Star!' and 'Evening Star!' and of course the Dogstar was often referred to.

Star had a human best friend. It was the new day-guard, Moses Nhleko, a handsome, smiling young man. If Moses was missing from the front gate he could be found in the puppy stockade, trailing a bit of stick on a string. He became chief puppy sitter and dog-runner and they were blood-brothers. They had boisterous games around the yard, while, of course, keeping a weather eye on the gate for any visitors. Moses said he was 'training Star for guard duty.'

Panda trained him too. At first the two dogs went together to the front gate to bark in the mornings, and did the rounds of the fences, to make sure no cattle came too close. Then one morning, Panda decided to stay in bed in her kennel under the dining-room window, waiting until the toaster popped. When she smelt the toast she sauntered into the dining room and the two of them sat down to wait for their four titbits. From then on she was still Senior Dog, but Retired Dog in the mornings, leaving Star to do the 6am watch.

On 10 November 1989 Star was going to the vet for his final vaccination when suddenly the sky turned black. Johannes Dlamini, the driver, said urgently 'Stones' and we took shelter. The storm broke and hailstones came down in every size from golf balls to tennis balls, clanging and bouncing off the roofs with a noise like kettledrums while thunder rolled around the mountains. Those twenty minutes created a panel-beater's heaven. Cars were dented and windscreens broken. The garden was strewn with branches, leaves and bark, and flowers that should have been standing up lay down in surrender. Hail stones tore through large-leaved trees like bullets, leaving clean holes. We wondered about the birds – were they knocked out by the hailstone or worse, battered into tatty feather dusters? We hoped they had a good early warning system. And then the storm turned its back and went growling away into the distant hills.

The storm was reflected internationally. 10 November was a day of international change. The Berlin Wall came down. The symbol of fear became a symbol of renewal, as the 'wall woodpeckers' began knocking lumps off it with hammers. Change had come to Poland, to Hungary, to Bulgaria. Prague would follow, and the fall of Ceaucescu in December. The shape of the world was different. We listened to the BBC news every morning with astonishment as the Soviet bloc disintegrated. Change, although we didn't know it, was also moving closer to southern Africa. Just as Gorbachev was letting some light and air into the stultifying atmosphere of the Eastern bloc, so de Klerk – curiously almost Gorbachev's physical double – was letting light and air into the stultifying atmosphere of apartheid-ridden South Africa. We listened and watched.

As always it took time to create a routine in the house. The staff made an odd team. Gloria was a stout, strong lady with a mind of her own. She had been a great favourite of her previous employer, and was very confident. Sometimes her estimate of what she should do was a little less than mine. She had days of black moods, when she stomped around with a face like thunder and the air in the house turned blue. We all went around on tiptoe wishing it was all over – whatever it was. Bona, on the other hand, was a young woman in her twenties with a joyous smile. She tackled everything with energy and good will. Beating carpets, playing with the dogs, running to open the gate, Bona did it all with her whole heart. And she loved learning to cook. There was no 'Dom Cook' course, but we cooked lunches together in the kitchen and she observed carefully.

Bona brought food in to the table with a proud smile and a polite traditional bob. She found new recipes in magazines and tried them out as a surprise. One day she announced with a beaming smile that she was making a cake and a pie at the same time in the oven.

'I thought,' she said, 'I would kill one bird with two stones.'

Gloria, on the other hand, didn't want to learn anything new and said so. At lunch time she cooked meat and rice or mealie meal for the staff. The drivers and Mr Mabuza didn't rate her cooking highly, especially on days when she was glowering at the world. Swazi traditions include poisoning, and they were far from sure.

Soon after we arrived Bona announced that she was pregnant. In Swazi tradition, as with the Zulus, the birth of a child is the necessary prelude to a marriage, since it proves the young woman's fertility, and binds the two families together. Marriage is a union of families, not individuals, but Bona did not seem sure whether this child would lead to marriage. She would have time off when the baby was born and Jane, from Zimbabwe, would come to Swaziland for a month, to help in the house. Jane was not working at the time. She had never travelled and she was excited at the prospect.

We did not bargain for the baby to be born early. One night at 3am there was an urgent knocking on our window. It was the night-watchman. Bona's baby had been born and I was to come to the staff flat with a razor to cut the cord! By now I had learnt many things during ten years in Africa, but midwifery was not one of them. Desperate measures were called for. Three in the morning or not, Theresa, a friendly Irish ex-nurse, was telephoned, and nobly came to help. Bona looked happy and serene, holding her damp, sleepy new daughter. It was a scene from a Madonna and Child painting. When asked what the baby's name was, the reply was 'Thabiso' – happiness.

Thabiso lived up to her name. She was a fat, laughing baby. Her first word was Star, and they grew together. Star would wait for her at the door of Bona's little flat, and as they ran together in the garden he would inevitably knock her over, causing shrieks of delighted laughter.

Jane Nyamararo came from Harare wearing a red felt hat. It was her first flight, and she saw the sea from the air. She was immensely excited and immensely self-contained. She fitted back into her old job and we did the shopping together in an easy relationship. At the supermarket she was given some strange looks. She was African, but not Swazi. When supermarket staff addressed her in Siswati she would answer in English. On one occasion this so infuriated the check-out clerk that she turned to me, as if Jane were not there, and said: 'What's the matter with her? Why won't she speak to me? Is she stupid?'

I explained that not all Africans speak Siswati or Zulu and that Jane came from a different country. The young woman looked very doubtful and still regarded Jane suspiciously. We advised Jane to be very proud of being Zimbabwean if it happened again, and to ask people if *they* knew how to speak Shona.

In the course of our official duties we went to a scholarship fund-raising dinner at Waterford Kamhlaba School. Dress was everything from black tie to boiler suit. The music was loud, the chicken was tough and the ice-cream was melted. We heard an address from the politician, writer and anti-apartheid campaigner Helen Suzman on what she expected of South Africa for the next five years. What a dynamic and courageous little woman, funny and fearless! I was amazed that she had come thus far unassassinated.

Waterford Kamhlaba (meaning 'of the world') was the southern African branch of the World Atlantic Colleges. Built on a mountain top outside Mbabane on land granted by the king, it housed 800 students from fifty-two nationalities, all on bursaries from their own countries. They studied for the International Baccalaureate, and followed a liberal curriculum, including a large amount of community service. The then headmaster, Dick Eyeington, was a tall greying man with bright, piercing eyes. His wife Enid, a smiley ex-nurse, ran the community service programme. Nelson Mandela sent his daughters there while he was still in prison; the children of Desmond Tutu, and Walter Sisulu were students, as was Ian Khama, now the President of Botswana. The ethos of the school breathed tolerance, integrity and egalitarianism. It sent a stream of open-minded leaders and thinkers back to their own countries.

(That was in 1989. In 1995 Dick and Enid Eyeington retired from Waterford, and were looking forward to life back in England but, ever idealistic, agreed to go to Somaliland for four years to re-establish an SOS Children's Village secondary school north of Hargeisa. In 2005 they were shot and killed in their house while watching television. The killers were Islamic extremists acting on the false rumour that the Eyeingtons were converting Muslim children to Christianity. Africa can be an extreme place.)

Education for rural Swazis was on a different scale from Waterford College. Not long after our arrival, KJ had to make his first speech at the opening of a school. It was a 'micro-project' – the donation of school furniture to a new primary school at the Mhlume Sugar Estate. Micro-projects would become dear to his heart. They were local undertakings – a school, a bridge, a small road, a village pump, vegetable garden or dam – and each project was specifically requested by members of a local community who themselves contributed. The input could be land, or labour, or brick-making. Whatever the community could offer, would be doubled in monetary value. Eager requests flooded in, and rural areas sprouted blue and yellow signs pointing to communities which had proudly co-operated in their own development. This would be KJ's first public speech and the king would be there. Spurred on by his friend, Chief Sipho Shongwe, the Minister for Education, he would give the speech in Zulu, and in the traditional way, beginning with a story. He needed a tale about community effort. Racking our brains one morning in the bathroom, I had an idea.

'What about the Ant and the Grasshopper?' I asked.

Webster's Bookshop, a little shop, like a Tardis inside, yielded a copy of *Aesop's Fables*. KJ translated the story into Zulu/Siswati and put it in the traditional format of 'Once upon a Time' that the people loved. The day came. We were seated in state near the school classroom. The king and his ministers were arranged on the platform, wearing their red, black and white traditional dress. Press and TV were there. No one knew that KJ spoke the local language. Almost no Europeans even tried. He began his speech: '*Kwasuka sukela . . .*' ('A long time ago it happened . . . ')

There was a shocked silence. He stopped, and said it again, this time cupping his hand behind his ear. Now there was a delighted childlike response from the crowd in the traditional manner: '*Cosi!*' ('Tell us, tell us!')

And the story was on its way. They participated in the tale, laughing spontaneously at the little high voice of the grasshopper and the rough voice of the ant. They clapped in agreement at the moral of the tale and agreed that community effort was necessary in these things. By the time we arrived back in Mbabane, the filmed event was already being relayed on the Swazi Television evening news. The story was played and replayed all week on the radio. The queen mother, in a speech, was heard to say: 'As that man said, we must work together.'

I was approached in the supermarket and asked: 'Are you the wife of "That Man"?'

KJ's reputation was made. He might be from Europe, but he understood the language and the people. From that moment work in Swaziland opened up. Applications for micro-projects flooded in. Village groups of local chiefs and elders wearing skins and carrying staffs came into town with their requests. A letter came inviting KJ to the opening of a new school, saying that if he did not come his presence would be 'miserably missed'. The problem was that every time a new speech had to be made, we needed another fable. We used the 'Three Animals', 'The Lion and the Fox', 'The Old Man and the Donkey'. Aesop was invaluable. Sometimes, in desperation I made up a fable or two. It may be that in years to come, when folk tales are told around Swazi firesides, and collected by earnest and puzzled young anthropologists, they will note that they strongly resemble some of the better-known fables of Aesop, and are always prefaced by 'As that man said . . . !'

As work progressed in the office, at home we were working to close down the old and mouldy house. Now permission to rebuild was through and it was time to go. We ferried carloads of possessions to one of three staff houses in Pine Valley.

During our last week in the old house, history was made. On 11 February, Nelson Mandela walked free from prison after twenty-seven years. He emerged clear-eyed, waving, and free from bitterness. I ran to the gate and called Moses to leave his guard post, and to come and watch it with us.

The houses in Pine Valley were mythical mountain dwellings straight from Tolkien. Clean and white, they perched on the hillside, each balanced at its own angle, on its own rocky out-crop, each politely turning a shoulder from the others for privacy. A dark front door gave onto a small, shadowy hall. The only way to go was down the black slate stairway. As one descended, brightness increased until at the bottom the darkness exploded into glass and light. A new vision expanded into awareness, a world of lawns and sunlit mountains. The miracle never failed. Each time the beauty of the valley overwhelmed us.

The Danish architect Sven Hvass had angled each house so that the sun was invited in during the winter, and excluded in the summer. Our predecessors had been gardeners and the rocky ground was terraced and planted with hundreds of Canna lilies in newly bred colours. Everyone loved the house. Panda loved chasing lizards around the rocks. Star loved to stand on a huge boulder barking, and he would listen, head on one side, as a mysterious dog barked back at him from across the valley, in a perfect echo of what he had said. Paddycat liked to lie on the warm black slate tiles. Bona adored her smart little flat with its own sunny courtyard and the laundry she could use whenever she needed to. I loved my big pentagonal, light-filled study with room for music and writing and sewing. And KJ loved the peace and quiet.

There were five acres of garden. Mr Mabuza was busy all day. Each morning, at 8am he reported to me for duty at the kitchen door. A tall, dignified old man, he stood there, silhouetted against the hill, and pulling himself up to his full height gave a smart military salute, barking: 'Sir!'

I loved it so much that I never had the heart to ask him to change.

One morning I was in the kitchen preparing breakfast when Star poked his small white head around the door. Once more I fell into 'puppy-speak' and said fondly: 'Hello, little whitey!'

And once more it happened. Tall African Mr Mabuza was on Star's heels for the morning greeting. It was even worse than the first time. Had he heard? What did he think? I was hot with embarrassment. How could I do it twice?

Despite Mr Mabuza's English and my Siswati, we usually managed to communicate. Then I bought some packets of wild-flower seeds to embellish the terraces. We sprinkled them around. But when they came up, say what I might, Mr Mabuza shook his head disapprovingly and laboriously weeded them out, one by one.

There were five acres of rocky hillside threaded with little paths for walks. Around the perimeter was a strong wire security fence. We felt safe. Until one morning there was a phone call from a neighbour to say that half the fence was missing. Fifty yards of wire had gone from the lower part of the garden, out of sight of the house. The thieves had laboriously detached the wire from the metal poles and one night had simply rolled up the fence and taken it away. It was a bit like stealing the night-watchman and the guard-dogs.

We never knew what we would see when we opened the curtains in the morning. The valleys might be shrouded in mist, there might be a blazing sunrise or brilliant sunlight shining on wet rocks. The folded mountains could be green or purple or brown or blue or grey. In the rainy season storms could bring a navy blue sky and brilliant shafts of white light. It was a photographer's and artist's paradise and I longed to record some of it in watercolour. Helen Moir, a Scottish artist, was offering art classes. It was the beginning of lively tuition and long, quiet times painting with friends. We met up in twos and threes, and would go out into the mountains to sit in silence for hours, struggling to put on paper the beauty that we could see. The first time a painting of Pine Valley came together I felt true elation. I still have it. It is not the best painting in the world, but it cemented a relationship with the landscape, and small successes became more frequent.

At about this time a new Rotary Club was founded in Mbabane – one that would accept women. The Mbabane Mbuluzi Rotary Club was one of the first 'bi-sexual' clubs, and KJ and I decided to join. We knew little about Rotary, but thought it would help us to integrate with the local community. The club was full of jolly chaps and determined women – perhaps we still feel we have to try twice as hard. We had not quite expected the elaborate system of fines for imagined misdemeanours, or the boy scout rubrics and rules. Sometimes it was hard to take seriously. But we solemnly wore our badges, and attended meetings and involved ourselves in local projects.

To raise funds for one of these, we volunteered to take part in a 'Donkey Derby'. There would be donkey-races, beer and soft-drink stalls, afternoon teas and face painting. We didn't know much about 'Donkey Derbys' but KJ knew donkeys from his youth in Ireland and liked them. He volunteered to be 'Officer in charge of donkeys'. The donkeys were brought in from a rural village by their owner, for a small fee. They were used to working, but not willingly, and the owner and his sons stayed at their rears with stout sticks which the donkeys stolidly ignored. They were to race along a home-made race-track ridden by able young riders from the local stables. The public would have their fun by placing bets on the donkeys who were named and numbered for the occasion. The only problem was that nobody told the donkeys. These animals had barely been ridden, and certainly had never taken part in a race. They were not impressed. Even with keen riders on board, the mounts just stood around and cropped the grass or wandered over to talk to a friend.

KJ and I thought we had the answer. We went out along the valley road to a vegetable stall and bought a box of carrots. It was such a big box that the stall-holder was planning to retire on the proceeds. We were confident that with a carrot in front and a stick waved behind, the donkeys would learn to race very quickly. Not a bit of it. They were Swazi bush donkeys. They had never seen a carrot, much less eaten one. They ignored them. The races were a shambles. The young riders did their best to get their mounts moving. KJ and I ran ahead with carrots, and the owner's little sons brought up the rear waving sticks, which they had been cautioned against using. Occasionally an animal crossed the finishing line accidentally. The patrons who didn't win their bets ended up aching with laughter anyway. The donkey owner had a profitable day, his sons ate a lot of hamburgers, and the donkeys, who never knew what it was all about, had one of the best meals of their lives when it was all over. They probably thought it had been an easy day. And we made enough money to put a roof on the school buildings of the current project.

Once more we were 'walking through Waterloo'. As we worked to make relationships, opened rural projects or made fools of ourselves at 'Donkey Derbys', the political scene in the world and in southern Africa was changing drastically. We may have been in a tiny kingdom in southern Africa but world events were reflected there and would ultimately change lives. We were beginning to learn to be flexible, to respond to whatever life and the job brought us in the place we were. Our time in Angola had taught us well, to know when to say '*E assim*' – 'That's the way it is', and to understand that, sometimes, the only explanation for events was 'This is Africa'.

14

The King and I – A Contrast of Cultures

After such a public introduction to the country, courtesy of *Aesop's Fables*, KJ was often summoned to the domed Palace at Lozitha, in the Ezulwini valley. There, following the tradition of his father, the king saw his people, his ministers, his counsellors and foreign representatives. KJ was accepted as an honorary Swazi. He was given a Swazi surname ('Kunene', meaning 'those of the right hand'), and known respectfully as 'Baba Kunene' (Father Kunene). The people called him 'The King's Friend'. In time the friendly young king would call him to the palace when he felt the need of objective advice. Swazis were expected to bow low and walk backwards out of the royal presence but this was not expected of foreigners. The king addressed KJ in Siswati, and greeted him with a handshake.

King Sobhuza, in his time, had gone on long walkabouts, visiting all regions of the country and holding small traditional courts of justice as he went. The Swazi system, however it may appear to outsiders, is one of person-to-person communication. Any Swazi citizen has the right to speak to the king and to request his judgment. The young King Mswati tended to stay up late at night for these sessions with the result that ministers and ambassadors were often called to the palace for discussions after midnight.

Swazi society in the past has treasured its traditions. In modern times, traditionalists who surround the king are in favour of keeping the status quo, and modernists, including young university-educated people, are all for reform and Westernisation. It is a state of uneasy balance. The queen mother, who rules in tandem with the king, is responsible for the spiritual welfare of the nation. She is – perforce – a traditionalist.

Although King Sobhuza, as the great chief in a polygamous society, had many wives and concubines, few apart from the senior wife stayed in the palace. The others lived on land in their own rural areas, and supported themselves by farming. The king visited them from time to time as he travelled the country.

Young King Mswati, a handsome, pleasant and well-intentioned young man, is constantly misunderstood by the international media for his polygamy. Initially, it is said, he wanted to take only one wife, his first. This could not be countenanced by the elders. In Swazi tradition, as king, he is bound to take wives from strictly prescribed tribal and family groups, to unify the kingdom and for ceremonial purposes. Various clans have age-old ceremonial functions and a wife must be chosen from each. These duties are not regarded lightly. The king has a position in society akin to the 'Divine Right of Kings' of historical Western monarchs. On his ceremonial actions depend the prosperity, wealth and fertility of the nation. At the 'Umhlanga' or Reed Dance, the maidens cut and bring new reeds for the queen mother's home and dance before the king. The 'Incwala' or First Fruits ceremony is a sacred and mysterious ritual which the king must undertake to ensure the next year's crops. The events are held on dates carefully chosen in consultation with Swazi diviners. It is a kingdom where myth and magic coexist side by side with a modern commercial and government structure. Fine western-trained doctors and hospitals coexist with African medicine: the Inyangas, or herbalists, the Sangomas, or diviners, and the Umtakati, those who work by night and cast spells. Swazis exist with one foot in each of these worlds, bound together by the old beliefs of ancestor worship and animism, and step across the borders between one and the other, depending on the needs and circumstances of the moment.

This was the world in which we were living and working. Foreigners, though aware of the exotic and 'primitive' culture around them, could spend an entire working term in the country unaware of the deep influence of the old ways on modern, business-suited Swazis. When life crises came, there were certain situations and illnesses that the European way could deal with. Western medicine was known to be excellent for surgery and broken bones, for instance, and injections could give strength, but there were problems, such as lingering illness or fainting fits, which in many people's minds required a more traditional, intuitive or mystical approach, and for these, traditional healers were, and still are, sought out. The depth of these beliefs and their driving power lie under the surface of the lives of ordinary people. Ancient religion is the powerhouse driving an entire kingdom and people.

Offerings are routinely made – pouring beer on the earth, for instance – to placate the ancestors and to maintain harmony between man and nature. In Swaziland, the energy is red and raw, powerful, primal and acquainted with the concept of blood and sacrifice. Here people are accustomed to death, and are more comfortable with its place in the scheme of things than we in our dislocated Western society. Swazis understand the exchange of energy when life is used as a spiritual bargaining tool.

This world-view, based on the traditions of an agricultural and herding people, might seem irrelevant to what we experience as a modern technological era. And yet the system, when it operates harmoniously, gives psychological security to people who know who they are in the tribe, in the clan, in the family, in the web of relationships. They know where their loyalties lie, what foods they should or should not eat depending on their family name, what rituals and sacrifices are needed to keep life ticking over in relative safety and harmony, and who to consult if there are problems. They are in touch with their deep intuition, and wisdom often comes in the form of dreams, when the ancestors or sacred animals may speak. In the rural areas which Westerners often deplore as materially poverty stricken, traditional people are happily free of the Western dependence on linear time, and have their own way of relating to the universe. It does not do to ignore traditional belief and the resulting social mores by assuming that Western ideas are better and should be imposed.

A case in point concerned the foreign service of a particular Western country which we will call Utopia. Intent on doing good, and spreading 'superior' ideas, the powers-that-be back at Utopian headquarters decided that the Swazi attitude to women needed to be changed. It is true that at that time Swazi women were minors, and subject to their husbands. In contrast to the West, however, when they grew old and became elders, their voices were heard and deeply respected. But by Western standards, younger women had a hard life and were apparently ignored.

It was the age of feminism, women's studies and women's rights. A decision was made back in Utopia to show these Swazis what was what. It was decided to send a woman ambassador, a woman first secretary, a woman in charge of Development Aid, and a woman in charge of volunteers. The results were predictable to everyone except those in the Utopian Foreign Service. For the next few years, the Utopian Aid Programme ground to a halt. From the Swazi point of view there was no one those in power could talk to on an equal footing.

One night KJ was called down to the palace for a meeting at 11pm. He noticed the car of the Utopian Ambassadress in the palace parking ground when he went in. When he came out it was after 1am. The Utopian car was still there, with its flag, and the Utopian Ambassadress called to him.

'I need to see the king urgently. Is he very busy tonight?'

(In Utopia, things are always urgent!)

'Oh yes,' replied KJ, being as kind as he could. 'He has a lot of important meetings.'

What he could not tell her was that the king had come to the end of his meetings and was laughing and joking with his advisors. He had asked one of his ministers whether there was anyone else waiting outside to see him.

The reply came: 'Oh no, Your Majesty, only an *ntom-batane*!' ('only a little girl')

The lady ambassadress, a senior diplomat from Utopia, would not have been pleased.

Time, too is a dividing factor. Time, for us Westerners is linear. We see our lives as a string of things to do, stretching from the time we are born to the future. We are always dwelling on the past, or looking at our watches and planning what we must do next, instead of attending to the present. Time in rural Africa is more like a dot surrounded by a circle of variable size. It is a 'now' which expands and contracts depending, not on what the clock says, but on the experience of the moment and the people one is with. We Europeans can be infuriated when people from other countries have a different concept of time, and turn up either early or late for our strictly controlled appointments. I was given an insight into this by an African friend, who confided that in Africa, where transport is fickle, and there is always a pot on the stove, it is acceptable to arrive two hours before or after a given arrival time. After that, though I still wanted people to arrive punctually (and to be fair most people did) I had more understanding.

Some ambassadors in Swaziland (and not only women) were finding it very difficult to operate. One of them asked KJ's opinion as to why this should be. KJ didn't know but, on an outing with his friend the Minister of Agriculture, decided to find out. He put the question, in the correct courteous form in which such questions are put in Siswati, saying: 'Supposing an ambassador were to be having difficulties seeing His Majesty, and getting things done, why might that be?'

Chief Sipho knew very well who was being referred to and laughed. He said: 'It is a matter of time. You know us Swazis. We take time. The first year a person is in Swaziland, we neither see them nor hear them. We don't know them. The second year they are here we see them but we do not hear them. The third year we begin to both see them and hear what they have to say.'

KJ nodded. Light dawned. The diplomats in question were sent to each country for precisely two years. What chance did they have? It was a conflict between 'We take the time we need,' and 'Let's get it done now!'

Weekends were often spent on duty in rural areas attending the opening of developmental projects. Sometimes the king would be there, a minister or local chief. We would be greeted by the chief and village elders and led to inspect the school or bridge or new village pump. We would then be seated with ceremony to watch the dancing. In Africa people celebrate with movement. We might hum going down the street if we are happy. A Swazi will perform a little dance. Dancing is essential to a celebration. Boys often performed a version of the men's Sibhaca dance. It had evolved from a dance for warriors, calculated to strike terror into the opponents, and was danced wearing goatskin armbands and leggings to make the warrior look bigger and more muscular. Nowadays, when battles are not so frequent, the dancers also wear a colourful striped skirt-like garment – a sort of male tutu. Gesturing fiercely with shield and spears, the young boys of the village would dance, lifting their legs alternately in the air, and crashing them to the ground, each stomp punctuated with the beat of a drum, as if the warriors' feet were shaking the earth. The dance accelerated, legs rising higher, stomping more fiercely, the drum beating louder until suddenly, at an unknown signal, the warriors collapsed as though slain.

When schoolboys danced, it needed imagination to see them as future warriors but they could not be faulted for their enthusiasm. Often on young, skinny legs, the goatskin leggings fell down, but undaunted, they kicked them aside and the dance went on. Girls of the village would come out and dance too, singing and clapping their own rhythms. Clad in colourful cloths, their dance consisted of alternate high kicks. As their feet rose above their heads, hands modestly held down their clothes so that nothing unseemly should be glimpsed. And then the old women would come, with little titupping steps, wearing heavy black pleated cowhide skirts, and *amahiyas*, their hair beaded into the married woman's mushroom-shaped head-dress. Flat-footed, they would sway and stomp, as they chanted and ululated.

When the dancing and the speeches (another Aesop's Fable) were over, refreshments would be served. If we were lucky it would be mealie-meal porridge and vegetable relish. Sometimes there would be the expensive luxury of a coke or a sweet sticky drink. The men might have some beer. If we were unlucky it could be something more exotic.

On one occasion a cousin of mine from Australia was visiting. Gabrielle was an adventurous Australian matron in her early seventies and came as a guest to the opening of a village pump. We solemnly inspected the pump, tasted the water, listened to the speeches and applauded the dancing. When the food was served immense tin trays were brought along. They contained two-foot long wooden stakes around which were twirled chunks of tough-looking grilled meat like lumps of blackish liver. Asking what it was, we were told: 'It is the stomach of the cow. It is very nice.'

Desperate to find a way to refuse, we backed away, saying generously: 'Do please eat our share, we are not very hungry!'

Other festivals were more elaborate. Celebrations of the king's birthday at Somhlolo Stadium were huge affairs. Cows would be killed to roast, schools would be bussed in from the rural areas, women in hide skirts and Swazi warriors would parade. As well as the Swazi chanting, the Manzini Choir, or perhaps the *Asihlabelele* ('Let us Sing!') Choir would perform, combining their innate musicality and superb voices with disciplined choral training and hours of practice. Moving and dancing as they sang, their versions of 'Shosholoza' and 'Stimela' brought shivers to the spine, long before Western choirs began to attempt their pale versions of African song.

At one of these occasions a vivid vignette came at the end of the long day. The Swazi air force in its entirety – one plane – had flown overhead in salute. The marching and the speeches were done. The Royal Swazi army had paraded and were lined up in formation in the light of the setting sun. In a wonderfully odd reversal of history they were wearing British redcoat military uniform. As we watched, a Swazi prince stepped out wearing skins, beads and a *beshu* – a loincloth of skins. He had long hair, and a beard. And he was carrying a sophisticated camera on a tripod. Laying down his spears and shield, he carefully set up the camera, peered through the viewfinder, and began to take shots of the Royal Swazi redcoats.

Building work on the new house overlooking the Ezulwini valley had begun. Bill Sterling, the jovial building contractor, and his team of workers had taken over the site. The old house was stripped down to its window-sills and looked forlorn. The dereliction was intensified by the presence of a large flock of chickens clucking around the garden – the property of the site manager who saw no reason why all those lovely snails and slugs should be wasted. Some of his workers saw no reason why those lovely chickens should be wasted, and from time to time, sad to say, a few were missing on a Monday morning.

There were tiles to be matched, and paint colours to be chosen, site meetings each week and exciting trips to Johannesburg clutching samples of cream and gold fabric and carpet in my hand. For anyone with an atom of creativity it was a dream assignment but a responsibility. I anguished over each decision, wanting to make choices that would harmonise with the natural materials, and would enhance life for all the families who would come after us. As anyone who has built a house will know, it is a constant balancing of the dream with the budget. Slowly the walls were raised, the floor plan became visible, and one day when we arrived, the team of Swazi builders were putting the finishing touches to the entrance. Perched on scaffolding, they were singing a rhythmic work song. The man on the ground took a spade-full of wet concrete, and tossed it onto the trowel of his friend balanced fifteen feet above. The rhythm never faltered, and the catch was perfect every time.

One day to my surprise, an invitation came from the palace for 'tea with the Queen'. The Palace of Lozitha was a mysterious domed presence in the Ezulwini valley. Like most ordinary people I had not had too many dealings with Royal palaces and I was secretly thrilled and curious. Dressed in my best and driven by Mr Dlamini, I set off down the mountain, in good time for the 10am appointment. The palace gates were guarded by a soldier with a sub-machine gun who waved us in. Halfway up the drive a Swazi man got up from where he had been sitting on the kerb, threw his toothpick into the herbaceous border and sauntered off. We waited for fifteen minutes, while a bearded youth, wearing camouflage trousers, a red shirt and pink trainers shouted and gesticulated. Small, round Mr Dlamini moved the car, and hovered nervously in several different directions at once. The phone rang in the guard box but by now the guard had disappeared. Three more youths ambled along a veranda, eating watermelon. It dawned on me that we had done it again. We had taken the time on a mere invitation card too literally and at 10am, Royalty was just stretching itself and opening its eyes.

At 10.30, a Swazi lady appeared. She did not introduce herself but just said: 'I have come to meet you!'

Not in the first flush of youth, she was fashionably dressed in a green and black dress bisected by a very tight belt. She wore black patent leather shoes with very high heels which swivelled her ankles and bent alarmingly as she walked. Her hair was rigid and staring from the trauma of a recent vicious straightening. She tip-tapped on ahead into a room marked 'Reception' and vanished without a word.

I was expecting something much more elegant than the house I was creating with such care up the hill. The Royal reception room was furnished with mustard leather settees. It had a royal blue carpet and disconsolate pot-plants. Housework had not yet begun. The cushions were where they might have landed after a palace pillow fight, and the carpet still had traces of yesterday's pebbles and sand. An umbrella stand stood inexplicably on top of a coffee table. In a glass cabinet in the corner there were eight spaniels made of mustard-coloured china, and two large fluffy toy poodles. On the reception counter the clock stood next to a telephone and a fire extinguisher. The hands of the clock had stopped at five past nine,

I sat and waited. An immaculately dressed young man in a dark suit walked past, looked in and went about his affairs. Then a large woman wearing a nylon leopard skin over her shoulders appeared behind the reception desk.

'At last,' I thought. 'Something is going to happen.'

But no. She drank a plastic mug of tea in silence, gazing into space, then disappeared, leopard skin and all. It was beginning to feel very Alice in Wonderland-ish. I kept wanting to say, like Alice: 'Curiouser and Curiouser!'

A guard dressed in khaki appeared. He looked around the empty room very, carefully, then turned to me and said:'

'Is there anyone here?'

Accepting that I did not at that moment qualify as 'anyone' I gestured vaguely and said: 'Well, there's no one else here. Who did you want?'

With some desperation he replied: 'A committee! I've lost a whole committee!' And backed out before I could sympathise.

At 10.40 the 'whole committee' entered, led by an elderly bearded prince, wearing the Royal red lourie feathers in his hair. He was followed by a group of six men in suits. As they sat on the settee, looking self-conscious, I felt out of place and kept my eyes down. And there in my line of vision were feet wearing white socks, brown socks, grey socks, and yellow socks all lined up neatly in a row. I wondered if the anxious guard would ever find them or if he would be condemned to spend eternity like a uniformed White Rabbit, forever scurrying after his 'whole committee'.

I would never know. The lady in green reappeared and we went up some steps into an entrance hall, flanked by a stuffed white lion and lioness on one side, symbolising the king's strength as 'Lion of the Nation', and two stuffed leopards on the other. They were all trying to look very fierce and pouncing, but as they had been stuffed quite some time ago, it was pretty unconvincing.

We went through a large round foyer, dominated by a vast modernistic chandelier of multi-coloured glass organ pipes, and came face to face with the leopard-skin lady once more, still drinking tea, still gazing into space.

Finally we came into a small cosy room, where the young queen was sitting on a sofa. She was a plump and pretty seventeen-year-old, dressed in flowered silk. She had shy eyes, and looked unsure of herself.

We sat down, the green lady on the floor and I on a chair. The little queen thanked me for coming. I thanked her for inviting me. The dialogue foundered. I remarked on how early a 10 o'clock appointment was, and she agreed that it was difficult to get ready in time. I could see that she had taken a lot of trouble with her dress. She was wearing a patterned blue cotton cloth over one shoulder, and a length of flowered silk tied around the breast, fastened with a glittering bird of paradise brooch; all set off with a diamante and pearl necklace and earrings and little green shoes.

We tried hobbies as a conversational topic. Queens, it seem, don't sew, but like reading fashion magazines like *Vogue*, and romantic novels – those where the heroine marries the prince perhaps? Living in the palace was exhausting. People stay up late, sometimes all night, to play videos and music and card games, and to sing gospel songs. Queens usually like to sleep during the day, like dormice.

The queen ordered juice, and in it came, borne by a ragged and barefoot little girl about eight years old, probably a small relative of someone attached to the palace. A tin tray with two glasses of granadilla juice on saucers and a plate of digestive biscuits was placed reverentially on the floor in front of the queen. After a few moments, while we all silently surveyed the logistics, a gilt and glass table was dragged over with imminent danger to its teetering Chinese vase.

Polite conversation limped on as we sipped the juice and nibbled a biscuit.

There was a sudden babble of Siswati outside and a great deal of unsubtle stage whispering. It seemed that the American Ambassador's wife had arrived for her 11.30 appointment.

'It has been nice to meet you,' said the queen.

Dismissed, I trailed out after the green lady and hovered awkwardly in the anteroom while she conducted a conversation with the leopard-skin lady and other friends. It was bizarrely reminiscent of a girl at a supermarket check-out, chatting to her friends as she rang up the till. Abruptly remembering that I was there she looked around.

'Come!' she said, making that hand gesture they teach in dog-training classes. Oh dear! And I had thought I was an honoured guest of the queen!

We emerged out into the sunlight. Mr Dlamini was waiting. I

felt that if I blinked the whole palace and its inhabitants might disappear and I would find, like Alice, that I had been dreaming all the time.

Life became particularly hectic for the next few weeks. The young king went to a Commonwealth Conference in Harare, and brought back with him Sir Lynden Pindling, Prime Minister of the Bahamas, and his retinue. The visit seemed to have been a sudden decision, and so with one day's notice, there was a string of invitations to dinners, lunches and receptions. Unfortunately in their haste, the printers had a little slip-up in proof reading. All the invitations invited us to meet – Sir Lyndon Piddling.

The dinner for Sir Lyndon didn't go entirely as planned either. The Conference Centre glowed with flowers and candles. A couple of hundred people arrived on time. However, the king was delayed for two hours, so we sat at the table staring at the smoked salmon starter as it slowly curled up at the edges. We were so hungry that we tried to steal little bits of bread from underneath our rolls without anyone noticing. Across the table, the Korean *chargé d'affaires* slowly subsided into his smoked salmon with exhaustion while his tiny wife twittered at his side and tried to wake him. All the while there was music playing. Obviously it was known that European people liked classical music – Mozart in particular – but unfortunately someone had chosen the Mozart Requiem.

'Requiem Eternam' boomed out, and we watched our smoked salmon expire to the strains of the 'Dies Irae'.

At the office, development projects of all kinds were forging ahead. There were projects at the university, in education, in agriculture, in land conservation and rural development. One scheme put forward was the development of a multi-lane highway which would ultimately link Mbabane, the government capital, with Manzini, the commercial centre. Near Mbabane was a steep mountain road, with hundred-foot drops and perilous sharp curves. Cows, horses and goats wandered across the road and when thick mists came down at night the only way to navigate was by fixing on the cats' eyes in the middle of the road. Slow trucks, smoking old '*bakkies*' and speeding drivers all took their toll, and there were many accidents. KJ had funds to begin developing the section between the Matsapha industrial site and Manzini, where traffic jams regularly caused chaos.

The king was anxious for the project to advance, seeing it as one of the keys to Swaziland's development. He had discussed it enthusiastically with KJ. All the studies and financing proposals had been done, the funding was available, and the project should have been under way but there were dissenting voices. There were some Royal graves near the road site, which could not be disturbed, there were people living on the route who could not be moved, it would take at least a year to move the electricity poles that stood in the way, there were water-pipes that would take even longer to change . . . the list went on.

One night the king called KJ to the palace to discuss the plans for the new road. They spent time looking at the options and talking about the benefits it might bring. The delays were discussed.

Early the following morning there was another summons to the palace. This was surprising, since the young man did not usually begin his meetings until lunchtime.

On arrival at the palace, KJ saw a cavalcade of cars drawn up outside. The Prime Minister was there, the Minister of Works, the Minister of Agriculture, and the Minister of Housing, together with their permanent secretaries and the directors of all these services. Something was up! As he got out of the car, KJ went along the line, and greeted each official with his respectful surname, only used to give real honour and recognition. The use of it is formal – something like saying 'Queen Elizabeth of the House of Windsor'. Few Europeans knew the names existed, and still fewer would have memorised them to give the greeting in the correct manner. As he went along the line there was a murmur of appreciation, and some amazed laughter.

A message came that the group was to go inside to greet the king. To KJ's embarrassment King Mswati insisted that he should sit beside him as he made a pronouncement saying: 'I have called you all here this morning, because I think this road is not happening fast enough! I thought Baba Kunene should be here with us as we look at it.'

The assembly set off up the mountain in a motorcade and first stopped at the place where the Royal graves represented bones of contention. The king had an announcement to make: 'There are some graves here of minor royalty. I have decided that there is a place of honour for them beside the Sacred Mountain.' No one could quarrel with that.

The next stop was at the spot where the electricity grid would block progress. The king merely pointed to the poles and lines and asked:-

'Who is responsible for this?'

The Director of Electrical Services scurried forward.

'These have to be moved!'

'Yebo (Yes), Your Majesty!'

'When can this be done? By next month?' An even lower bow.

'Yebo, Your Majesty!'

The Director of Water Services received orders for his water pipes, the Director of Posts and Telecommunications found himself agreeing to move telephone lines in an unimaginably short time, and the procession of cars moved on to the homes that were in the way of the new highway.

Here the king's tactic was different. He simply reminded people that an agreement had been made to move these homes to better housing in a new area. No one seemed to remember such an agreement, but there were many wise looks, and much nodding of heads, and people agreed that this was indeed so. It would be a rash government official who would contradict his king or admit to a slip of memory.

It was well past lunchtime when the procession reached the top of the Malagwane Hill – the end of the projected road. Everyone was hungry. The Minister of Works sidled up to KJ and suggested that everyone should be invited back to our house for lunch. KJ was in a quandary. He'd never tried surprising me with the king and his entire cabinet for an impromptu lunch. And in addition, for the king to come to a private house would require weeks of planning, palace inspections and permissions. KJ thought on his feet. He quickly replied: 'It would be a great honour to invite everyone, Minister, but I am just a guest of His Majesty like everyone else. I cannot invite His Majesty, because he has invited us!'

The Minister of Works retired, disappointed. Emissaries were sent ahead to the Swazi Inn at the top of the hill. They were informed that the king and his ministers were coming to lunch. By the time the cars arrived the inn was in a state of panic, waiters scurrying everywhere, carrying trays and emptying freezers. To add to the confusion Swazi TV, in the manner of the media everywhere, had got wind of the unusual goings on, and had arrived with their cameras.

At lunch the king made a speech about the new road. KJ made a speech. The prime minister made a speech. The new multi-lane highway would be built. The young king's benign leadership would assure it. When it was all over, those present at the pilgrimage up the mountain went home scratching their heads, and wondering how they had said 'yes' to so many impossible things before lunch.

15

Whirlwinds, Witchcraft and Warriors

The renovated house was ready at last and we were leaving Pine Valley. I ferried car-loads of possessions. Our neighbour, colleague and friend, Gloria Pinto Teixeira, was helping with a pile of dresses one day, when she began to laugh.

'So many dresses!' she said.

Oh no! I thought. It's 'Madam-you-have-too-many-shoes' all over again. But this time I knew there *was* a word for 'too many' in Portuguese so she was serious. I resolved to clear out the wardrobe yet again.

We had been making these trips in sunny weather. One of the joys of southern Africa is the beauty of the seasons. It is sunny all year, even in the winter, with few grey days. One can be lulled into thinking that it is just like southern Europe. But Africa holds fierce surprises.

On the afternoon before the final move, the sky darkened. Remembering the previous storm when Mr Dlamini had warned us of 'stones', I rushed about closing windows and doors and checked that the dogs and Paddycat were safely inside. The heavens opened. The rain came down as if someone was emptying buckets from the sky. The wind roared, funnelling up the valley of folded mountains in a peculiarly localised way. People on the road were running for cover. Leaves and branches of trees went flying through the air, and window frames were rattling and banging. As we watched, heavy veranda furniture from next door flew into the air and landed halfway down the hillside, a swinging seat swung off its hinges and a canvas gazebo turned itself into a parachute. Something large and dark flew past the front door and landed with a crash above us. This was a tornado! Then the rain came down in earnest, with hailstones. Cars were battered once more, roofs and windows broken. When we went to investigate the crash at the front of the house, we found the solid concrete guard house from next door. It had been lifted and carried halfway up the hillside. The day-guard who was inside it at the time, had felt himself airborne, and had jumped out with nothing worse than a cut shin.

The following day (once more, April Fool's Day) we moved back into the renovated house. Waking up in a new house is like waking up on a different planet. All the angles are different, the light is different, the sounds are different – even the direction of the birdsong is different. We might have felt as if we were on holiday if it were not for the amount of work to do. It seemed that when a house was built that was not the end of it. There was a three-month maintenance period when fine tuning was done under contract. Every morning at 7am there was a crackle of intercom in the kitchen and we were told: 'Madam, the chaps are here to plaster the wall,' or paint the balcony, or go up on the roof to test the alarm, and the day exploded into a Breughel landscape of little figures with ladders. Just like the first days in Luanda.

When the house was being wired, we had been plagued with an extremely distrait electrician. His name was Beaver, and he beavered away, crossing wires, putting in light fittings upside down and in the wrong rooms, following me around, maddening me by calling me 'dear' and asking a lot of very unelectrical questions. As a result, all the upstairs plugs tripped when there was thunder, and when that was fixed, either the fridge or the TV immediately went out of operation.

We had ordered a dining room suite in 'pale ash' but when it came it was bright salmon pink. We re-ordered a table and chairs to be made in a sustainable golden wood called 'saligna', a kind of acacia, from a local factory. After three returns to the factory we eventually succeeded in furnishing the room. And just when I thought I had things under control I found Star in the main reception room, amid the cream curtains and pale upholstery, staring fixedly at an air conditioner and singing a plaintive little song. He refused to be moved and insisted that there was something up there. After a day or two, a terrible smell proved him right. The Swaziland Pest Control Services came and removed a dead rat. I was handed a solemn invoice for 'Expert removal of deceased rodent'.

There followed a dramatic weekend. On the Friday night there was another magnificent storm. We sat out on the upstairs balcony as the sky crackled and exploded. At 10.15, as we were stupidly watching a video, forked lightning shot across the screen and the lights went out. So we went to bed with candles. At 2am there was a crack of thunder which sounded as if it was in the house, and at 2.30, another one which set off the alarm system. We ran to turn off the alarm then waited to explain ourselves sheepishly to the armed response guards from Guard Alert. At 6am we got up and stepped onto the carpet, squishing in an inch of water. The entire upper floor was awash.

The house was built on top of an iron mountain which attracted lightning. The lightning had jumped the lightning conductors to a copper pipe in the bathroom wall and had blown a joint. Such a lightning bolt could have caused an explosion and taken off the roof. From 2am until 6am the wall and floor cavities had been filling up with water which was now running down the curtains into the room below. As it was the last weekend of the month, when people received their pay, all the plumbers were hung over or out of town. A kindly Dutch carpet contractor brought his industrial vacuum cleaner and siphoned out buckets of water from the brand new cream carpets.

Mr Mabuza, the gardener, was padding around in his very

holey socks, thanking God that we were not killed in our beds. As hundreds of people are killed during storms each year in Swaziland, it was not an unreasonable thought – the wet roofs of grass huts are prime lightning conductors and in a storm, everyone runs to stand for safety under the nearest 'sausage tree'. (Nobody has ever been hit by lightning under a sausage tree. As they are quite rare, this is not surprising.)

Bona looked very serious. She came to us in the dining-room with a solemn face and asked for a staff meeting with 'the Boss' after lunch. KJ agreed, and there in the kitchen was Bona, looking uncharacteristically stern, Moses in his uniform, Gloria, wearing her trademark red felt hat, and tall Mr Mabuza, stooping slightly and twisting *his* hat round and round in his hands. The conversation was conducted in Siswati, since this was Swazi business. Bona was the spokesperson. The staff were convinced that the house had been bewitched. Since there had been three lightning strikes the previous night, it was obvious that someone was really out to get KJ, and had employed extra-strong *muti* – medicine or spells – to destroy the house. If this was so, Bona, who lived on the property, was not going to stay around. It was too dangerous, and she had her children to think of.

'What are you going to do about it?' she asked.

KJ thought on his feet. He assured her that we would go to church on Sunday to thank God for protecting us so that, try as they might, even the strongest spell could not harm us. That seemed to satisfy Bona. She went off for the weekend, and after exchanging glances, the rest of the staff decided to stay on too.

Strange as this may sound to Europeans, to anyone who knows Africa well it is not strange at all. We westerners like to believe that we are largely responsible for what happens to us, and we think we are, or should be masters of our own fate. When things go wrong, we tend to attribute it to something we have done, or not done. We blame ourselves, feel guilty or get depressed. In general, African people do not suffer in the same way from depression, but rather from paranoia since in southern Africa, illness and misfortune are thought to be due not to something I do, but to something that is done to me. It is brought about by someone who ill-wishes me, and has had a spell put on me to do me harm. When one lives, as people have lived in Africa for hundreds, even thousands of years, in a culture dependent on climatic conditions for survival, one has no illusion of control. Life can be wiped out by a drought, a flood or a famine at any time. Herdsmen and planters like the Zulus and Swazis have always felt it necessary to use all possible means to influence the spirits and the weather in their favour, to bring about good fortune rather than bad. This includes a firm belief in magic.

The purveyors of magic in the society are the Inyanga, the herbalist, who heals physical ailments, the Sangoma, or seer, who 'sniffs out' the culprit responsible for illness or misfortune, and the Umtakati, the one who deals in dark sorcery and spells and works only at night. All have power which can be drawn on in times of sickness or crisis. Each of these practitioners has undergone a long period of training, possibly a lifetime, in his or her own field and is the heir to generations of accumulated knowledge. Since long experience has shown Swazis that external circumstances can destroy them, it is a short step to seek help from those who might have the power to control those circum-stances, be they sickness, misfortune or climatic disaster. Despite Western cynicism, most thoughtful people who have been in Africa for any length of time have stories that defy explanation.

The following week, when the carpets were dried and re-laid, and the bathroom was repaired, we went to a function at the home of the UNICEF representative. Among the guests was the head of the Traditional Healers Association. He was a tall strong man in middle age, with opaque black eyes, his matted long hair tied back with a strip of hide. He wore a *beshu*, or loin cloth made of skins and monkey-tails, a sports jacket, and brightly coloured football socks. During the cocktail party one of the government ministers came over to me. Dressed impeccably in white shirt, dark suit and designer silk tie, the minister leant down for a confidential word: 'I believe you have been having some trouble at your house with storms,' he said. 'I should have a word with that chap over there' – gesturing towards the head of the Traditional Healers – 'He's the man in charge of all the thunder and lightning in Swaziland.'

While all of this was going on my two refuges were the watercolour painting sessions, and riding. I had always wanted to learn to ride. At a small ramshackle stables in the Ezulwini Valley, Jojo, a tall South African blonde with long legs, a cheeky face and a short back and sides haircut, gave riding lessons. I clambered up onto Madonna, a broad, slow-moving black mare. Madonna seemed too large, it was too high up, and I was terrified. I jolted around the ring, feeling idiotic in a bright pink track suit, and tried to look as if it was enjoyable. Soon things improved. I bought jodhpurs. We went on 'outrides' into the valley, and occasionally a second of pleasure arose amid the terror. Jojo was a strict teacher and sent us round in interminable circles on the lunge rein. At first I thought she was saying the 'lounge' rein and couldn't see anything lounge-like about it. Most of the time I was crouched like a monkey, waving my arms, or desperately trying to stay balanced without stirrups.

Then Jojo of the long legs and the Akubra hats closed down her stables, and I joined another stables called Nyanza. It was in the Malkerns, a valley of pineapple fields, lying like a cushion of green in a frill of purple mountains. Nyanza was run by two sisters, Wandy and Nandi Williams, and a team of African employees. They had fifty-six horses, six Alsatian dogs, four whippets, six Siamese cats, a flock of geese, a flock of peacocks, and a small herd of dairy cattle. The stables were a magnet for four-footed waifs and strays. There must have been a hidden notice outside in all animal languages, like the signs left by tramps, telling creatures in distress that they would be taken in and cared for. And as if that were not enough, Wandy periodically went into South Africa and brought back retired race-horses with psychological problems. It was a happy paradise, full of small children riding Thelwell ponies, playing games of fox and hounds among the pineapples, holding fancy-dress horse-shows, and having the sort of good time they would remember for the rest of their lives.

Still the 'nervous lady rider', I was put on TJ, a stocky little pony who was as steady as a rock, graduated to beautiful black Natasha, and then to Jester who was 'mine' whenever I was there. Jester, when I met him, was dark grey – almost black. He was a teenager in horse terms, with a shaggy winter coat, gawky legs and big ears. I heard with incredulity that one day he would be pure white. He was the son of my first mount, black Madonna, by a Percheron, one of a team working in the timber industry in the Mhlambanyatsi forests. Jester's broad back was like an armchair. He had a puppy-dog-like quality, and would trot docilely behind me to the field after our ride. When his face was brushed he closed his eyes in ecstasy. He had feet the size of dinner plates and didn't know his own strength. Once he inadvertently stepped on a peacock, and he frequently walked through fences and let out all the other horses. I had a fantasy that the others egged him on, then left him to face the music.

The best thing about Jester from my point of view was that he was almost bomb-proof. We rode round the pineapple plantations, along wide grassy passages between the rows. Other horses may have been spooking and dancing because there was a dog, goats, a wild pig, or even a shadow. Jester plodded on unconcerned. We went harvesting wild guavas – we humans stuffed ourselves and the horses liked them too. The only thing Jester really didn't like was butterflies. That year there were hundreds of them – black and white with flashes of metallic turquoise, brown and yellow with red spots, tiny orange and red and yellow ones like flying petals. When a butterfly flew into his big face, this huge ton of a horse leaped a foot into the air as if he had seen a tiger.

There was always something happening at Nyanza. We went on out-rides in the valley, among the pineapple and turmeric fields, Alsatian dogs running alongside and whippets streaking three dog miles to every one on horseback. There was the day Jester let all the horses out and they stampeded. We flattened ourselves against the nearest tree while Wandy and Nandi stood in the middle of the road, arms outstretched in the path of the galloping herd. There was the day a flighty Arab jumped into the river, rider and all. There was the day Wandy went to collect wood shavings from a local furniture factory and her *bakkie* blew up and burnt to a cinder. There was the day I went for a twilight ride with my friend Judith. Arriving back late, the stables were closed, and Judith jumped through a window to get the tack-room key – into the gaping maws of seven Alsatians.

But perhaps the best story about Nyanza and one that illustrates the pioneering spirit of the Williams family and their crew is the tale of the Jo'burg Tsotsis (criminals). Nyanza was isolated from neighbours, but reachable from the road and across pineapple fields. One night after the family had gone to bed a group of robbers – surely a gang of Tsotsis from Johannesburg, decided that this farm run by mere women would be an easy place to terrorise and rob.

In a little room off the tack room, some distance from the house, an old family retainer sat every night, well rugged up, working as a night-watchman. Umdala had been with the family for many years and was fiercely loyal. He kept an eye on the animals, and would patrol during the night, and rouse the family should there be any problems. On this night the Tsotsis crept into the stables and found him. They put a knife to his throat, threatening that if he made a sound it would be the last sound he would ever make. Reasoning that he was dead anyway, the old man decided to go like a true warrior. He opened his mouth and uttered the loudest, longest and most blood-curdling Swazi war cry he could. The sound must have carried for miles. It certainly carried to the house where the two girls were sleeping. They didn't know what was going on, but Wandy grabbed her rifle, and Nandi crept out to the old Land Rover. They saw shadowy figures flitting around the stables. Nandi angled the lights of the Land Rover, while Wandy, a crack shot, began to shoot low – to frighten the intruders without endangering any of her beloved animals. The dogs, who were already barking, were let out. The horses began to neigh. The flock of geese were awakened and began cackling. The peacocks began to scream like demons perched in the trees and the herd of Jersey cattle began to moo and bellow.

No one seems to know what happened to those Tsotsis, but they were never seen again. The skelums probably didn't stop running until they got back to Jo'burg, vowing never ever to go near Swaziland again! Is it any wonder, with such stories, that I loved going down to the stables? Not only could I leave the correct diplomatic world behind, and get dirty and scruffy, but I never knew what might happen next.

But now that the new house was finished, the garden had grown and the lights were fixed, it was time for the Official Opening to demonstrate that the European Commission was seriously committed to staying in the country and helping with its development.

We began to plan.

The house had been built for just this kind of occasion, and we were about to test it out. Invitations were sent and the guest list mounted. It was not quite feeding the five thousand, but the numbers were impressive. One of the hotels in the valley would do the catering. Speeches would take place inside, with a public address system for those outside on the verandas. If the queens came they would not be allowed to mingle with the crowd (there were men present) so they and their escort of police-women would stay apart, and emerge for the opening ceremony. KJ slaved over his speech. I kept a million details in my head, worked with friends to create huge flower arrangements and, just for fun, manufactured a blue and yellow ribbon to be cut at the Grand Opening.

At the eleventh hour it was announced that the king would not attend, since that might imply favouritism, but would send a senior prince as his representative.

We woke up on the morning of the great day and looked out. It had been raining heavily all night. It was still raining. The sky was dark grey and there was the sound of water dripping onto the glass roof of the hallway. The grass was squelching. Heels and trouser legs would be sodden. We looked glumly at the skies every three minutes for signs of blue. Gloria in her best red felt hat was energetically mopping the tiled steps and the entrance. We had visions of dignitaries slipping and sliding their way into the party, broken royal limbs and law suits.

Caterers arrived, and moved their tables to a drier place. The King's Protocol officer arrived and announced that the bar could not be upstairs as planned, because 'no one could be higher than the King's head.' As the princely representative was 'King for a Day' this applied equally to him. The bar was therefore repositioned. Food was organised for the guests, for the drivers, for police, and for soldiers and guards. The queens and their retinues had their own buffet, and the king's representative and ministers would have a special meal served in the dining room. We juggled a hundred balls at once.

We needed background music – something European. Mozart – too quiet. Beethoven – too complex for wallpaper. Chopin – too fragile. Then we were loaned a tape of Strauss waltzes. It sounded gorgeous echoing over the garden and down into the valley. We just hoped no one would point out that Austria was not yet part of the European club.

The rain kept us nervous up to the last moment. It eased off and stopped just before the first guests were due to arrive. No one slipped on the stairs. The king's representative arrived. The queens processed into their little private room and I divided my time between Royal Conversation Duty and the hundreds of other guests. The seven young queens were like a group of sisters; chatting, giggling, swapping make-up and doing all the things that young women in their late teens and twenties do when they are out together.

The noise inside the tiled hall was a roaring hum. The crush inside and out was intense. I managed to wriggle through sideways, and spoke to almost everyone. Somehow the waiters filled their trays and carried them around. I was thankful that it was not Adelaide & Co.

When the time came for speeches KJ told the story of the Treaty of Rome and the founding of the European Community. It was dramatic and made sense, and there was a moment of appreciative silence at the words: 'No more war, No more hunger.' The blue and yellow ribbons were cut by the king's representative. During the speeches I noticed the queens. They were standing in a row by the wall, looking bored, the youngest having trouble with the giggles. But my eyes were drawn to a little boy about eight years old who had come with them – who knows why? He was a roly-poly little chap, like a little Swazi Billy Bunter, wearing a grown-up suit with a shirt and bow tie, and grey flying-socks from a plane, which rolled down in folds over his ankles.

The sun came out at the end of the function, just as people were drifting off back to work. Moses, the young day-guard, Star's friend, sent urgent word down from the gate, saying: 'The caterers are stealing the food.'

KJ and I dashed up to the gate, as a large catering vans was driving out with a cargo of happy and jubilant waiters. Doing his imitation of an angry rhino KJ demanded that the van should be opened. There inside was a festival of food, salvers piled high, whole hams and turkeys, all put aside so the staff could have a feast. We had no problem with the staff eating – we always took care that they should eat very well. But did they have to put aside enough food to feed the whole of Mbabane? Having made his stand KJ had to do something, so he compromised by retrieving a large ham from the van and stalked back to the house with it in his arms.

Then Moses struck again.

'The French chef is stealing the wine!' he said.

In French, KJ challenged the chef who threw up his hands in innocence. When the boot of the car was opened, it was filled with cases of wine. Protestations about taking things back to the hotel were fruitless, since the hotel had not supplied the wine – we had. The chef too, saw his booty ferried back to the house.

After the effort, the post-mortem. We were all tired and triumphant. Our feet were burning and painful. Together with the staff we relaxed and ate up scraps, feeling that the new house was now truly open and could do its work.

In the middle of the reception there had been a phone-call from Nyanza stables. Someone had brought a portable phone but in the crowd all I could gather was that Wandy and Nandi would not be able to come.

'OK,' I said. 'That's fine. Thank you for letting me know!' At that point in the scrum two people more or less made no difference at all.

Now as we relaxed there was another phone call. Had we heard that Rob Williams, the father of Wandy and Nandi, had died last night? We knew he had cancer – KJ had sat with him and they had had long talks. But what had I said? What must they think of such a callous reaction? Still in our finery we squashed shoes back onto our feet, grabbed a basket of flowers and set off on the 25 kilometre trip to the Malkerns valley to visit the family.

Everyone was sitting around the farm living room, strewn, as usual, with tack and saddles. We were welcomed as old friends. There was half-hushed talk of their dad's last moments. Voi, his wife, took KJ aside and asked if he would conduct the funeral. They didn't want a church service, she said. Rob had not been a church-goer but he liked what KJ had said in their conversations.

This would not be our first Swazi funeral. Nor would it be our last. Several had been on farms, the body brought home and buried lovingly in a precious place, close to the homestead or overlooking a valley. The community came in great numbers, to help dig the grave, to throw earth into the grave, and to sing.

Rob was buried on a hill overlooking an expansive view. He was a good man who had helped many people in his time though he would have denied that he was in any way 'religious'. KJ read from the New Testament: 'Lord, when did I ever feed the hungry?' And spoke about what he knew of Rob and his work. I sang 'The Lord is my shepherd,' and people joined in, African voices rising over the hillside. Once the singing began, it went on in a seamless stream of music, traditional harmonies rising up spontaneously while the coffin was being lowered, the earth thrown down, and the filling-in of the grave begun. He was truly laid to rest by the family, by friends and by the whole community. Everyone went back to the farm and food of all kinds appeared out of cars for a feast as the talking went on; old stories, reminiscences, fond and funny anecdotes of the family's long life in Swaziland.

For every funeral in Swaziland, the earthy humanity was the same. People knew death, and accepted it in a way that is rare in our sanitised Western culture. Whether it was a funeral on a farm or homestead, African or European, the community flocked to give support, and sang the soul to its rest.

Despite the beauty of this place, tragedy was often no further away than a bend in the road. Too often it struck young people in their teens and twenties. The lethal combination of young drivers, tiredness, long distances, and treacherously winding roads left families bereft and inconsolable. At several of these funerals KJ was asked to speak, and sometimes I was asked to sing and play the harp. It seemed that, at these times, people wanted deep reflection and music. KJ's past vocation as a priest, and my old Celtic songs, seemed to help. It was a validation, not of the official role but of deeper realities.

Death from Aids had not yet come to Swaziland. It was known to be a possibility, even a probability. In Zimbabwe deaths were already occurring, and cases were being denied in hospitals. Pioneering research was being done on how best to spread awareness. But Africans from rural areas were not used to deciphering three-dimensional photographic images so that Western Aids Awareness posters and messages did not make much sense. And much Western propaganda was complex, lecturing on what *not* to do, or what did *not* cause Aids, leaving listeners bewildered.

In Swaziland, at the industrial site near Matsapha Airport, where many South African firms had branch factories, a young English medical doctor and his wife, Geoff and Penny Douglas, had opened a clinic and were pioneering one of the earliest Aids Awareness campaigns in southern Africa. 'Man Talk' posters and flyers appeared everywhere. The two young professionals spoke and gave workshops incessantly. In a polygamous society, sexuality was an accepted part of life. Condoms were regarded as unnatural, 'like eating a sweet with the wrapper on' or 'having a shower in a raincoat'. How many sexual partners were 'too many'? People found it difficult to believe that an act so normal, that had been performed since the human race began, could actually make them ill. It could not be true. It must be just another Western plot to limit African population growth. And besides – symptoms might not appear for ten years. Who could say what had caused them? The southern African talent for living in the present moment was a hindrance to belief in the coming crisis. Penny and Geoff felt like the prophets in ancient times, voices shouting in the wilderness, as they tried to warn the Swazis of the plague to come.

Slowly the Aids epidemic would spread southwards down the main truck routes through Tanzania, Zimbabwe, Malawi and Swaziland and into South Africa. The problem, as we now know, would be exacerbated by the breakdown of traditional values, as traditional systems of courtship and morality decayed, by the return of infected migrant workers from the mines to a polygamous society, and by the tradition that women should be acquiescent to men. The stage was set for the HIV holocaust that would come later. Even people who had read all the studies and knew the predicted statistics could not begin to visualise the devastation and hardship that would ensue.

16

Moses da Vinci, and a Dinner fit for a King

Our cheerful young day-guard, Moses Nhleko, was the friend of everyone in the house. Particularly Star. Every day Moses made toys out of sticks, string and old tennis balls and patrolled the fence at a loping run so Star could chase them. He went on leave for two weeks, and Star tried without success to entice a series of uninterested temporary guards to play. In the end I put on running shoes every evening and jogged around the perimeter fence, to siphon off some of that excess energy. To use up even more energy, Star invented a special bull terrier mad-fit which consisted of running hell for leather in a wide circle, doing pirouettes and helicopter jumps as he went. We were relieved when Moses and his toys returned.

When we came back from leave in Australia, we noticed that the 'Beware of the Dogs' sign on the gate had gone. To dissuade intruders, I had bought a selection of ferocious signs all featuring bull terriers. If only burglars had known, they would probably have been kissed to death! In place of the fierce sign, there now hung a life-like portrait of the two dogs, hand-painted and wired firmly to the gate.

'Who did that?' I asked.

'I did,' said Moses, as he opened the gate.

This needed following up. In the next few days, I asked Moses if he liked drawing, and what he drew other than dogs.

'I draw everything!' was the reply.

Intrigued, I bought a box of coloured felt-tipped pens, and a drawing block. A natural artist, Moses drew naïve scenes of Swazi life from memory, full of atmosphere, bright colours and movement. Asked to draw a lion, he could immediately produce a picture of a lion killing a cow, or two lions fighting. He drew yellow fields of ripe corn in perspective, scenes at the bus station, and herds grazing by the river. Asked to draw the house, Moses sat in his guard-house at the gate but, for a wider perspective, imagined himself further up the hill. Both cars were included, and because trees were in the way of the very important flag that was his responsibility, he made the trees transparent. He tried water colours and acrylics, entered the local Art Society show and won a prize. We were so proud of him and his smile grew even more cheerful.

His real job as a guard brought different adventures. Several mornings a week I went riding early. Moses would man the gate, locking it securely after I went out. One morning as I waited to join the traffic at the summit of the mountain road, a thin, ragged young Swazi man with matted locks made a sudden dart at the car, opened the passenger's door and jumped in. Fearful for my handbag I placed it under my feet. Now saddled with a wild young man in the car, I told him to get out in every language I knew and some I didn't. I hooted the horn, hoping for help from passers-by. They merely looked incuriously and went about their business. I desperately hoped for a policeman. There were none. As fast as I unlocked the doors and told him to get out, he locked them right back again and sat tight. I wondered if he had a knife.

I turned the car and drove as fast as possible back to the house, to enlist Moses' aid. As the car roared down the hill to the front gate, hooting in a maniacal fashion, Moses emerged from his guard-house with a surprised expression and opened the gate. I wound the window down, saying: 'Moses, get this chap out of the car!'

Moses summed up the situation perfectly. He had a friend at the time, a young guard working at the house next door. Now this guard was extremely bored after two weeks of guarding an empty house. He came running to see what the commotion was, happy for action at last. The two of them set to work. My unwanted guest sat tight. As fast as the young guards opened a door, the wild young man locked it again.

Finally, combining distraction and fast movement, they wrested open the passenger door, grabbed him and he tumbled out. The neighbouring guard was so thrilled that he swung his baton wildly at the young man's head. The wild young man ducked and the baton hit Moses instead.

Bona arrived on the scene just in time to see a strange, wild young man on the ground, and Moses being attacked by the guard next door.

She dashed inside and rang KJ, who heard a wild story of Madam's car, Moses bleeding, and a lot more, all delivered in very fast Siswati. He telephoned his friend the Chief of Police to say that there was an emergency at the house then swung around via the police station hoping to pick up a policeman or two. What he found was the Chief of Police himself, with two black vans of uniformed and armed officers, all ready to go and fight for Baba Kunene. Like the Charge of the Light Brigade they roared up to the house. And what did they find?

Moses with a cut lip, a repentant guard next door, and a very meek and subdued young wild man sitting on the ground.

The young man was taken away but not charged. He was a harmless chap who liked riding in cars, and did so at every opportunity. After his release he had a brief and glorious career in town. He leaped into the car of a woman who was so frightened she jumped out, leaving her engine running so he locked himself in and blocked town traffic for half a day. He jumped into the car of the Portuguese Consul, locked the doors and sat, wearing the consul's coat. He was last seen walking down the mountain towards Manzini, no doubt looking for more cars to sit in. In Swaziland people like the wild young man are given food, and accepted. They are a source of mild amusement, and everyone knows that they are harmless – even a bit magical. I wish I had known that at the time.

March 1992. 'The TV has been on all day. White South Africa is voting on constitutional reform, province by province. Every time a new "yes" comes in I phone KJ at the office to rejoice. One newspaper described it as "Turkeys voting for Christmas"!'

I had bouts of dissatisfaction with all that I didn't achieve and all that I had to do and did not choose. I had volunteered to help at the annual Swaziland Animal Welfare Dog Show, and was quietly getting on with it when KJ was called down to the palace at 7.30 in the morning. He came back with an unheard-of request from the king to come to dinner on the same day as the dog show. I was briefly annoyed but if it was a choice between a dog show and entertaining a king, there was not much competition.

It would be a big affair. What did the king like to eat? Steak, it seemed, and ice-cream. Who would be the other guests? He would bring some officials from the palace, we would invite whoever else he requested and others we would choose – a mixture of ministers, diplomats, and business people. We also decided to invite Father Larry McDonnell and Sister Judith Dean, a Salesian priest and a jolly Anglican nun who were great friends, and famously 'worked the room' at functions on behalf of their projects with street boys and the disadvantaged. They could talk to the king about their work. There would be palace guards and security men, police and army personnel to feed.

Armando was 'borrowed' for the occasion. Armando was a wise old Mozambican retainer who worked for Portuguese colleagues. He was an experienced cook, and a gentleman. He did tend to finish off the leftover wine from the wine glasses at the end of the evening but that bit of jollity was a small price to pay for good cooking. It just meant that by the time he was paid for the evening, he was so happy he hugged and kissed KJ on both cheeks, bless him!

On The Day, the table was decked with flowers and candles. Armando, Bona and I set to in the kitchen. The soup was made, the steaks were in their marinade, vegetables prepared and in the saucepan.

At 4pm, KJ smelled a rat. Why had no one from the palace come for security checks? Things were suspiciously silent. He phoned a contact at the palace.

'Oh Baba Kunene, didn't they tell you? His Majesty has been called to attend special memorial ceremonies for his late father King Sobhuza. He cannot come to the banquet.'

In Swaziland, the king himself cannot apologise. Royalty can do no wrong – although at that particular moment, it was a close run thing in my kitchen.

'Stop!' I shouted to Armando who was just about to do something irrevocable to a mountain of potatoes.

Surveying the preparations, I was in no mood to undo all the work. KJ took off to give the news in person to Swazi guests with non-functioning phones. One of them was his friend Sipho, the Minister of Education. To make things worse, as KJ stood at the front door, the minister's little dog crept up and bit him on the behind.

Fourteen people had to be told that dinner was off. They would understand, but . . . I looked regretfully at the flower arrangements and the glittering table setting.

'Bona, let's just turn the plates over and leave the table as it is. Maybe we can get someone tomorrow to come and help us eat all this food.'

The next morning KJ rang from the office. The Australian Ambassador from Pretoria was in town, saying his farewells before he left for a new posting. A big, bluff, likeable chap, we had met him before.

'Aha!' I said.

'Shall I?' said KJ. It seemed a good idea.

The Australian Ambassador found himself invited to an 'impromptu' farewell dinner in his honour that night. Last night's guests were re-invited together with a few interesting additions.

The ambassador was amazed at the lavish table, the company and the food, all assembled for him, as far as he knew, since that morning. The soup, the steak, the home-made ice-creams, were all perfect. The king would never know what he had missed. And it was a triumph for Europe-Australia relations.

But there was a sequel. Three years later we were in Suriname, ex-Dutch Guyana, on the north coast of South America. Once more we planned to visit Australia for Christmas but KJ's Australian visa had expired. We had the choice of trusting the Surinamese postal service – never a wise idea – or we could stop off, passport in hand, at the Australian Consulate General in Hawaii. We opted for Hawaii.

Arrived in Oahu we set off for the centre of town. The palm trees were waving, the sun was shining, and the traffic was crawling with twenty-foot limousines. We were trekking across a street as wide as a football pitch when, behind me I heard KJ say, 'Oh no!'

'What is it?' I asked.

'The elastic in my underpants has just snapped!' he said.

With male garments this is not as disastrous as it might be for a girl, but it is still precarious, particularly when about to pay a visit to the Consul General of Hawaii. In a hobbled sort of way we reached the consulate, handed in the passport and with smiling Antipodean efficiency it was stamped and handed back in less than half an hour.

As we left I suggested that a pin and a few running repairs might be in order.

'No, no!' was the reply. 'We're going back to the hotel!'

We got into the lift. As the door closed a large foot was thrust in to block it, followed by a muscular leg and a solid body. The owner pressed the ground floor button with authority and then turned around. Simultaneously he and KJ said: 'I know you! You're the EU man from Swaziland / the Australian Ambassador from Pretoria.'

The ambassador so royally treated at his 'impromptu' farewell in Mbabane, now treated us royally to a sightseeing trip around Oahu and lunch at the Country Club, underpants and all. This time we confessed. We told the story of the king's dinner that never was.

It sounds as though life was nothing more than a succession of dinners, functions and cocktail parties. In the popular imagination that is how diplomats are seen. And because, for most people, dinners and parties are regarded as pleasure, not duty, it seems to be a life of sybaritic indulgence. But for diplomats this is work added to working hours. The dark suits, the silk dresses, the pearls and high heels are the working clothes. At social functions contacts are made, information exchanged and useful relationships formed. Eating together has been, from ancient times, the accepted way of making and confirming friendships, sealing pacts and ending wars. 'The man who has taken salt at my table shall not then make war upon me.' And when a guest has enjoyed an evening of good food and good company, the next meeting will go smoothly. I was beginning to see my role as not only one of support, but of enabler and facilitator.

Nowadays courtesy, protocol and social rules are often ridiculed. But they have valid purposes. A written invitation is useful when there may be five or ten invitations coming in at the same time. It says clearly when and where the function is, what to wear and what time to arrive, when an informal phone-call can easily be forgotten. Seating arrangements are a courtesy to government, and to the countries represented, who are seated according to their seniority in post. It is clear and impersonal.

Everyone knows who they are and where they should be. As the rules became second nature, entertaining changed from a nerve-wracking duty to an exercise in creativity. I began to play games with different background music to encourage easy conversation, experimented with the colours of food and flowers for different effects, and we put together more daring lists of guest who would be useful contacts and would genuinely enjoy each other's company.

Some social events were more memorable than others. Dinners given by banks could be difficult. All too often the hostess seemed ill at ease and conversation languished. On one unforgettable occasion I was seated next to a high-ranking executive from a now defunct international Asian bank. Since most people like to be asked about themselves, I asked my neighbour a leading question about his work. He told me. At length. Through the starter, the main course and the dessert, needing only the occasional interjection of: 'Did you really?' or 'How wonderful!' from time to time.

It was an endless flow of self-adulation. At the end of the meal we parted company and the bank executive made a bee-line for KJ, saying: 'Your wife is such a wonderful conversationalist!'

As I had not said more than ten words I wondered what his definition of a conversation might be.

At other times an evening can be the victim of an innocent saboteur. One night at the American residence there was a gathering of diplomats and aid workers. The UN Representative was there, with his Portuguese wife. Like many people for whom English is a second language, Maria had difficulty pronouncing the sound 'th'. Whatever she did, it always came out as a hard 't'. This caused no problems while the conversation was on neutral topics such as thought, themes or theories. It was only when the discussion turned to Swazi politics and the king in particular that a problem arose. We struggled to maintain straight faces as Maria joined energetically in the discussion, delivering her opinions on the doings of the king, who, unfortunately for her was called: 'King Mswati the Third.'

People reveal unexpected sides to themselves at social occasions A German colleague comported himself with heel-clicking correctness in the office. But after a meal and a few glasses of wine he would dance with maniacal intensity, arms and legs flailing like an octopus in a blender. There was the visiting French count who, at a party, leapt up and performed a hilarious version of the 'Chicken Dance'. A revered American ambassador's wife, a clone of Barbara Bush, danced a wild solo Charleston one evening in our hall after dinner, just to show that she could. And at an Easter morning brunch, I had carefully prepared and labelled non-pork sausages for the benefit of the Israeli Ambassador. As I explained this to his wife I glimpsed, out of the corner of my eye, the Israeli Ambassador creeping furtively away with a huge plate of eggs and bacon.

I, too, could let myself down. There were a number of game parks in Swaziland, all cared for by Ted Riley, Swazi born and bred, who was the king's Game Ranger. Ted was only happy in his old khaki shorts and *takkies,* * swerving around the bush in his Land Rover and cherishing his beloved rhinos.

One evening we were invited for a meal at the Mlilwane Game reserve – to celebrate the arrival of a new hippo, donated by the Diplomatic Corps – known jocosely as the Diplo Hippo.

We arrived at the park after the gates had closed to the public. The light was dimming in a warm tropical sunset, animals and birds were settling down for the night, and there was that smell of African earth after a hot day.

There would be an evening *braaivleis* or barbecue, and Swazi dancing. The game rangers aka the dance troupe were late. We waited as the barbecue sizzled. The men arrived in a roar of

---

* Takkies – soft white gym shoes, also known as plimsolls in England and sandshoes in Australia.

Land Rovers. They had been out chasing rhino poachers. They donned their dancing gear and gave some spirited rounds of Sibhaca dancing before supper.

By the time we sat down we were ravenous. Food was put on the plates including some of Ted Riley's 'wildebeest sausages'. Inhabiting vegetarian high ground at the time, I was not keen to eat these animals. I allowed myself a small taste of one corner of spicy wildebeest sausage. The next time I looked, the plate was empty. From that day to this, I don't know who ate them.

Game parks were a fringe benefit of postings in southern Africa. Apart from the three small parks in Swaziland itself, it was only a two-hour drive through spectacular mountain scenery to the Kruger Park, an area as large as Wales. We could pack a picnic on a Friday, and take off for a weekend in the wild.

We decided one weekend to drive north as far as possible up through the Eastern Transvaal Highlands, and then into the Kruger Park. We entered at the Phalaborwa Gate and went to Shingwedzi camp which is good elephant country. Out by 6am we could see the herds coming down to water holes. As we drank coffee in the morning light, we watched toddler elephants playing and slithering in the mud. There were giraffes, the 'Indlulamithi' – 'the one who passes over the trees'. Their delicate horned faces appeared above the topmost branches, like giant sea-horses swimming in the sky. The babies were only as tall as a man and moved with the balletic gait of their mothers, blinking eyelashes which would be envy of any Hollywood starlet.

The bush was dry and empty. Game spotting is like gambling in that rewards can come at any time. We had a 'talking book' cassette in the car, a detective story that we had been playing on the drive from Swaziland, and switched it on to finish the story. As we rounded a corner an impala came at full speed across the road. He saw the car and jumped, clearing the vehicle with extraordinary grace and judgement. Well, almost – as he went, a hind hoof touched the windscreen and shattered it, leaving behind a few tufts of fur in the shards of glass.

We stopped the car. KJ got out to see if the impala was hurt, forgetting that the reason for its flight might have been lion-shaped and hot on its heels. At that speed he was probably half a mile away already. But the windscreen was shattered, crazed and opaque. We made a small hole in it so that we could see to drive, and carried on, shaken. Windscreens are not easy to come by in the wilds of the Kruger Park, and this type was not even available at PG Glass in Phalaborwa. We would have to spend the last three days of the trip peering through crazy patterned glass.

Shamefacedly we crept back to the game lodge with our shattered windscreen, expecting to be summoned to the Chief Game Ranger, and reported or fined – or worse – for having hit an animal. It was a nasty nervous drive back. As we came in the gate of the lodge, a ranger was there, attending to his vehicle. He straightened up and saw the windscreen. Summing up the situation, he let out a big Afrikaaner laugh and said: 'Eh man, what hit you?'

'An impala!'

'It jumped, eh! I'm glad for your sake it wasn't a kudu! It probably came off better than your windscreen!' He went on tinkering with his truck. And that was that.

Back in Swaziland we planned a large Christmas party to pay back a lot of official invitations all at once. It would be a traditional Christmas dinner – except that here, in contrast to Angola, I wouldn't have to ferry the ingredients halfway round the world, nor cook for half the night. This time the Swazi Inn would cater for the occasion. KJ knew the new Swazi manager and felt the local staff needed a chance to prove themselves.

It was a rainy day. Rain in southern Africa often happens at midday, and comes down in solid sheets of water at a moment's notice. Just as lunch was about to be served there was a clap of thunder and the clouds split. Well-dressed guests scrambled for shelter on to the verandas. Tables were retrieved from the garden at a run and reset. There was just room for everyone. The main course went well. There was plenty of ham and turkey to go round. To keep it simple for the caterers I had ordered mince pies, ice-cream and fruit salad for dessert, followed by coffee.

The waiters were smartly dressed and moving around efficiently. I spotted the catering manager and suggested that it was time to serve the dessert. A strange expression crossed his face, and his eyes swivelled round as if he was absolutely sure I was talking to the person positioned just over his right shoulder. I repeated the question. Unable to vanish he managed to say: 'What dessert?'

There was none. One hundred and fifty guests had finished their turkey and were waiting with their mouths open for more to eat. It wasn't going to happen. I must have spoken with conviction because the manager and several waiters disappeared in a cloud of exhaust in the direction of their hotel and re-appeared a very short time later with enough mince pies and ice-cream to serve the more elevated guests. The rest made do with coffee.

17

Suspicion, Sadness, Somalia, and Celebrations

After the Christmas party came overseas leave. Mountains of staff food to be provided, lists of tasks, meals and vitamins for the pets – it was a case of stay up all night or it would not be done. On the last morning, we said goodbye to all the staff, except for Mr Mabuza who was nowhere to be found. Dashing out the door we raced down the mountain to Matsapha airport. In the airport building I realised, with an icy contraction of heart and stomach, that my passport was not in my bag. KJ phoned the office and Jean, programme officer and friend, drove to the house, and found the travel wallet on the bedside table. She gave it to Sam the driver to rush to the airport. He sped down the mountain to such effect that he was stopped by the police. They were so impressed with his explanation that they stopped whatever they were doing to provide a police escort for Mrs Baba Kunene's passport. My Aussie documentation arrived at the airport with several police cars and a full panoply of sirens wailing. We caught the plane.

In the middle of the Christmas leave we heard that there had been a burglary at the house but that things were taken care of; there were no details but it sounded depressing. Like Scarlett O'Hara in *Gone with the Wind*, I decided to think about it tomorrow.

When we arrived back Bona was waiting to greet us. She had discovered the burglary, reported it and cleared up the debris. A dyslexic policeman had taken her statement, calling her the 'chicken girl' instead of the 'kitchen girl', which made her sound like a character from Hans Christian Anderson.

'I am so glad you didn't see it, Mrs Pamela,' she said protectively. 'It was a terrible mess.'

There was a dreary time of checking up on what had been stolen. The thieves had not been discerning. Like the biblical story, one was taken and one left. A pair of binoculars was taken, but KJ's small typewriter, and my sewing machine nearby, were left. An ioniser from my desk had vanished and I wondered what they thought it was?

And my electric typewriter was taken. This thrilled me. It was a horrible machine. Made just as computers were beginning, it was neither typewriter nor computer. It had arrived with Danish and Chinese instructions, which hardly mattered, since even with an English handbook it was incomprehensible. The next owners would have hours of frustration. I wished them well. The one thing I wished they had not taken was a little silk roll containing jewellery, full of memories of grandmothers, aunts and first romances. Jewellery insurance being what it is, there was not a lot to be done. It was a lesson in the ephemeral nature of possessions.

Bona and Moses were mortified that it had happened on their watch. They had been sitting near Bona's house at the time, eating their lunch. The dogs had been asleep on their cushions in the kitchen. The two young staff went round at their own expense on days off, inspecting goods for sale. They also consulted a diviner who was said to be able to 'see' stolen goods. I was impressed at what he 'saw' – he described a drawer full of little gold boxes, which was exactly how the jewellery was kept. Not so impressive was the 500 emalangeni he would charge to take us to where the jewellery lay – in a house in Manzini, he said. KJ decided it was a racket and let it drop.

Suspicion fermented inside the household. How had the thieves known when the staff would be at lunch? Why had the dogs not barked? Every afternoon Gloria of the felt hats walked to the bus with Mr Mabuza. She told Bona that Mr Mabuza was angry with us because we had not said goodbye, and because he had not had the balance owing on his new glasses. He was going to send his sons back to take all the things they had left last time. Bona relayed the information to me and I relayed it to KJ. Mr Mabuza was interviewed and dismissed. He had a generous pension and was paid off in full, glasses and leave included.

But for once I felt nervous. I drove around with a gorilla steering-wheel lock, and thought dark thoughts about alarms, and bird-scarers on the fence. I lay awake wondering about joining the gun club. It is easy to see, in retrospect, how defensiveness leads to 'higher walls and more boiling oil'. Once fear takes over, trust goes out the window.

Shortly after Christmas, KJ received an offer he couldn't refuse – to be the EU Special Envoy to Somalia. He accepted it as a temporary assignment. Excited by the challenge he spent every spare hour researching the politics, history and background of that country, riven for centuries by feuding factions, vendettas and civil wars.

In 1969 after a military coup, Mohammed Siad Barre had become the leader of Somalia. He in turn was overthrown in January 1991 by a coalition of two clan groups, one led by Ali Mahdi and the other by Mohammed Farah Aideed. Siad Barre's exit was marked by a scorched-earth policy in the fertile valley of Juba. The ensuing inter-clan warfare cost the lives of 20,000 people during 1991, and accelerated the destruction of Somalia's agriculture.

Food in Somalia became Power. It was hijacked, used to bribe clan leaders and exchanged with other countries for weapons. In the early 1990s up to 80 per cent of the food provided by international aid organisations was stolen, and this continued as KJ would find out to his cost. While all this was going on, some 300,000 Somalis died of starvation and another 1.5 million suffered hunger and privation. In all, sixteen separate clans were fighting viciously for dominance.

In July 1992 UN military observers were sent to monitor food distribution, and Operation Provide Relief (UNOSOM-I) officially began. UN agencies were struggling to deliver food and supplies but relief flights were often looted at gunpoint as soon as the planes taxied in.

In December George Bush proposed that United States combat troops should lead an intervention force. Twenty-eight thousand US troops were deployed to Somalia. The objective of Operation Restore Hope was to secure and open the trade routes in Somalia as quickly as possible so that food could get to the people. It was confidently expected to be a short assignment, over in the New Year.

It was into this situation that KJ was called. Since the EU was one of the biggest food aid donors, his task was to get food to the starving population and to persuade the Somalian warlords to co-operate He was also mandated to talk to the warlords together with representatives of EU member states, in the hope of a negotiated settlement. He left at two days' notice to meet the Spanish commissioner in Nairobi, where the office of the special envoy would be based.

On arrival in Mogadishu, the first thing he noticed was the encampment of US troops around the airport. Operation Restore Hope stretched for half a mile either side of the airfield. With its hardware, tents and trucks it looked more like an invading army. There were no customs to pass through since Somalia had no government, only warring factions. The only way to get from the plane to the city was by arrangement with local militia men who acted as guards, travelling in *bakkies* armed with light machine guns.

Because it was so dangerous, KJ and his team members stayed in Mogadishu for only a few nights at a time. Most of the work could be done from Nairobi. He left filled with resolution in mid-January. He would be back in Mbabane at intervals of approximately one month, to oversee the office there.

Meanwhile in Swaziland I was holding the fort. All seemed peaceful. On 13 January, I wrote to my friend Mary:

> As I write I am surrounded by the soft black southern African night, and the sound of dogs barking in the distance (and closer, too, if Star takes in into his head to guard from the security of the kennel). In the garden there is a chorus of crickets, all keeping time in waltz rhythm. From time to time a belated Christmas beetle shrieks and crashes into something. In the morning it will be found on the floor like a bizarrely beautiful death's head ornament. I remind myself that here and now, in this place, there is so much to be thankful for.

I was in a particular mood of gratitude that night. Not only was it a beautiful and peaceful place, but Panda had returned from what seemed like the jaws of death. She had been operated on for a large tumour and after a day of dread she was back. It was strange to go through all the process of grieving for a member of the family only to have her restored. She would be thirteen at Easter – ninety-one in human years. We knew we couldn't keep her forever, but loved her unique combination of soft-eyed fidelity and Sylvester Stallone toughness. Were she a Swazi or Zulu chief she would have had praise-names shouted out to her as she approached: 'Panda, catcher of thirty rats, Panda, slayer of the mighty cane rat, barker in the night, mighty eater of peanuts, devourer of kitchen trays, redoubtable cheater of the gates of death!

As soon as she awoke she was given an antibiotic wrapped in mince. With a disgusted expression on her face, she staggered straight out the door to bury it in the garden. It seemed she would be busily lizarding in the garden again before too long.

Panda recovered quickly. She resumed her morning position by the car, lest I should go to the shops without her. We went to the supermarket and visited the ice-cream parlour. One night, ten days after her operation, she was uncharacteristically loving.

She climbed onto my lap and sat there for the whole evening. When the time came to go out, she pleaded to stay inside. So she slept in 'her' armchair. In the morning she was not hungry but accepted a little dish of cut up liver. As the day went by she was obviously not well. The phones were down. There was no way to call out the vet. Finally, after lunch I put her in the car and took her to the surgery. She was haemorrhaging internally but he did what he could. On the way home in the car she suddenly propped herself up. I took her paw, she looked at me intently, and died.

I carried her into the kitchen and laid her on her cushion, still warm, still Panda. Star came in and barked loudly at her to wake her up. It was a strange night, wondering where her little spirit was. She was there, but gone.

I telephoned KJ in Nairobi, to tell him. He had barely arrived and was between meetings. There was nothing he could do or say. His mind was on the task at hand.

When the staff came in the next morning I told them she was gone, using the beautiful and dignified African expression: 'Panda has left us.' They nodded in sympathy, and came to stand by her body for a few moments. Mr Dlamini said: 'That's life.'

It was true. Africans are in touch with the unity of life and death in a way that we Europeans, with our overlay of emotionalism, are not.

We buried her. Moses dug the grave, near the rock where Polar Bear lay. As he was digging he stepped on the place where Polar Bear's squeaky toy was buried, and leapt a foot in the air from fright at this squeak from beyond the grave. Staff and friends gathered around and we buried her with the little tin tray she adored. We read the Walt Whitman passage again: 'I think I could turn and live with animals . . . ' – and said our farewell. Wrapping her in her blanket and putting earth on the grave was comforting, as if I were tucking her in gently for eternity.

The house seemed empty. It was the first week that KJ was in Somalia. It was hard to get the corners of my mouth turned up again. Memories of Panda were present at every turn. As I wrote once more to Mary: 'Don't get animals unless you are prepared to have your heart torn and your life reduced to ashes when they leave. It is a little better than it was with Polar Bear, since at least I had done everything I possibly could for her last days and I was holding her paw in the car when she actually died. There is no doubt that death is awful for the survivors. I don't quite know how it is for Panda. As joy-filled as her marvellously exuberant little life, I would hope.'

It was difficult to be interested in anything. I hoped that in a few weeks I would have organised a timetable and would be more at peace. It had been raining for a week. My friend Judith, a dog person herself, phoned every night for a talk. One night she came around for a meal and we repaired a lavatory cistern together A good basic bit of therapy. By the time we finished it was probably the only thing in the house that was not dripping. The water was running down the walls in the hall, the dog was dripping, the cat was damp and the gardener steamed every time he came to the kitchen to ask a question.

It was very odd having KJ away for an indeterminate length of time. I had learnt to be a 'supportive wife'. It felt particularly useless when there was no one to support, only a huge entertainment hall and a diplomatic number plate. But what good would it do KJ, me or anyone else to go into a decline and stop doing things?

However, life was not without incident. One evening the following week, there was a mighty crash at the front gate. Bona raced up the stairs, and together we peered through the study window.

'It is Sam!' she said. 'He has crashed our gate!' and together we ran downstairs and across the garden.

There was the official car, slewed sideways, its nose wrapped around a tree. Sam Dlamini, the young second driver, was slumped in the driver's seat. We telephoned the second in command at the office, sensible Dutch Mr Schroeder. An ambulance was called. Sam was dazed and had no idea what had happened. By the time the ambulance arrived he was sitting on the ground.

'Get in!' said the ambulance driver impatiently, gesturing to the vehicle. It was a mini-van with hard benches.

'Aren't you going to help him?' I said, shocked at this cavalier treatment.

'No!' said the driver. 'He can walk.' So Sam got up obediently and walked to the ambulance, to be taken to the hospital. What if he had really been injured?

When Sam's memory returned, he recalled a brief nightmare. As he came down the hill leading to the gate he had put his foot on the brake, but the car accelerated. He had no control. He imagined Moses coming to open the gate directly in the path of the speeding car, so turned at the last moment and crashed into the tree instead. He may well have saved Moses' life by endangering his own. Fortunately only the car was damaged. The cause was never resolved. Similar stories came from all quarters – of cars that had taken on a life of their own and raced through red traffic lights in Johannesburg, or into garage walls There were dark hints of speed-control gadgets jamming. The garage provided an embarrassingly visible interim car – a bright red hatchback about twenty feet long – and the insurance saw to the rest. But since that day I will have no dealings with a speed control lever.

A concert had been pre-arranged in the house's big entrance hall, with a string quartet from Johannesburg. It was a distraction from the loss of Panda. The hall was designed for large gatherings on rainy nights, but was also useful for fund-raising events. I found myself the President of 'Friends International', the usual association of expatriate ladies that exists in every country. We supported organisations like the Cheshire Homes, and one of our projects was to buy wheelchairs for the local hospital out-patients department.

Many disabled people were stranded there – children in particular. They were restored to health, but had no mobility. Hospital funds were stretched and wheelchairs were expensive. European wheelchairs were useless on African bush tracks, but in Manzini there was a mission complex, a large orphanage sheltering hundreds of children, many of them disabled. It was run by Father Ciccone of the Servite Order, a charismatic Neapolitan, rotund and joyous. The children were given self-respect and interdependence in this orphanage – the lame led the blind, and those who could walk helped those who were in wheelchairs. When there was building work to be done, they insisted on taking part. A wooden plank would be put across the armrests of a child's wheelchair. Strong children would lift two or three stones onto this shelf, and with great pride, helped by their friends, even the weakest could make their contribution to the new building and join in the fun.

The mission workshops produced a wheelchair that could cope with the rocks and bumps of African rural life and it was these that we supplied, helping the hospital out-patients and Father Ciccone's orphanage at the same time. For such functions a local hotel was happy to lend chairs for the night. We invited musicians to play, cooked our best for a buffet supper and charged a reasonable amount for tickets. This time too, planning paid off. There were no hitches, it was the one beautiful balmy night of the week, the quartet was a talented group of young woman from Johannesburg. Even Paddycat scratched at the door, chose a lap to sit on, and settled down to listen. Everyone including the cat enjoyed themselves and we made enough money for twenty more wheelchairs.

In contrast, back in Somalia, KJ was working on two fronts: in Nairobi, and in Somalia on fly-in fly-out missions. Mogadishu was a place of indecipherable chaos unlike any normal living environment. The entire city was a haphazard market where people were coming, going, running, shifting, with no evident pattern. Some areas were empty and sinister. From time to time, the city would erupt into a state of riot. It was divided between different clans and warlords and had invisible barriers that were dangerous to cross. One morning, travelling with Patrick, an ex-British army officer, the team found themselves in a mob of people. They turned into a side road to escape. Soldiers materialised on each side of the truck. They heard the click of guns. Patrick, experienced, said very quietly to the armed guerrillas riding shotgun on the truck: 'Don't look, just keep driving slowly!'

The line of soldiers separated and allowed them to pass. They had driven past General Mohammed Aideed's house unawares and had been mistaken for the opposing side.

They visited the regions of Baidoa and Bardera, the epicentre of the famine, to monitor food distribution. It was a camp where tens of thousands of displaced people were being cared for by aid agencies such as Medecins Sans Frontiéres, and UNHCR. Air transport of food was a last resort – it was expensive and brought little food in comparison with road haulage. But as yet there were no safe routes by land. When they arrived a transport plane was due to land. The local warlord had his troops and anti-aircraft guns on the tarmac. The guns were trained on the plane. The food could only be unloaded on his terms.

It was tense. As they stood there a man died before their eyes. What could a human being do? People were starving to death. Unbearably moved, KJ gave the OK for the plane to land, despite the warlord's presence. As they watched, sacks of food were unloaded. Half was taken off by the warlord at gunpoint. Only half the food was allowed to go to the starving population.

KJ's mission to Somalia came to an abrupt end. By the end of

June, after six months of unrelenting effort, a project had been finalised to resettle 30,000 refugees in the Juba Valley – the fertile area denuded by Said Barre so many years ago. Arrangements were in hand with UN agencies to implement the project. It was minutely planned by the aid organisations, all anxious to lessen the sum of human misery in the country. Tents would be provided, bedding and cooking utensils, agricultural implements and seeds; everything that would enable people to start a new life.

KJ was in Mogadishu. He was called to the house of warlord Mohammed Farah Aideed, an unsmiling man with dead, impenetrable black eyes. The project was explained to him. KJ expected to be complimented on the plans to help the Somali people. Mohammed Aideed had only one comment: 'You've forgotten one thing,' he said.

KJ replied carefully: 'With respect, General, I have personally checked all the lists and I don't believe anything has been omitted.'

Back came the answer: 'Yes, there is an omission. You have forgotten to pay me.'

There were 30,000 people to be transported together with all of the equipment. The total pay-off demanded by the general amounted to one million dollars.

'If that isn't paid I'll blow up the trucks.'

Shocked, KJ said: 'But they are your people!'

And the reply was: 'So?'

'And what if we don't agree?' asked KJ.

At a gesture, a man standing by the wall silently opened his jacket and showed the pistol nestling in its holster.

'We have strong arguments to convince you,' he said.

'I find your arguments very convincing,' said KJ, and left.

When the incident was reported to HQ a decision was made to pull him out of Somalia as special envoy. He was not James Bond, and the risk of KJ or other aid workers being killed was too great. The thought of Mohammed Aideed blowing up 30,000 refugees was too terrible to contemplate. An envoy with a death threat on his head cannot function. For the moment, other ways would have to be found.

For several weeks KJ remained in Nairobi awaiting developments. He lived with great care. There were known representatives of the Somali factions in the Kenyan capital who could carry out the assassination. In the weekends he left the city and went to the coast, staying somewhere different each week – just in case.

At the beginning of July, after a new special envoy had been appointed, he returned to Swaziland, to resume life there as head of mission.

The whole world knows what followed. October 1993 would bring the incident of 'Black Hawk Down' and affairs in Somalia would hit world headlines. Indirectly those events would have a crucial influence on later events in Africa, as we will see. In July 1996 Mohammed Aideed would die as a result of gunshot wounds received in a fight between opposing factions. The refugee problem continues to this day.

The contrast between KJ's life and mine could hardly have been greater. My lot had been administration, meditation groups, painting, riding, and charity concerts. My handsome pilot cousin Steve had visited Swaziland with his bush pilot father and, in a hired Cessna, we had danced across the skies of southern Africa to Victoria Falls. KJ meanwhile had been in an environment of danger, starvation and misery and had witnessed sights that even in imagination I could barely share. The return to the order and safety of Swaziland must have been surreal for him. But it was not fully a return to normal.

We had been in Swaziland since April 1989. Our term of duty was up. During the months when postings were allocated, KJ had been in Somalia. Now there were few vacancies left and no word from HQ. We were entering the long, sleepy time of

European summer holidays, when there was little enthusiasm for decision-making. KJ took the opportunity for a well-earned two week break in the UK.

At 8am on the first morning of this brief post-Somalia vacation, the phone rang with the news that he had been appointed to one of the world's least sought-after postings – Equatorial Guinea. After making a few 'Are you joking?' phone calls this threat was removed, to be replaced over the next few months with the Solomon Islands (a Pacific paradise thirty-six hours from anywhere), Nigére (I was thrilled to hear that the delegate used to go to work on a camel), South Africa (which went to a pleasant Irish chap who knew Mexico well), Mozambique (which went to a Portuguese candidate) and Zambia (which went to who knows whom or why).

On a lighter note, we came back to a period of frenzied activity in Swaziland. There was going to be the Reed Dance, another SADCC (Southern African Development Coordination) Conference, a southern African ministers' meeting, and a trade fair, plus celebrations for the king's twenty-fifth birthday and the twenty-fifth anniversary of Independence all rolled into one. It was a major bundle of events for a small country to organise. Other places might quail, but we felt that Swaziland, with its large hotels and facilities in the valley, would cope.

When the arrival list was received, all twenty heads of state were scheduled to land between 10am (Prince Edward) and 16.45 (the representative from Belgium) at precise fifteen-minute intervals. Thinking of the minuscule size of Matsapha airport, we paled when we read it. The possibilities for collision seemed tremendous. Fortunately the list bore no relation to reality, being a figment of some local official's imagination. He or she just thought it would look neat and tidy produced that way.

The Reed Dance itself was the usual Cecil B de Mille event, with its swaying, singing, dancing, roaring cast of thousands. This time the ranks of 10,000 scantily clad Swazi maidens were augmented with a regiment of Zulu maidens wearing even less. The warriors crashed their spears and shields on the ground, the mature women ululated, the drummers drummed.

That evening we met the wife of the new South African Ambassador. It had been their first Reed Dance. Afterwards their son of nine demanded to phone his older brother at school in Pretoria. Remembering all the bare breasts and buttocks he had seen, his mother felt nervous. She hovered around the corner as he made the phone call.

'We've just been to the Reed Dance,' said the nine-year-old. 'All those Swazi girls! I've never seen anything like it! You should have seen their . . . knives!'

There was a day of celebration at Somhlolo National Stadium. With so many guests the Master of Ceremonies did his best but got a bit bamboozled as people arrived. As the cars drew up at the VIP stand, he doggedly read out whatever he had on his list. Hence the Swedish Ambassador looked decidedly African in appearance, and Zambia's Prime Minister appeared to be Chinese.

Among the real VIPs were Prince Edward, ex-President de Klerk of South Africa, President Mandela, Pick Botha, the South African Minister of Foreign Affairs, the Crown Prince of Morocco and the Sultan of Brunei. The King of Zululand was there, plus warriors, President Masire from Botswana, President Chiluba of Zambia in his platform shoes, President Mwinyi from Tanzania, President Sam Njoma from Namibia, and President Arap Moi from Kenya. Among the 'civilians' was Tiny Rowland, tycoon and chief executive of Lonrho with his wife. A statuesque woman, Mrs Rowland wore a white bull-fighting cloak, surmounted by a white sombrero of monumental proportions and resembled a very tall mushroom.

All of these dignitaries were accompanied to the dais by armed escorts. After the first five I began to suspect that it was the same pick-up truck with the same guards and the same sub-machine gun on the back, just doing a circular run. But perhaps the best moment came with the advent of one of Swaziland's local celebrities. Mr Goldblatt-Grant, a small wizened octogenarian who owned much of Swaziland, chose for the occasion to drive the longest and whitest Cadillac anyone had ever seen and was dressed as a Chicago gangster in white silk suit, white Stetson and enormous white winkle-picker shoes. He was so impressive that he received a special round of applause all to himself.

The king wore the traditional Incwala headdress of glistening black feathers, his young brown chest shining in the sun. When he arrived, we were treated to a real spectacle. Specially brought in from South Africa were sixteen motorcyclists straight from Toytown. They had white uniforms and white motorcycles, with two red flashing lights at the front and two blue flashing lights at the back. They were every little boy's dream. At the crucial moment the Swazi air force flew over and its one plane streamed forth smoke in the red, black, blue and white of the Swazi flag. The colours blended in the wind, and we were bathed in a heavenly cloud of baby pink which wafted and floated for some time. Only the angel choirs were missing.

There was a long programme of entertainment. The Manzini Choir and the *Asihlabelele* Choir sang, swayed and jived, there was an orchestra of Jew's Harps, diminutive drum majorettes, and a thousand or so schoolchildren taught by the Taiwanese Embassy waved squares of coloured paper on command, to fill the arena with the Swazi flag, and the king's portrait, and Happy Birthday in bright colours. Or rather, the schoolchildren scheduled to do this had not turned up for practice, so in desperation, the Taiwanese embassy marshalled 1,000 scantily clad Reed Dance maidens at the last minute, clothed them in white T-shirts and drilled them fit to bust instead.

There was marching aplenty, skin-clad, spear-carrying warriors by the thousand, tripping Reed Dance maidens wearing bead belts and brilliantly coloured skeins of wool and a few thousand married ladies, vast and pendulous in cowhide skirts brandishing terrifying knives and wooden spoons. The Swazi army did precision marching in their bright redcoat uniform, with a great deal of gold braid, accompanied by military band music which was only very occasionally off-key. At the finale everyone was arranged around the circumference of the stadium. The small Commanding Officer in front seemed unaccountably to have exchanged trousers with someone at least a foot taller. His uniform was impeccable but he wore trousers that flapped and concertina-ed round his ankles like Charlie Chaplin.

We arrived home hot and tired, but there was still the State Banquet to attend. At the Royal Swazi Convention Centre 400 people were seated at long tables. Each table was decorated with metre-high glass vases, so that roses and ivy cascaded above the guests' heads. Silver and glass sparkled and the army brass band played loudly.

On the stage sat the king and the many VIPS. Five of the queens were there, wearing identical slinky Las Vegas dresses of white sequins, identical straight black wigs, identical tiaras, and identical red ribbons across their bosoms with identical saucer-sized diamante Orders attached. But since they could not socialise with men, the poor girls, in their finery, were relegated to a side table with ladies from the palace and spent the evening admiring each other.

The food was abundant, and the puddings a delight – delicate sunflowers of chocolate and crunchy marzipan, with centres of fruit mousse. I wondered what the lusty police and bodyguards made of them? Coffee came with hand-made chocolates, including a chocolate model of the young king's head. No one quite dared to bite into one of those – it seemed vaguely treasonable.

President Chissano from Mozambique made a speech full of references to 'Colonial Oppressors' and 'Freedom from Yokes'. He seemed oblivious to Swaziland's history since 'Our African

Brothers' had not come to help in the 'fight for Independence' as he asserted – it had all come about very peacefully. But it made a fine speech.

Then the army bandsmen really outdid themselves. The entire band of very large men in elephantine trousers and red jackets, stood and played at full volume, dancing vigorously with their instruments in a deafening finale.

Eight thousand of the king's subjects were invited to the Royal Garden Party the next day and queued for several hours for their bit of barbecued beast. As we waited the buffet tent was raided by harassed chefs accompanied by armed guards to refurbish the buffets in the Royal tent. When the buffet finally opened there was a scramble for food. I emerged from the fray triumphantly bearing one prawn. Swazi Royalty comes out in force on days like this. A few elderly princes firmly clutched bottles of Dimple whiskey. King Sobhuza's wives, now getting on in years, were there in their cowhide skirts and cloaks. As in the old days, some brought along shopping bags, for anything that might be encouraged to fall from a table or a jiggled tray.

It was a colourful occasion. Women were requested to wear hats, and most of us produced something resembling garden-party headgear. The variety of dress was startling. There was safari gear, morning dress and full tails. And I noticed one Japanese guest who seemed to have reasoned that a garden party was a very British thing. She had therefore donned the full British national dress for foreigners from Burberry, and sweltered in tartan wool from head to toe.

The festivities lasted a week. We danced a jig of relief as motorcycles wow-wowed down the mountain escorting twenty departing VIPs.

Thinking back to KJ's description of Baidoa, the starving crowds of people, the dying man, and the struggle for food, the contrasts were sobering and bewildering. But both are Africa.

18

Uprooting

After the festivities, we went to South Africa to find a companion for Star. I was dubious about getting a puppy, since we would be moving again, but Star was moping. In any case, we would be transferred to another African country and, with vet certificates, the pets could come too.

It was August. Winter in southern Africa is not the time for puppies, but Star's breeder had a young female, a year old, dainty and friendly who sat on my lap all the way home. Star fell in love. They were inseparable. They slept on the same cushion and got stuck in the kennel door trying to get out in the mornings. Her name when she arrived was Major but we changed it to Magic instead. She had tiny dainty feet, and trotted, as Bona said: 'Like a little mouse.'

The rest of the year was happy. The first year in an overseas posting is a time of uncertainty, looking through one's fingers at the possibilities. The second year is the beginning of comfort, and in the third year one is living fully. We had been in Swaziland for four years. Now it was 'home' more than anywhere else in the world. KJ was 'the Friend of the King' and an icon to the Swazis. I basked in his light, but had my own identity and many friends. I was involved in the community, in love with the beauty of the landscape as I committed it to paint and paper, and textile art was becoming a passion. Life was good. Too good.

The new road was under way. Government officials had done their work as the king requested. The flood of micro-projects, the schools, dams, bridges, roads, and other co-operative ventures had not abated. Blue and yellow micro-project signs sprouted all over the rural areas, and more communities requested help every day.

The only person for whom things were not good was Moses. He had lost his smile and looked depressed. He came to KJ saying that he was not well and we arranged for him to see a doctor. After a week he came back to see KJ. He wanted to leave. And the reason?

'*Lendawo iyangizonda*' ('This place hates me').

Despite four happy years of being a son of the family, his fun with Star and his painting, nothing else would do. For Moses it was serious. The spirits of the place were making him ill and if he did not move he might die. I was disappointed, but tried to understand. After all, there had been – and still are – places where I too might say: 'This place is not good for me.'

We had to let him go. Occasionally we met him in his security guard uniform, working around the town and exchanged smiles and greetings. He was still painting, and sold his work from time to time. We hoped that he had recovered and had found places that were more harmonious.

There was no news of our next posting. The Solomon Islands, Niger, Mozambique, South Africa and Zambia had come and gone. Now there were murmurings about Rwanda. We opened the Atlas again. There it was, squeezed in between the Republic of Congo, Tanzania, Uganda and Burundi. 'Awarded to Germany' at the Berlin conference it was, after World War I, 'given' to Belgium by the League of Nations with equal high-handedness.

We had lunch with the Belgian Consul in Swaziland. Trudy was a tiny redoubtable lady in her eighties who bred huge Rhodesian ridgeback dogs, and kept a pearl-handled pistol in her handbag 'just in case'. She had lived in Rwanda for years and loved it: pleasant little place, mountainous like Swaziland, nice people, mild climate, excellent residence and gorillas as well. We left for Christmas in Australia feeling confident about what 1994 would bring.

The first inkling that 1994 might have unpleasant surprises in store came two days before we returned to Swaziland. Our beloved Paddycat was dead. We finished the holiday in a daze, behaving well to keep each other's spirits up and hoping, each morning when we awoke, that perhaps it hadn't happened. Our first pet, and friend of fifteen years, had bizarrely caught a tooth in a crack in my pine desk – perhaps chasing a moth – who knows? In trying to pull free, he did irreparable damage to his mouth and jaw. The vet, who knew him well, felt that it was hopeless, and euthanased him. He was a good vet and I trusted him. Had I been there I would have pleaded for Paddycat's life, and nursed him night and day. But perhaps that would not have been kind.

13 January Once more I wrote to Mary:

My friend Judith stood in for me at the little funeral. She had been with us for Panda's funeral, and arranged for Paddycat to be buried with the dogs nearby, on the rocky outcrop overlooking the valley. We will now leave three little graves behind when we go. My throat aches as I write. I cannot tell you how much I miss him. I sense his shadow everywhere in the house. Surely if I turn quickly I will see him. I feel his weight on the bed at night. We were telepathic. At night I only had to think his name and he would be back through the window with a 'prrt'. He loved parties and made repeated entrances until he was noticed. He was a Geiger-counter for character – the two or three people he detested were all slightly shady characters. He loved meditation and came into the room each Monday night to join the meditation circle. At the end, there he would be, swaying gently with his eyes closed. On nights when we did Tai Chi, he wove patterns around our legs – a small furry dancer.

A couple of days after we arrived home, as I was sitting on one of 'his' chairs and thinking about him, I felt overshadowed by a huge cat above my head. It is said that every type of plant and animal has its Deva or nature spirit. Perhaps this was the 'Great Cat in the Sky' sending a message that Paddycat was all right. And of course he is – they all are. Life and death are so hard to understand.

News came that KJ's successor had been appointed. He announced that he was coming to 'inspect' his new realm. KJ, meanwhile, had not received his letter of appointment to Rwanda. We were neither here nor there.

Packing again. We tidied and threw out and worried late into the night, sandwiched between days filled with all it takes to wind up an office, plan a move, and say farewell to all the people who had become so close. KJ developed symptoms of an ulcer and the dogs had a fight. A summons came from HQ to report there on Good Friday – forgetting that the entire office closed down over Easter. When it was pointed out that the only airline tickets available at that time would be in first class, HQ had an attack of Institutional Parsimony and said: 'Well, you can leave on 5 April after all.'

While this was all happening, the Swazi people made their love felt. They organised farewells. One of them was given by an unknown group called 'The International Friendship Association'. They met irregularly, it seemed, to make speeches about International Brotherhood and Friendship. The invitation said that it would be a sausage-braaivleis in the valley. We dressed accordingly. When we arrived, we found that plans had swung 180 degrees and it was now all roses and candelabra in the Royal Swazi Spa Hotel. On the way in, we noticed some members of the stunning Manzini Choir.

'Must be something else on!' KJ muttered, 'Wish we could hear them instead!'

When we sat down to dinner the choir was there, all sixty of them, to sing a full programme in KJ's honour, including a special song composed about him. We had to go on stage and dance with them for the TV cameras. I was not too thrilled by this. My clothes for the supposed barbecue included a pair of comfortable shoes that didn't stay on very well, and a fairly unexciting dress with buttons that popped with exertion. It is no easy feat to dance in the beam of TV cameras, trying through the back of one's head, to follow the movements of an entire choir dancing behind.

We must have done reasonably well, because back at our table, a small bearded Swazi prince said: 'You guys can really swing!' – then subsided into his beer like a dormouse, sound asleep.

We had to find space in our suitcases for bizarre last-minute gifts – a Swazi spear and shield, book-ends of petrified wood, and copies of all the books about Swaziland ever written. Local chat shows and newspaper letter columns were full of regrets about the going of Baba Kunene.

Moving day came. The packers arrived, and the dogs were, as usual, incarcerated. All doors were sealed except the one through which boxes would depart. At lunchtime the seven jolly packers disappeared to eat, leaving the half-packed van parked close to the house.

When it was time for the dogs to have a break they burst joyously out of the bathroom, and we galloped round the garden. It was a long walk with a lot of sniffs. By the time we turned back to the house, the packers were approaching from the opposite direction. Star and Magic saw them too. Ever eager to make new friends they accelerated. The seven packers saw them just too late. They accelerated too, and with a concerted 'Aieee!' they achieved instant levitation, arriving as one on top of the giant lorry in a single gigantic leap.

Star, Magic and I gazed up at seven wide-eyed Swazi packers peering over the side of the van, convinced that they had narrowly escaped being torn limb from limb by two grinning and panting bull terriers.

Eventually, his ears burning, KJ left on 5 April as his eager successor swept in on the incoming plane. A month's briefing at HQ was planned while I stayed in Swaziland in a tiny guest cottage at the far end of the garden, packing, organising and trying to be invisible. The dogs and I would wait until KJ circled back to Africa to pick us all up, en route for Rwanda.

That was 5 April. On 7 April, with an American friend Emily, I was teaching a day's course on 'Counselling in the Workplace' for local community leaders. We glanced at the TV in the conference room. A plane had crashed in Rwanda, presumed shot down, killing all on board, including the President of Rwanda. What we did not know was that it was the last piece in a carefully orchestrated campaign. Within an hour roadblocks were mounted all over Kigali and Radio Mille Collines made its announcement: 'The Time has Come.'

There was no television in the little flat, but on my minuscule radio news from Kigali poured out every hour. On the BBC World Service, Lindsay Hilsum from the 'Hotel des Mille Collines' detailed the nightmare of slaughter as the genocide unfolded. She painted pictures of piles of bodies in the streets, and swollen corpses floating down the rivers. My emotions zigzagged between disbelief, horror, compassion and extreme cowardly thankfulness that we were not caught up in the middle of it.

In a hundred days, at least 800,000 people were killed, mostly by machete. 'During this peak period, one murder was committed every two seconds of every minute, of every hour, for sixty days. It went on non-stop for three months as doctors killed patients, teachers killed pupils, clergy killed or assisted in killing their congregations, neighbours killed neighbours.'

KJ was stranded at HQ – the field man's nightmare. To know that these horrors were going on and there was nothing he could do was torment.

There was no phone at the flat. I crept out at night to

telephone KJ from the homes of friends. Affected by the tension, the dogs had a fight. They only stopped when I slipped and fell on top of them and we sat there looking at each other in astonishment. In the beautiful house that we had built, the new incumbent was making a clean sweep. Fumigators were called in, bougainvilleas landed in the dust-bin and bathroom fittings were thrown out. When the cream and gold house was painted baby pink it was time to move. Best not to know. I would go to England, and the dogs would have to go into quarantine kennels.

In the remaining weeks strange things began to happen. I had always liked Swaziland and the Swazi people. Now I realised how much I loved them. As I walked around Mbabane, my heart opened and filled with love for everything and everyone I saw. Africa had worked its magic. And although I neither said nor did anything different, people reacted. In the post office and in shops I was now greeted and called 'Sissi' – 'Sister' – which had never happened before. I had conversations sitting on stone walls with Swazi people I didn't know. Bona and I had sisterly cups of tea in her little flat. Buying vegetables became a warm social event. KJ had told me how intuitive his African friends could be – how on arrival, people would be given a nickname that was perfectly descriptive of who they really were. Now my love of all that would so soon be lost, was mysteriously visible to the people I met, and they responded from the heart.

American Emily invited me to meet two Swazi health workers who were interested in the counselling course that we had taught on that fateful 7 April. It seemed to me that they were extremely well trained from their Aids counselling course in South Africa and didn't need more courses.

'What do you *really* need?' I asked.

'Somewhere to do our work,' was the reply.

The local Aids clinic was tiny and full of queuing patients. Counsellors were reduced to seeing their clients in corners, or outside in all weathers. There they would break the news of the illness, trying to soften the fact that there was no permanent cure, that it was probably a death sentence, that families could be without a breadwinner, and children could be orphaned in a relatively brief time. They needed privacy and comfort to give support and advice.

'What if we could find the money to build a proper counselling centre?' I asked. Their smiles were an answer.

I went to see the head of the clinic, a strong Dutch Salvation Army officer. Bona told me that she had the complete trust of the people. No one was ever turned away but they could do so much more with bigger premises. I had a plan. It concerned the 'Women of Europe' in Brussels who raised money to support projects for women and children. It was a match made in heaven. Forms were filled in, and the project was agreed. Even better, the building contractor was our old friend Bill Sterling. He doubled the size of the new centre out of the kindness of his heart. A few months later, photographs arrived. This was not reflected glory from KJ. This was my project. I had done something for the people of Swaziland. It was one of the best moments of my life.

The dogs and I left Swaziland on 9 May. It was Europe Day and KJ's successor was revelling in his first lunchtime function. We quietly left the flat and prepared to leave the beloved country early next morning. The dogs were pre-booked into a quarantine kennel near Dover. We drove all together in a van to Johannesburg and handed them over at Jan Smuts airport, wondering if we would ever see them again. They went jauntily towards their long, long flight, tails waving. We phoned the Dover quarantine kennels on arrival. A cheerful English voice said: 'Yes, they've arrived. They're having something to eat and Magic can't stop wagging her tail!'

KJ went back to work. At HQ the staff from Rwanda had returned in a state of shock. All of them had seen death and terror at first hand. One colleague had sheltered his domestic staff in the house for as long as he could, until they were seized and killed before his eyes on the front lawn. I thought of Bona and her children. Another wanted to go back to rescue his girlfriend, and a third to search for his great Dane. And with that bizarre irrationality that can afflict all of us when circumstances are just too overwhelming to absorb, one woman was bewailing her lost recipes.

History can repeat itself. In August 1994, just six weeks after the massacres, KJ arrived in Kigali as the 'Special Envoy of the Commission of the European Union'.

He wrote: 'My first feelings on entering the Hotel des Milles Collines were of foreboding and dread. Over 1,000 people had been crammed in there for weeks in daily expectation of being murdered. And death was never far from our thoughts. One day the Administrator returned to the office in a state of shock. He had heard that there were vegetables for sale in the newly re-opened market. When he went, there in the middle of the cabbages, as through they belonged there, were human skulls.'

But his abiding memory was one of utter desolation. 'On a trip to the Burundi border for supplies at the end of August we stopped the car at the side of the road. I can still remember the absolute silence. This small country of a thousand hills and seven million people was completely deserted. Houses were abandoned, doors hanging open like gaping mouths; no animals could be seen or heard, no birds sang and what strangely struck me most of all, no insects hummed. Utter eerie silence! It was as though nature itself had been rendered speechless at the atrocities which had been committed.'

The aim of the mission was to oversee emergency aid and to rebuild the infrastructure of society. The team set up in the looted office. Computers had been destroyed and all records lost. Still worse, it had been the scene of murders. Michel, the administrator, had had the distress of discovering the evidence of this. Heroically he had set about restoring things to order single handed.

There were traces of the massacre everywhere. A rocket had hit the delegate's house. Packs of abandoned dogs roamed the streets. People still lived in fear and few went out after nightfall. The office messenger disappeared one day, never to be seen again. After that young Rwandan staff were carefully escorted home each evening. A small stray dog wandered into the French Embassy and was adopted by the staff as a symbol of survival and hope. A cockerel was given to KJ's team. He was intended for the pot but he was such an engaging fellow that he was kept as a pet. He sat on top of the satellite telephone dish and crowed his optimism every morning. There were horses roaming loose around the city. With Michel, KJ rounded them up, placed them securely in the field of a riding school and arranged for someone to care for them. All these tiny movements were sprigs of hope after a season of death.

After the initial shocked disbelief at the images on their TV screens, the world was clamouring for answers. Few people understood the complex roots of the genocide, roots which went deep into the history of the region and were closely inter-twined with its colonial history.

Until Europeans came, Rwanda was a closed state. It has been called the Tibet of Africa. Like Tibet, it was a mountain kingdom, and Rwandans maintained no outside relations, made no conquests and allowed no foreigners into the country. They believed their country was the centre of the world. 'God might visit other countries by day but every night he returned to rest in Rwanda!' Rwandans are not two races, Hutu and Tutsi, but one, the Banyarwanda, a single nation of one language, one faith, and one law, divided into three casts by occupation. The Tutsis, though the minority, were the ruling class and the Tutsi king, the Mwami, ruled with his court of nobles. The Hutus, 85 per cent of the population, were peasants and herders, and governed their own hillside communities. The Twa, just 1 per cent of the population, were labourers. A workable system between the groups had prevailed for hundreds of years.

Differences polarised in the early twentieth century in a mirror image of European racial discrimination. New attitudes, combined with erosion and land shortages, contributed to racial tension. Noses and foreheads were measured by the colonial government. 'Ethnic Identity Cards' were issued, and one group, the Tutsis, was given political ascendancy. But when democratic movements swept Europe, the Belgian colonial government abandoned their favourites the Tutsis, and the Hutu majority was encouraged to seek power. The final betrayal of the Tutsis was the enforced abolition of the age-old monarchy and the election of a Hutu president. The stage was set for bitterness and discord between groups of people who had lived in harmony for centuries.

Why was the massacre allowed to continue unchecked for three months? Many books have been written trying to understand how, in an era of mass communications, the world could stand back and watch. And in particular, how it was that the UN peacekeeping force had no power to keep the peace? General Romeo Dallaire had pleaded strenuously for sufficient forces and a mandate to intervene. In 1998, before the International Criminal Tribunal for Rwanda, the general choked back tears as he said that, with a well-armed force of just 5,000 men and a proper mandate,

'The UN could have stopped the slaughter of hundreds of thousands of Rwandans.'

But no such mandate was forthcoming. Why?

The United Nations is just that. A club of nations. Some members of the club carry more weight than others. The violent deaths of 800,000 innocent Rwandans were closely linked to events in Somalia, less than one year before, just after KJ's stay there. On 3 October 1993, eighteen American rangers were killed and TV images of their bodies being dragged through the streets of Mogadishu were beamed around the world. Americans were outraged. This could not be allowed to happen to American citizens ever again! 'Presidential Decision Directive 25' was passed by President Clinton, imposing strict conditions on any peacekeeping operation before America would give its approval.

So despite all that was happening in Rwanda, the USA refused to admit that a genocide was taking place. Had they done so, they would have been obliged, as signatories to the UN Treaty on Genocide, to intervene. On 10 June 1994, in the midst of the killings, the US State Department spokesperson, Christine Shelley, was asked by reporters to clarify the American position.

'We have every reason to believe that acts of genocide have occurred,' she said.

'How many acts of genocide does it take to make a genocide?' a reporter asked.

'That's not a question that I'm in a position to answer,' she replied.

Since the UN operates by a system of veto, unless it was agreed that 'genocide' was occurring, no full UN peace-keeping operation could be put into motion. Because there was no mandate, had UN peacekeeping troops made any armed intervention, they would have been court-martialled. Their hands were tied. And so the killing went on.

Pictures were beamed around the world at the end of the genocide, when processions of refugees streamed across Rwanda towards the Congo. Finally the world's conscience was aroused. Aid and aid workers flooded in to the area – too late to save the Tutsis. But the processions of 'refugees' for whom the world donated so much help included thousands of the killers.

KJ stayed in Rwanda for talks with the new President Pasteur Bizimungu on how to repair the shattered society, how to get the city functioning again, how to deal with the unspeakable social problems that such a human catastrophe leaves in its wake. It would be vital to rebuild the physical fabric of society, to restore the social structure, to heal the psychological wounds of survivors, and to build in attitudes and safeguards against such an outbreak happening again. It would need to be tackled at every level of society.

While KJ was engaged on these weighty matters, I was back in England, living in East Kent. It was a far cry from life in Swaziland, Angola or Zimbabwe. After sixteen years away, I re-experienced the bucolic nature of English country life – the greenness of the countryside, modest chirping birdsong on cold mornings, the grey rain, the chilly sunshine, the sleepy local population, grimy trains where passengers were too polite even to say 'Good morning'. No one sang or danced in the streets, except once a year at the Hop Festival when there was a lot of beer. Summer strawberries and raspberries, cherries, late summer plums, and the autumn apple harvest; red winter sunsets against black trees – the seasons rolled past. It was all very English but was this the England I had dreamt of during all those years in the tropics? It had changed – and so had I.

The dogs were in quarantine kennels in Dover. Their run looked out on fields of sheep, cows and horses. There were good smells and plenty to bark at. They were fat and happy and grew thick fur coats like small polar bears. Once their quarantine was over they could have come home. But we lived in Lees Court, an old stately home divided into apartments. It had acres of grounds, but no proper fencing. It also had old stately English residents who demanded that rules be observed – and a poodle who lived on the ground floor. Two rambunctious bull terriers could have caused havoc. They stayed in the kennels and we went for walks in the fields.

During the year I enrolled in some adult education classes. After years spent painting in the mountains of Swaziland, the local nonagenarian watercolour class was a little tame. Sitting round a bare table in the freezing village hall of Old Wives Lees, painting a single lemon didn't set the heart racing. More interesting was the course in Creative Writing. It was taught by a young woman from Whitstable, a small coastal town. She had once worked for a woman's magazine in London. Janice was creative in her teaching and authoritative in her critiques.

One of our assignments was to write a short play. I wrote 'Revolution in Banjuta'. Set in Africa, the characters included a British Ambassador of the good-looking and effete kind, his wife, her lover – a handsome game ranger – and members of domestic staff, all with strong personalities. The action took place on the eve of an insurrection in which the game ranger and the domestic staff were involved. At the climax planes flew overhead, guns were fired and men in military uniform appeared. Scenes included a formal dinner, white linen, glittering silver, candelabra alight. There were snatches of dinner-party conversation as a background. That was easy. I had heard it many times.

When the work was handed back our teacher from the wilds of Whitstable was incredulous.

'It's so far-fetched,' said Janice, 'so nineteenth century. It couldn't happen. *No one* lives like that any more!'